CW00336623

The Feminine in Management Consulting

The Feminine in Management Consulting

Power, Emotion and Values in Consulting Interactions

Sheila Marsh

for Marion
(I feel I know
you !)

[signature]

2.12.08

palgrave
macmillan

First published 2009 by
PALGRAVE MACMILLAN
Houndmills, Basingstoke, Hampshire RG21 6XS and
175 Fifth Avenue, New York, N.Y. 10010
Companies and representatives throughout the world

PALGRAVE MACMILLAN is the global academic imprint of the Palgrave Macmillan division of St. Martin's Press, LLC and of Palgrave Macmillan Ltd. Macmillan® is a registered trademark in the United States, United Kingdom and other countries. Palgrave is a registered trademark in the European Union and other countries.

ISBN-13: 978-0-230-20716-5   hardback
ISBN-10: 0-230-20716-2   hardback

This book is printed on paper suitable for recycling and made from fully managed and sustained forest sources. Logging, pulping and manufacturing processes are expected to conform to the environmental regulations of the country of origin.

A catalogue record for this book is available from the British Library.

Library of Congress Cataloging-in-Publication Data
Marsh, Sheila, 1954–
   The feminine in management consulting: power, emotion, and values in
   consulting interactions / Sheila Marsh.
      p. cm.
   Includes bibliographical references.
   ISBN 978-0-230-20716-5 (alk. paper)
      1. Women consultants. 2. Business consultants. I. Title.
   HD69.C6M375 2008
   001–dc22   2008030083

10   9   8   7   6   5   4   3   2   1
18   17   16   15   14   13   12   11   10   09

Printed and bound in Great Britain by
CPI Antony Rowe, Chippenham and Eastbourne

For my father, Tom.
(1916–1990)

Contents

List of Tables and Figures

Tables

Figures

Acknowledgements

I wish gratefully to acknowledge consistent, motivating, stimulating and always helpfully questioning support from Michael Reynolds and Sharon Turnbull at the University of Lancaster; and the unstinting, generous and challenging involvement of all my colleagues featuring anonymously in this book – you know who you are! I could not have achieved anything without you.

I owe enormous thanks to my good friend, Susan Weil, whose encouragement helped me contemplate this work in the first place and see light in sticky moments. And not least I owe a great deal to the consistent and uncomplaining support of my partner, Sue, in affording me the space and time, in putting other things on hold for six years and not least for checking all my references – definitely a labour of love! My love and thanks to you.

Introduction

A notorious 'amusing' anecdote about management consultants concerns a dead horse and how many stupid, worthless, desperate and absurd approaches to tackling it (including of course flogging it) the consultant formulates, while ignoring the immutable fact that the horse is indeed already dead.[1] This story, and others similar, which circulate unchallenged and are endlessly re-told (readers will undoubtedly have their own examples) are part of the complex and ambiguous process whereby the consultant achieves her identity or sense of self and forges her sense of worth or value.

How can we make sense of our identity in the face of derision, denial of worth, the butt of endless jokes and internet 'stories', and indeed of pejorative academic work? (see for example Fincham 1999a) Somehow being a consultant is not a 'proper' occupation to own up to – certainly not in critical academic circles. 'Proper' is an interesting word – definitions include: 'appropriate, usual, suited to a particular purpose, correct in behaviour, vigorously or excessively moral' (Collins 1989). So I have wondered what is this impropriety, what is the consulting process and what space there is for a 'critical consulting' practice – since that what is what I think I do or at least aspire to do.

Despite the ubiquity of consulting as an acknowledged growth industry (Kipping and Engwall 2002), the consultant remains an ambiguous being, a shadow identity. The management consultant, in her relationships with those commissioning her and with her consulting colleagues, is nevertheless a site where identity is produced, perceived, and questioned.

Here I will first explain how this book, and the study that informs it, came about and the journey this represents, before describing the structure of the book and how you may want to use it.

1

Starting points

The triggers for the study presented in this book were in some ways always present for me, as an independent consultant[2] working in the public and not-for-profit sectors since 1987. I have periodically agonised over feeling I needed to ('ought to') return to a management post to maintain my credibility in working with managers, to have up-to-date 'knowledge about' management. My extremely strong feelings surprised me and raised for me how I was constructing my own sense of self.

The managers who commission me work in tricky terrain, and I often doubt what I offer them. Sometimes we seem far apart. Sometimes it is hard then to see how we can work together. Sometimes I feel I know exactly what to offer and can see things they do not. The intractability of their situation is often striking: they experience rhetorics of change yet battle the inertia and stuckness of their organisations; they want, as I do, to work with the public to improve publicly funded services, yet so much can get in the way. I was also struck by how variously I could conceive the distance between us: about time and space; about different viewpoints and perceptions; about the skills of a consultant, as opposed to their 'knowledge'; about values and intentions. Equally important is the place of the manager in these dilemmas, not passive but crucially part of the emerging dynamic.

In all this I wrestled with the constant dilemma of how then to act. What bridges distance? What fosters connection, integrity and legitimacy in the midst of pressurised practice? What creates change, difference, learning? Can we challenge power and inequality? How can a 'critical consultant' work? These dilemmas then triggered my research.[3]

So I began by noticing the impact on me of my personal experiences of consulting work. Looking back to that time I now see I held an essentialist view of self: my previous identity of 'manager' had gone and was now 'consultant' or maybe 'learning specialist'. I was convinced that I was distant from the managers I worked with and that this was negative – I thus aspired to closeness. I felt there was a relationship between us and yet its process and nature was hard to grasp. Paradoxically, my earlier work (Marsh 1992) had highlighted that, in choosing a consultant, the chooser can feel less concerned about the relationship than about the consultant's track record and needing that reassurance that the work will go well. Interestingly all the consultants in that study were more concerned about processes and relationship building. So were my renewed concerns about identity, role and worth once more missing the point, in relation to managers' concerns? Or were they a new starting point to explore consulting? I decided the point was to study the actual consulting process and enrolled for a doctorate.

This book is thus about my work, the people I work with and the work we do.

> I hope to blur the boundaries between rhetoric and theory, personal and political, self and society through an account which constructs the multiple ways the 'experiences' of my friends and co-workers exceed, yet in some form inevitably, ironically, reproduce the culturally specific forms and metaphors that shape their lives and to which they themselves give meaning. (Kondo 1990:48)

As for Dorinne Kondo, the complex experiences of my 'friends and co-workers' are at its core. I intend the book to open up to view the different concerns, stories and insights that we experience as consultants and that I shall characterise as a 'feminine'[4] discourse of management consulting.

> ...feminine, is that a good word? Doesn't it just make people think "pink lipstick"? (a consulting colleague)

Inevitably the 'feminine' is tricky terrain as this comment suggests but it encapsulates the ways in which my work unfolded, transforming my understanding of my starting dilemmas.

The unfolding 'feminine'

The issue of gender came up consistently as my research unfolded. I was confronted with its centrality and ubiquity, 'the shadow negotiation ...beneath other interaction' (Kolb 2003:129), although I resisted this. I had not wanted to focus on gender. I had 'been there and done that', as it were, over two decades of working on and around equalities issues in the workplace, both within my consulting practice and in previous work experience both paid and unpaid. I deliberately tried to edit these issues out of my planned study on consulting interaction. I did not reckon with how 'we end up "doing gender" whenever we "do" anything else' (Ely *et al.* 2003:7)

While accepting the need to 'beware the impulse to confess' as a woman (Metzger 1990), the issue of gender chased me through the first three years of my work until I acknowledged its centrality. My colleagues and I are, with few exceptions, women. It gradually became clear to me that my starting points expressed what are seen as gendered concerns. I see now how gendered are issues of closeness, of the primacy of relationships and the connected desire to make a difference for others: all are identified with women (Marshall 1994; Miller 1976, 1982) and the 'feminine'. These starting points privilege notions of connection over distance; show doubt of self-worth in the public sphere of work; assume empathy with managers in their dilemmas; and reflect a struggle to make sense of assumptions stemming from traditional models of management knowledge and linear career paths. They are riven with what emerged as the core themes in the study: power, emotion and values, each of which connect significantly to gender. All this signalled that gender reverberated within my inquiry and my consulting work, whether I wished it or not. This immediately raised major challenges.

> ...we live in a gendered world, that gender is masculine and is importantly also misogynist ... Gender is both called forth and masked. (Davies 1995:61)

For gender is not simply about women – what questions does a focus on women beg about men? The 'feminine' initially offered me an alternative to the largely male and 'masculine' view of consulting in existing research and writing – very little work exists on women consultants or concerned with gender in consulting. But I have come to view the 'feminine' as a coherent way to express not only experiences of consulting that are not generally visible to a broader audience, but also as a critical term with which to explore all consulting processes in new ways.

So, in privileging the lens of femininities,[5] the better to illuminate consulting processes more broadly, I ask you, the reader, to suspend disbelief in order to consider where the notion of a 'feminine' discourse can lead in exploring the process and interactions of management consulting in general – what can it illuminate? The themes of women in consulting and the 'feminine' are key outcomes of my work, unanticipated – and, as I mentioned, unwelcome! But they brought together the core themes of the study: power, emotion and values in particularly compelling ways that for me inform the framing of a 'feminine' discourse of 'critical' consulting.

'Critical consulting' practice?

Aspiring to 'critical consulting' contrasts with the public image of management consultants, as agents supporting a managerialist agenda for purposes of profit (Fincham 2003). I identify my values and commitment as falling within 'critical management studies'[6] terrain where 'responsible management consulting may make a difference' (Parker 2002:131). I struggle to translate this into 'critical consulting', that is, consulting practice which aims for progressive goals of social change through both its (potential for) *influence* on public policy and *how* the consultant works with organisations and individuals.[7] It draws in notions of ethics, of problematising managerial norms in prevailing organisational contexts, of challenging inequalities of power and of enacting democratic principles. It aims for reflexivity without a narcissistic focus.

What the managers I work with do, and so potentially what I do, has some impact on the broader world. Our work affects, for example, health and social care, inequalities of health and how public services are organised: those things matter to people. As a colleague put it in discussion (1 June 2005): 'If you are being paid out of the council tax from some old lady with a leaking roof and the council hasn't mended her roof, then why should the council pay you, if it then couldn't repair her roof?'

Our consultancy work needs to matter then, to make sense, in order to be justified as a use of public or donated money. 'Critical consulting' practice is therefore about how consulting work can contribute positively. For me what difference my work does or does not make is important to those I work with and to me, and, ultimately, to people who use public services. I recognise, however, that a notion like 'critical consulting' is inevitably flawed:

> like all oppositional discourse, the opposition can never be pristine or transcendent, but it is always already situated within other discourses, reproducing conventions even as it problematizes them. (Kondo 1990:302)

We may try to change power relations as we work, but there are no 'pristine' places of power or resistance: we are caught in contradictions.

Kondo's linking of power, identity and resistance is thus a helpful framing for creating discursive space for 'critical consulting'.

What am I aiming to achieve?

My most important aim is to make sense of what I and my colleagues do. The justification for this potentially narcissistic focus resides in our collective interests which provide broader valid purposes:

- in being paid public money for our work it is in everyone's interests better to understand this rather hidden aspect of consulting
- the sheer lack of work exploring what happens inside consulting, despite the growth in consulting and spending on it, including within the public sector
- to explore the effects of consulting processes in public policy terms
- to consider interaction between consultants and managers as professional and managerial discourses shift and develop interdependently
- to inform the future work of myself, and people who work with me, both those commissioning and those carrying out work, and others engaged in similar arenas

As a reader I hope you can identify your own interests in one or more of these reasons.

In tackling my inquiry I tried to avoid obvious built-in assumptions: for example I did not reify the consulting process from the outset by focusing on, for example, its 'effectiveness' or on the 'client relationship'. I intended to illuminate consulting processes from the inside out, through exploring consulting interactions.

The shape of the book

As I have indicated, my journey took me from a focus on consulting (reflected in Part I) to a focus on women consultants (using my own work as research material in Part II) and further to crystallising the key themes of the study, power, emotion and values, within the notion of a 'feminine' discourse of consulting, which I develop in Part III. Throughout the book I include '*reflection*' boxes which contain my thoughts – and some insights – from my consulting as well as those triggered in my research and as I wrote this text, and also excerpts from my research journal. Such boxes form a concurrent but different voice layered on my writing.

Part I opens the terrain of consulting and advice-giving to organisations to question and (re-)conceptualisation. It shares my journey across the terrain of management consulting, initially setting the scene for the study with my own context, but crucially offers the broadest framing of consulting from premodern times to contemporary research and writing. It ends with my overall conclusions about consulting as a discursive practice.

Chapter 1 begins with my own terrain. It sets the context for the study I undertook of my own consulting work and explains why it took the shape it did. I offer my definition of consulting and describe my work setting in small scale public and not-for-profit management consulting and how it differs from the setting of most prior research on consulting. This helps me review key questions, such as: what is 'small scale'; what is the context for my work in the public and not-for-profit sectors; what is the nature of the work people commission; what are its politics and challenges? I chart how my network of colleagues collaborates and describe the six pieces of work that I studied. The chapter links the issues of context to my research approach. I chart how I designed my research both to make the most of being an insider and also to produce a rigorous study.

I had been astonished to read that consulting 'began' in the early years of the twentieth century. This did not make sense to me given what I knew about certain historical figures, such as Machiavelli or (even earlier) Plato, and how they worked with public leaders. I set out to read more and ended in uncovering fascinating material about a wealth of figures before modern times who were involved in what we would now call management consulting. Intriguingly these figures, both men and women, show us ways of advice-giving that illuminate our present day approaches to consulting. This novel 'genealogy' of advice-giving (after Foucault) in Chapter 2 sets a challenging frame for viewing contemporary writing and research about consulting, what has influenced it and what still does. This Foucauldian approach helps us to expand our thinking about what consulting activities may comprise and how these activities have been construed and carried out over centuries. It certainly helped me transcend my daily work setting and broaden my concepts of consulting. It is a substantial chapter as I need to share at length the actual words of premodern advisers that need both context and a fair degree of commentary. Here too, the issue of women advisers gradually emerged as importantly different and a special section about them also grew. Since prior readers of this chapter have been especially excited about this material, I was loathe to cut it and hope you will be similarly excited!

Chapter 3 creates a framework of six images of consulting drawing on contemporary writing and research about consulting. I found that despite others viewing this work in two strands ('mainstream' and 'critical management'), I could identify images they both share that propound powerful discourses of consulting. These are: the economic transaction; the service; the advice industry; the profession; the knowledge industry; performance and rhetoric. Chapter 3 explores each image and uses them to characterise our current perspectives on (studying) consulting. This raises sharp questions for the 'critical consultant' to which I return at the end of the book.

Part I ends with Chapter 4 which draws together the conclusions from the genealogy with the images of consulting I identified. Here I show how consulting is best seen as a discursive practice, shaped by a series of discourses of consulting. I set out the discourses of consulting I see operating. These not only sharpen our view of the ambiguous shadow that is the consultant but also provide material to help explore actual consulting practice. Again I have been astonished that no one else has explicitly taken the view that consulting is rich in discourses that shape its processes, so that the discourses I set out here represent a first attempt to chart them explicitly.

Part I thus frames the consulting interactions I explore in Part II, providing discursive resources with which to consider and explore my material. I hope Part I will interest those already involved in practising, researching or commissioning consulting both through its historical material that challenges some current thinking on the origins of consulting, and through its characterisation of discourses of consulting that shape us and our work – as indeed we shape them.

Part II presents a view inside consulting work, first setting out in Chapter 5 my research approach. I discuss here my theoretical base in relation to discourse, how I used an autoethnographic approach in gathering material, and how I applied Critical Discourse Analysis (CDA) to make sense of the interactions. I am keen to share the insights that using CDA brought to my work. It helped me gain a distance from my own work that was crucial, as well as helping me keep the broadest social/political issues in view. Little is published that shows CDA in use for working with interactive material so I hope this will interest a segment of readers and inspire some to use the method. Readers who only have a passing interest in the details of methodology need read no more than Chapter 1 and may wish to ignore this chapter. Chapter 6 presents 'live' material from the six pieces of consulting work that I first introduce in Chapter 1; Chapter 7 presents reflective pieces from

discussions or stories collected in the course of the study from my colleagues, other consultants (including men) and from myself. These
chapters give a flavour of the material I gathered and offer a view into
the hitherto hidden world of consulting interactions. The material
from live consulting work and from reflective stories was so rich and so
vivid in expressing the themes of the study that I have retained as
much of it as possible within the confines of length. Chapters 6 and 7
are therefore substantial, but, I hope, gripping. Both chapters end in
charting the issues raised and commenting in relation to the discourses
identified in Part I, thus setting the scene for exploration of core
themes of power, emotion and values and for sense-making in Part III.

Part II thus offers a case study of the use of CDA on interactions
which is not commonly seen. I intend the layout and commentaries
offered to help those interested in using CDA to see its tools in action.
Readers are able, and may of course choose, to read these chapters
simply as material and my commentary on it, disregarding the whole
issue of CDA. Similarly you may wish to skip the detail of the material
presented and simply read the commentaries or the end of chapter
summaries. As you read Part III you will find I refer to elements in the
material presented and it may be that only then will you want to dive
into the detail: it is for you to choose. In discourse analytic work it is
important to keep choices open and to set out the work transparently
for the reader to examine as you wish.

Part III begins with Chapter 8 which considers the meta-themes of
power, emotion, and values which surfaced from the material in Part II.
In developing these themes and their paradoxical implications for
actors in consulting processes, I identify critical linking issues which
are entwined with these three major themes: relationships, identities
and the nature of the commercial process itself. Chapter 8 takes us into
different territory than hitherto: our construction of power, using a
Foucauldian approach; emotions at work, especially for the professions;
and the nature of the commercial process, especially the role of values
and morality in economic activity. The chapter culminates in offering
a mapping of consulting interaction showing these themes in connection to the broader social/political context, mirroring the process of
critical discourse analysis. It concludes that the gender-inflected nature
of all the elements of the mapping holds major significance in understanding what is going on in consulting interactions.

Chapter 9 takes up this challenge in exploring femininities and consulting. Here I draw on the enormous literature on gender and work to
explore how the study as a whole (re-) animates a 'feminine' discourse

of consulting linked to the genealogy in Part I and contrasting with competing contemporary discourses. I re-examine the themes of power, emotion and values from the perspective of the 'feminine' drawing especially on Joyce Fletcher's concept of 'relational practice' (2001), but also on concepts of the female entrepreneur and her discourse of 'worthwhileness'. From this discussion I set out the elements of a 'feminine' discourse of management consulting, which privileges processes, privileges social purposes and embraces emotion.

Chapter 10 draws together the threads of the book. It takes an overview of the journey in the previous nine chapters, setting out my conclusions about where we have reached in relation to power, emotion and values; to consulting as a discursive practice; and to the 'feminine' in management consulting. It discusses what we can learn from a 'feminine' discourse of consulting and how this can contribute to developing 'critical consulting' practice. It therefore addresses the implications of (re-)animating a 'feminine' discourse of consulting for people doing consulting and for those commissioning consulting. In acknowledging some limitations to my work, I end with practical research ideas for those studying consulting. Thus in concluding the book I offer ideas that can be applied to practical work, relevant to all readers, that will contribute to what I hope will be a continuing lively debate about 'critical consulting' practice and how the 'feminine' can advance it.

Part I

Consulting: Exploring the Terrain

1
Studying Consulting from the Inside: What Do I Mean by Consulting and How Did I Research It?

Introduction

This chapter sets the context for the study I undertook and explains why it took the shape it did. I offer my definition of consulting and describe my work setting in small scale public and not-for-profit management consulting and how it differs from the setting of most prior work on consulting. This helps me review key questions, such as: what is 'small scale'; what is the context for my work in the public and not-for-profit sectors; what is the nature of the work people commission; what are its nature and challenges? I chart how my network of colleagues works together and describe the six pieces of work that I studied. The chapter then links these issues of context to my research approach. I chart how I designed my research both to make the most of being an insider and also to produce a rigorous study.

Defining consulting?

The simplest and commonest definitions of consulting regard it as the giving of advice.

> Almost by definition, a consultant is someone who offers advice (Griffin 2001).
> Someone – mostly a specialist – who is *asked* to give expert advice or information (Bohm 2003:21 his emphasis)

One succinct definition from a professional body reads:

> the provision to management of objective advice and assistance relating to the strategy, structure, management and operations of an

organisation in pursuit of its long-term purposes and objectives. (Institute of Management Consultancy 2008).

Sturdy considers training (in which most consultancies engage) within a definition of consultancy, since this *'advise[s]* managers and other employees on how to think, feel and act' (2002:131 my emphasis). Clark and Fincham (2002), as editors, comment that the 'constantly changing nature of the consultancy industry' makes definitions difficult (2002:2). However in their book's subtitle they too espouse advice as the core concept: *New Perspectives on the Management Advice Industry.*

Kieser sees consultancy as 'maximising client satisfaction' (2002:214) highlighting its aim as profit through the selling of time. Its success criteria include simplification and the 'reformulation of complex decisions so that they appear simple to decision makers' (*ibid*:212). He also describes official and unofficial side-functions of consulting: to legitimise management activity/decisions; stimulate acceptance of change; provide weapons for politics; foster careers of sponsors; provide an interpretation process for top managers.

Sturdy takes a broader and more theoretical view of consulting as:

> a feature of the process through which management knowledge is constructed, reconstructed, negotiated and substituted is a dialectic between consultants and clients mediated through particular managerial labour processes and the individual preoccupation with existential and material security. (1997b:532)

Here he is signalling both key processes of interaction, links to broader issues of the construction of management knowledge, and the importance of subjectivities within the consulting process.

The multifarious nature of consulting emphasises the need for a situated definition; Kipping and Engwall (2002) also underline the importance of context to consulting. So for my study I took consulting as encompassing:

> a range of processes to offer external advice and related support activities to help leaders/managers in the public and not-for-profit sectors to meet their goals, within a values framework for public service.

The context of my consulting work

Kipping and Engwall (2002) advocate exploring consulting within a three level analytical framework of 'industry, firm and project'. Next I discuss the kinds of work I carry out ('projects'); the broader social, political and discursive environment that frames this work ('industry'); and the network of colleagues and contacts with whom I work ('firm'). The industry and firm context concerns the practice and interaction of independent (mostly women) consultants in small-scale public sector and not-for-profit consulting. This contrasts with typical studies of consulting, which are overwhelmingly concerned with the corporate sector, especially with large-scale IT and accountancy consulting work, and dominated by consideration of the large consulting firm (for example Alvesson 1993; Clark and Fincham 2002; Fincham 2006; Kipping and Engwall 2002; Sturdy 1997a).

The dimensions of small-scale consulting

The work of sole traders like me, and the aims of those commissioning us, are not easily categorised according to traditional labels, such as management consulting or organisational development. While our consulting work remains *small scale* in terms of value (typically less than £10,000), duration (usually 2–6 months), consultant input (1–3 people for around 5–20 days total), its *reach* may be significant for commissioning organisations. Such work includes: policy development and advice, with the attendant research, public consultation and report-writing; advice or direct help with policy implementation, piloting and trials; review and evaluation of the impact of policy/innovations. This may be in national, regional, local or neighbourhood settings, from large, formal bureaucracies to small, informal community-based organisations. It can involve work with one individual, with a team or group, with a whole organisation, with a group of organisations working in partnership, or with a 'whole system' such as a community, or a local health economy (Pratt *et al.* 1999). Any or all of these can be combined and may involve running a series of events involving dozens of diverse people.

So small scale consulting work in public sector environments crosses policy and practice divides, involves diverse organisations and agencies, and may connect to local, regional and national levels of government. Government departments, universities, local authorities, health trusts, multi-agency partnerships and community-based organisations all commission us. We work with many different professionals not only with managers – these are both on-the-ground practitioners and policy developers – and often directly with elected politicians, service users and/or the public at large. This is multi-faceted work that draws on strategic thinking and planning, organisational development understandings, systemic analysis and facilitation skills, as well as requiring sector-linked knowledge of policy/practice and politics – both developed over time and immediate 'hot topics'.[1]

The public and not-for-profit sector context

The discourses of public sector management within which this work occurs are fundamental, along with the importance of broader political and social issues. This context is significantly one of dilemmas, where, with those who commission us, we aim to improve public services, combat social exclusion, and promote health, equality and empower-ment, but within tight policy, performance and resource strictures which stem from both the discourse of managerialism within public management and the operating environment of charitably funded organisations:

> [Managerialism] increases both direct and indirect methods of control in order to enhance productivity, increase profit and/or reduce costs. [It] gives managers the right to manage. It incorporates .....both control of the body and control of the mind. Through its own sleight of hand, it intensifies the labour process while at the same time col-onising progressive concepts such as 'empowerment'. (Macalpine and Marsh 1999:1)

This pervasive discourse produces immense pressure on managers who face the spread and growing sophistication of managerialism at the same time as growing demands to achieve improved social outcomes. The growth of consumerism has led to localised demands for better services and awareness of institutional discrimination has led to legit-imate demands for services to meet the needs of diverse populations (Macalpine and Marsh 1999).

The 'modernisation' project of the UK Labour government since the late 1990s reinforced this emphasis, such that if public bodies were seen to 'fail', other policy priorities, such as increasing local democracy, were overridden by government teams sent to take over. The impact of such managerial approaches is well known, for example 'modern-isation' plans and targets in health, league tables in education, the 'star rating' or 'traffic light' systems for hospitals and councils, bidding systems for funds. In this way top-down pressures for improvement add to the spread and intensity of managerialism (Lister 2005). The dom-inance of managerialism has also led to the growing use of consultants explicitly to bring private sector approaches into the public sector.

Saint-Martin (2000) demonstrates how the growth of consulting parallels the take-up of managerialism by governments and comments on the ideological backdrop to this:

> political factors and not technical expertise alone are an important part of the reason management consultants are brought into government to reform public administrative practices. (2000:198)

For the voluntary sector too managerialism has penetrated. Contracting to deliver an increasing proportion of 'public' services subject it to similar performance management systems and pressure to move to 'social enterprise'. In addition the sector has to meet performance management regimes for its funders.

This discursive context of targets, performance, consumerism and assumed public sector 'failure' produce: cynicism in the workplace, emerging privately where it does not endanger people's careers; 'the notorious difficulty of turning progressive policy into practice' (Macalpine and Marsh 1999); the challenge of being critical of managerialism while at the same time trying to improve services. This latter double-edge cannot be ignored in the public sector arena where, working with vulnerable people, action is required. Mere critical commentary is not enough. Public sector *values* demand action and improvement for public benefit. The political context and pressures are thus equally important whether in health services, central government, or local government where situated political dynamics are in play (Jarrett 2001).

Working in a network

This institutional and political context, and its discursive power, contrasts with the isolated, solo practitioner: the independent consultant. However, in common with many other independent consultants I have always worked in a loose connection with similar colleagues. I work frequently with one or more others, drawn from a network of colleagues (and friends) who do similar work. We have shared interests as independent consultants and hold a common set of values about working with the public sector. The group aims for an ethical practice of consulting within the public and not-for-profit sectors, as well as to work to democratic ends and against exclusion and inequalities. This approach raises the notion for us of 'critical consulting' and what it might mean.

My network is overwhelmingly made up of women, mostly people with whom I have worked in the past. Others are friends and colleagues of such people. We open up our own networks to each other. This widening circle of contacts embraces not only consultants, but also people who commission us, again overwhelmingly these are women. They may be former colleagues who stayed within the organisation and became more senior or who moved to a succession of more senior posts. They may be friends or contacts of friends.

This way of working contrasts with consultants who publish, or on whom contemporary research focuses. These consultants are overwhelmingly engaged with (large) private sector organisations, and are employed in extremely large commercial consulting firms, often those working globally. The few exceptions are consultants who both publish and have their own business, but who have effectively reached the status of 'management guru', for example Peter Senge, Peter Block, or those who are primarily academics, such as Barbara Czarniawska. Our network is an evolving set of informal relationships, fostered by monthly meetings that I call 'the development group' in this book. These discuss work-in-progress, support and help each other, and act as a source of colleagues actually to take on work or find possible work through our mutual contacts. This network was a key source for my study, both of the pieces of work explored in Chapter 6, and in generating reflection-in-action as pieces of work unfolded, presented in Chapter 7.

The consulting work I studied

I gathered material on pieces of work as I did them, aiming for a range of settings and different kinds of consulting work. The book draws on six pieces of work, summarised in Table 1.1.

The *National Policy work* aimed to bridge national and local government (tensions) to improve health in local communities. The commission was to research and produce a 'resource' to help people implement the new policy. This work linked to the beliefs and values held by my colleague and me in terms of learning, skills and local democratic processes. It ended in apparent success in delivering a highly regarded (by the potential users) 'resource'; however, this was not published by the government department as events and key people moved on.

The *One-to-One work* continues at time of writing and concerns a small, vibrant, national charity working with extremely marginalised people. Working with its second most senior person offers me the chance to influence and contribute to developing this organisation, in a setting where my ideas and advice are often taken up.

Table 1.1 'Live' consulting work drawn on for the study

Title of work	People commissioning	Who was involved	Type of work	Material generated
The National Policy work	Senior Policy Adviser in a civil service department leading on the new policy implementation, her manager and their advisory group	Myself, Michelle and Ros. Colleagues Madge and Sam took part at bidding stage	Researching and writing a 'resource' to be used by local authorities to assist in implementing a new government policy	Email correspondence between all actors over 5 months; contemporaneous personal notes of the project; taped reflective discussions held later with Michelle and Ros
The One-to-one work	Head of Research and Development for a small, developing national voluntary sector organisation	Myself only	Individual help with shifting roles and organisation development	Tape of one consulting session December 2004; continuing email correspondence on session issues/outcomes over a year
The Strategic Health Authority work	SHA Head of Modernisation with senior policy & executive colleagues, two local mental health trusts and three local authorities	Myself, Michelle and Karen	Assisting with mental health strategy development with local trusts and service users involving series of multi-stakeholder workshops	Tape of a meeting of consultant team in October 2003. Contemporaneous reflections and email correspondence between consultants over four months
The Local Authority work	Senior Policy Officer acting for the Chief Executive and leading Members of the local authority	Myself, Michelle and Alice	Development of a new policy document in consultation with key stakeholders	Tape of meeting between myself and the senior policy officer September 2003; three months' email correspondence between all of us and local authority staff; contemporaneous reflections

Table 1.1 'Live' consulting work drawn on for the study – *continued*

Title of work	People commissioning	Who was involved	Type of work	Material generated
The University work	The Head of Administration and the Dean of one Faculty of a university	Myself and Mel	Facilitation of process for team leaders to re-organise administrative teams to align more closely to student support needs	Tape of a discussion with the Head of the Faculty in July 2004; email correspondence between Mel, myself and university personnel over six months; contemporaneous reflections
The Voluntary Sector work	Policy and research leads for an established national voluntary sector organisation	Two consultants, Ros and Sally	A brief to undertake policy development including a literature review of the issue and a programme of participatory events	Email correspondence between Ros and lead commissioning person; taped reflections from Ros and written reflection from Sally

The *Strategic Health Authority work* involved a team of three consultants, working in a setting new to me (whereas my colleagues had a track record in mental health). It involved a great deal of direct work with service users, in order to influence service design and organisation. We helped managers work positively with users in active strategy development beyond traditional consultation. We ran a series of workshops across the health authority area to develop the mental health strategy, involving all the organisations in the local health economy and importantly the networks of service users that were developing strongly locally. The work was well-regarded by all the parties and the mental health user networks subsequently set up new, self-run projects.

The *Local Authority work* offered potential to contribute to community cohesion policy and local action to address social exclusion. It was challenging since the consultant team did not have a natural affinity in terms of values and beliefs with the local councillors. However work with a broad set of community stakeholders to develop the policy engaged the councillors very well and the difficulties seemed rather to be with officers inside the council.

The *University work* focused on a 'cinderella' part of a large faculty: the administrative staff. The aim was for us to develop a more student-focused administrative function with team leaders and their staff, alongside senior administrative managers. I carried out this work jointly with Mel for Laurie (with whom we had a long-standing consulting relationship) and her administration/IT manager, Stella. This was the first contact we had with Stella, who wanted support to review and re-structure her department.

The *Voluntary Sector work* did not involve me. I wanted to include a 'live' piece of work outside my direct experience. Ros and a colleague, initially Michelle and then Sally, worked with a national voluntary sector organisation to help develop a new policy on a core area of their interest. The agreed plan was for the consultants to do a literature review and run a series of participatory events around the country, then a big national event, all of which would inform the development of the new policy by the organisation. The material tracks a series of misunderstandings fuelled by time and changes in personnel which left the consultants paid less than their contract, as the people commissioning felt they had not got full delivery.

How I approached the research

I recognised early on that viewing consulting as a 'client-consultant relationship' which could be studied would not hold up as relationships

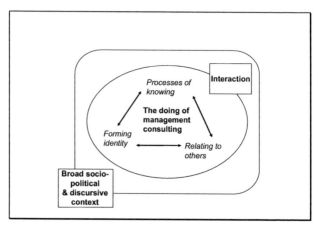

Figure 1.1   Initial framing of the consulting process

within consulting are multiple and shifting. I therefore initially considered the doing of management consulting as framed by three key processes: *relating to others, processes of knowing*, and *forming identity* (see Figure 1.1), that together constitute the interaction where/when consulting is enacted. This interaction is in turn framed by and helps constitute the broader socio-political and discursive context, that is, processes of power, culture, capital and the public policy sphere. I developed my research drawing on theory that reflects this framing: the *situated* nature of interaction and *localised* processes of power and discourse.

Researching processes

I shaped my research to explore consulting interactions by bringing a *process-based* world-view (Rescher 1996), which I felt was vital to achieving a study of interaction, together with feminist and poststructuralist approaches to the construction of meaning (Butler 1999, Fletcher 2001, Gherardi 1994, Smith 1988). This work helps escape binary thinking (Knights and Kerfoot 2004) such as male/female and draw on our more complex and multifaceted lived experience and its political context. Thus I focused on accessing daily *interaction* and explored it in discursive terms. Table 1.2 offers an overview in a nutshell.

Adopting the primacy of processes over entities offered me a powerful way to explore the doing of consulting work, a clear path to the social construction of knowing and to a focus on interaction. The process approach or 'becoming-realism' (Chia 1996) privileges *connecting acti-*

Table 1.2   In a nutshell: overview of the study

'What am I investigating?'
I am concerned fundamentally with *processes*, such as emerging relations between a variety of actors, and the ways these co-construct knowing and power, and the 'becoming' of subjectivities in interaction. I view these processes within, and contributing to, broader socio-political processes.

'What might represent knowledge or evidence of these?'
Tracking these processes over time taking account of the nature of their emergence and its impact on the actors involved. Reflexive work and contextualised material were key. Examining *interactions* was fundamental. Therefore *discourse* was taken as a key concept: involving both 'discourse' and 'Discourse' (Alvesson and Karreman 2000).

'What topic or broad substantive area am I concerned with?'
Small-scale management consulting in the public and not-for-profit sector and the interactions inside it between consultants and with those who commission us.

'What do I wish to explain? What are my research questions?'
I wanted to 'take the lid off' processes from the *inside* to explore the notion of 'critical consulting' and consultant identity. The questions I pursued are:
– What goes on in consulting interactions?
– What does it mean for (women) consultants?
– What does it mean for discourses of consulting?
– What does it mean for how (critical) consultants do their work?

'What is the purpose of my research? What am I doing it for?'
I want to understand the work processes I am enmeshed in. My broad aim is to illuminate the practice of consulting within the public/not-for-profit sector, *credibly and from the 'inside'* as a consultant myself. I acknowledge too the potential impact, both positive and negative, of pursuing this study on me and my work as a consultant – and that to achieve a positive impact was also part of my purpose.

Adapting Mason's 'difficult questions' (1996:18)

vities. It sees that these *create* actors and entities such as 'client', 'consultant', 'project'. It does not assume actors and entities are a fixed starting point, simply affected by connecting processes such as interaction, contracting and so on. In turn this sharply raises language and discourse as key to what happens, to exploring and understanding it. Critical thinking about identity also draws on discursive practices and the mutual shaping of the 'constitutive outside' in the identification process (Hall 1996).

Focusing on discourse also means taking a position on power and knowledge (Foucault 2002). So the notion of *discourse* seemed fundamental to making sense of consulting. Discourse, as expression of both language and social practice that shapes our conduct, and which we (re-)create through what we do and say, sums up much discussion about consulting that uses concepts of impression management, of professionalism and of 'knowledge work'. No contemporary studies of consulting have taken a thorough-going discourse-analytic approach to consulting work, although some have drawn on the concept of discourse to inform their theoretical position (Deetz 1998; Werr & Styre 2005).

This reinforced my choice to explore consulting processes using a discourse analytic methodology, predominantly on 'live' interactive material, researching consulting from the inside-out.

This discursive focus and the limited view of consulting history in contemporary literature also led me to develop a *genealogical review* (Foucault 1984c) of advice-giving to organisational leaders in pre-modern times, in order to give a more grounded historical perspective and illuminate present-day discourses of consulting. Building on this I used *critical discourse analysis* (Fairclough 1989, 1992, 2003) to work with my own contemporary material from consulting interactions. This approach explicitly starts from broader social and political issues in studying discourse, resonating with the politicised environment of my work in public policy and my aims for 'critical consulting.' More detailed treatment of this method is set out in Chapter 5. As you will see demonstrated in Chapters 6 and 7, critical discourse analysis (CDA) offers tools for textual analysis, while working within the broader inter-textual and socio-political context.

'Insider' research

This autoethnographic work (Hayano 1979; Reed-Danahay 1997) capturing consulting interactions as they happened in my own work is a novel approach since consultant writers have not subjected their work to such micro-analysis but simply describe it in quite broad terms (see Block 2000; Senge *et al.* 1994). Researchers into consulting also do not examine consulting processes from the inside, as they occur, but through studies based on retrospective interviews,[2] and consider that work by consultants themselves can hardly be critical (Clark 1996; Sturdy *et al.* 2006). This major gap in terms of empirical work on the *doing* of consulting is acknowledged by those in the field (Fincham and Clark 2003; Sturdy 2002; Sturdy *et al.*

2006). Thus 'insider' research (Coghlan and Brannick 2005) is potentially very important, especially of and by women, given the relative absence of women's voices in the consulting literature (see Chapter 3).

Therefore the depth of my own reflexivity was crucial for my study. For instance, I was surprised and confronted by material showing the pivotal role and proliferation of personal networks in the actual carrying out of the work, not simply in getting work; and by the power struggles and contradictions visible in my work and that I could see across our network. This encouraged me to continue to study my own practice with my colleagues, critically, reflexively, despite the dangers of producing self-referential material.

Reflexivity

The challenge in achieving an edge of productive reflexivity without sinking into self-obsession was live for me. Throughout I have commented on developing a reflexive approach, building on my personal starting points. Such 'self-conscious reference to the author by the author with the intention of disrupting the notion that texts are transparent carriers of objective truth' can be seen as a 'safe' or 'benign' way to be reflexive (Perriton 2001:36). Hertz defines reflexivity as 'an ongoing conversation about experience while simultaneously living in the moment.' (1997:viii) My journal enabled this for me, helping me look back and further reflect, the time gap helping my consulting and research work to become de-familiarised. Foucault notes (1984a:363) the ancient tradition of writing as part of formation of self, for example the ancient Greeks' writing-books that collected 'the already-said' and so constituted the self.

Reflexivity in my study aspired also to more trenchant 'textual guerrilla warfare' (Perriton 2001) in order to open my insider work to the external eye and engage in 'critical reflection'.[3] I tackled this through:

- including my contemporaneous personal reflections (or what Fairclough terms 'member resources ... what people have in their heads and draw upon when they produce or interpret texts.' (1989:24)), analysing them alongside the primary material.
- discussing the pieces of work and the insights of my analysis with colleagues.
- taping myself talking about my work, to examine my own discourse. Excerpts feature in Chapter 7.

– including 'reflection boxes' throughout this text to signal my sub-
jective thinking and reactions as I wrote and to include journal
entries.

But I also acknowledge the dangers of reflexivity in our self-obsessed
world, where this can be a highly limited form of inquiry, avoiding difficult questions in favour of 'the author's being loudest voice' (Hughes
1999:294). Holding my focus on the purposes of my consulting work
in the public and not-for-profit sectors helped me balance the focus
on self through the notion of 'critical consulting' (see Sen 1999) and
Perriton's 'socio-political' reflexive type (2001). On the other hand this
emphasises the 'local situatedness' of the study and so the limits of its
possible claims (Chia 1996).

So reflexivity is a double-edged sword: Bourdieu says of his female
students they are 'socially disposed to be too modest, too prudent, too
pernickety, taking refuge in empirical detail, minutiae'; they need to
have 'more audacity, theoretical chutzpah' (Bourdieu *et al.* 1991:256). I
aimed my reflexivity therefore to do both!

Researching women

I joined the process-based worldview to feminist work as mentioned
earlier. A feminist perspective brings a more material cast to this discourse-based study. It reflects my concerns regarding work in the
public and community sectors and the notion of 'critical consulting'
for progressive and inclusive ends. It also makes important links to
work on gender-identification and shifting selves, key to my starting
concerns. I plunged into the contested and crowded space that is the
gender literature to create a study that is:

- *not essentialist* – gendered difference is not pre-determined and
  cannot be attributed unproblematically to all men and all women
- *poststructuralist* – multiple meanings, here multiple masculinities and
  multiple femininities, co-exist and are socially constructed. Kamuf suggests we must abandon the feminine subject in favour of exploring the
  'complex forces of femininity' drawing on a Foucauldian approach to
  power and discourse (1988 cited in Metzger 1990).
- *feminist* – alongside the socially constructed gendering of society
  are clear material impacts: gender in a patriarchal world affects women
  and men differentially, and crucially affects women negatively – fem-
  inists take up the challenge of changing this power relation.

- *discursive* – acknowledging the process of gendering and gendered practice, and its situated enactment (Martin 2003); it is more than a set of skills to be learnt but must be co-created with others (Ferree 2003), and gendered 'masculine' or 'feminine' based on what a person says/does, within the constraints of the (negotiated) societal system of gender relations (Kondo 1990).
- bringing the '*sayings and doings* of gender' into theory and research (Martin 2003) about, in this case, management consulting.

As a woman consultant studying consulting interactions in my own work, my autoethnographic approach, where my insider status is 'obvious and important to [my] self identity' (Hayano 1979:100), enables women's experience to become a lens for examining what is going on in consulting. So I focus on exploring 'femininities' rather than 'gender'. For Butler, 'women constitute the *unrepresentable*. ... the sex which cannot be thought, a linguistic absence and opacity.' (1999:14 her emphasis) Here this has meant a focus on women in consulting in their own right and not solely in relation to men, drawing on Smith's feminist sociology that 'creat[es] a way of seeing, from where we actually live, into the powers, processes, and relations that organise and determine the everyday context of that seeing.' (1988:9)

Research from this perspective, termed feminist standpoint or 'women's voice' research (Calvert and Ramsey 1992, Fletcher 2001), situates critically at the line of fault between two subject positions (Smith 1988), such as woman and manager, woman and consultant. As Fletcher (2001) points out, this must be joined with a poststructuralist approach, which sees the marginalised voice as challenged and silenced by the dominant discourse and the power relations it constructs. I accomplish this joining through the autoethnographic study of actual interaction of (predominantly) women (their voices) but explored using critical discourse analysis. Martin has commented on the value of studying gender 'relative to situated interactions that occur in rapid-fire fashion and are informed by liminal awareness and nonreflexive intent' (2003:345); 'live' interactions of women in consulting fit this description. In this way I both name marginalised experience and (re)present that experience to create new discursive space (Fletcher 2001). Calvert and Ramsey emphasise the potential of a women's voice perspective for women and men:

> examination of concepts ... from the unique perspective of women's experiences can not only illuminate issues that are important to

women, but also can bring a different understanding of these concepts to men. (1992:83)

Calvert and Ramsey also carefully note the concomitant dangers of reinforcing stereotypes. Importantly such work may also change, redefine and/or completely re-cast the concepts themselves. As will become clear in Part III, this approach has indeed helped re-cast notions of what consulting work involves for women and men. But first I will turn to exploring the terrain of consulting more fundamentally.

2
Consultants, Confidantes and Consorts: A Genealogy of Consulting and Advice-Giving to Organisational Leaders

'the greatest trust between man and man is the trust of giving counsel.' (Bacon 1986:259)

Introduction

This chapter reviews historical material about/by those we can construe as consultants or advisers to organisations in the pre-modern, following Foucault's concept of 'genealogy' (Foucault 1984a, Rose 1999). Principally but not exclusively I consider individuals who advised the rulers and leaders of their time, employing 'the counsel of manners',[1] but who were not their employees. This provides me the nearest equivalent to management consulting in the public sector given the definitions explored in Chapter 1. I want to identify enduring discourses or important shifts in discourse which may illuminate current consulting interactions and the construction of consultant identities. I want to learn about women in these roles also. I am exploring the idea that consulting has existed for a lot longer than usually thought, stimulated by the rather ahistorical approach of much contemporary writing on consulting – and by my sense that at least public sector consulting has much older roots than the beginning of scientific management in the private sector, which is typically seen as the starting point for management consulting (Kubr 2002).

Contemporary writing implicitly or explicitly takes the view that consulting 'began' in late nineteenth to early twentieth century and developed alongside/in response to corporate growth, importantly post World War Two, and especially strongly from the 1980s to the present day (see for example Tisdall 1982; McKenna 2001). I question this very limited historical perspective and here explore pre-modern figures who pre-figure consultants in how they offered advice to the leaders of the most complex organisations of their day. White comments, for example, on Machiavelli that he worked with 'men who in their day were the Renaissance equivalent of Bill Gates or the Sultan of Brunei.' (2004:5)

Recently the notion that organisation studies should pay more attention to history has gained ground (Clark and Rowlinson 2004; Kieser 1994; Mutch 2005), suggesting 'more interpretive and inductive analyses' (Clark and Rowlinson 2004:332) going beyond the usual assumptions. Kieser stresses the importance of examining 'past choice opportunities' to avoid historical determinism (1994:611). This encouraged me to take a much broader view of what might constitute the genealogy of consulting than other authors have done[2] in order to unearth the discursive forebears which may illuminate contemporary thinking and my own material.

The chapter therefore examines my key concerns but from a historical perspective. That is, it views emerging relations between actors in advice-giving, the related co-construction of knowing and power, the construction of subjectivities in interaction; and links these to broader socio-political processes. It also uses situated material, the actual words of advisers where possible, in order to explore these processes. Equally this chapter holds and expresses my position that discourse is a key concept for understanding consulting processes. It also begins to explore advice gendered 'feminine' and look for traces of women's activity in the past which may illuminate the present.

There was a burgeoning premodern literature of advice to 'princes' from classical thinkers such as Aristotle, Seneca, Cicero, as well as throughout the medieval period and into the Renaissance. All the advice proffered from ancient times was twofold: how to help the prince to stay in power and how to be a virtuous leader. In drawing on their work today we must ask how far keeping power is the goal of modern managers, and how far virtue or an ethical stance is important. For many my experience suggests that survival *is* a key issue, whether in terms of surviving turbulent change and re-structuring, where keeping a job may turn on chance or favour (similar to Machiavelli's notion of 'fortuna'), or in terms of keeping a sane balance for life and work. Equally questions of ethics and where your personal 'bottom line' lies in terms of your approach to work and what being a manager or leader requires you to do in the modern organisation has produced a growing literature on business ethics, including for consultants (van Es 2002). This to some extent mirrors longstanding values of the public sector, such as service to communities, social justice.

I first set out the concept of 'genealogy' as developed by Foucault especially and how I chose to pursue it; I then present relevant material, chronologically up to the 18th century. I then turn to considering women in advising or consulting roles from queen consorts and confidantes to early women consultants.

Developing a 'genealogical' review

Burrell (1998) in considering the work of Foucault stresses the importance of:

> ...historical understanding, stemming not from an interest in the past, but from a deep commitment to understanding the present. ... concerned with genealogy ... locating traces of the present in the past... (1998:18)

Following this concept of 'genealogy', Carabine comments that Foucault examined 'the history [of the topic] for the purposes of writing 'a history of the present' ...he asks what it was in earlier periods and what it has become today.' (Carabine 2001:277)

Foucault makes clear this approach is not simply about tracing a given topic through time, assuming it exists throughout and simply evolves, but is about understanding history such that '[we] arrive at an analysis which can account for the constitution of the subject within a historical framework.' (Foucault 1984a:59) Here I am exploring the pre-modern in order to understand better how consultant as an identity is constituted and how consulting discourses may have emerged and become what they are today.

How far may a genealogy map and/or challenge taken-for-granted discourses of consulting today? Rose sees genealogy:

> ..try[ing] to trace, in very concrete and material forms, the actual history of those forms of rationality that comprise our present, the ways of thinking and acting with which they have been caught up, the practices and assemblages which they have animated, and the consequences for our understanding of our present, and of ourselves in that present...we can question our present certainties...by confronting them with their histories (Rose 1999:x)

He lists methods to uncover this socially constructed history: 'problematisation' or the criteria by which things or people, in this case consultants, come to be seen as problematic; examining how things are explained, designated, evidenced; considering techniques, apparatuses and means of doing; identifying who has authority or expertise, how they get it and keep it; exploring the selves involved, how they see the world, how they are known, what they seek to be or to achieve, what techniques of self they use and their strategies. Such work presents a genealogy which aims to provide a 'de-stabilisation or de-fatalisation of our present' (1999:xii):

> ... opening the possibility that things have been different, could have been different, ... If the history of our present is more accidental than we may like to believe, the future of our present is also more open than it sometimes appears. (1999:xii)

All this echoes Foucault's distinction between how in the past certain *acts* were criminalised, such as sodomy, rather than the modern construction and condemnation of *identities,* such as homosexual (Sullivan 2003). Butler similarly sees genealogy helpfully:

> 'investigate[s] the political stakes in designating as an *origin* and *cause* those identity categories that are in fact the *effects* of institutions, practices, discourses, with multiple and diffuse points of origin.' (1999:xxix her emphasis)

My distinction is that between *acts of advice-giving* in the past and the shift to the modern notion of '*consultant*'; to understand more about how the past has inscribed that present construct. Sullivan (2003) helpfully sums up:

> The task of the genealogist is to examine the random, provisional and often discontinuous ways in which power has functioned or been deployed and to analyse the forms of subjectivity that have been discursively constructed as a result ... to understand the present in terms of the past(s) that inscribe it. (2003:1–2)

What follows represents a first sketch of a genealogy of advice-giving to organisations. As Foucault points out (1984b), his kind of genealogy can only be sustained through tremendously detailed knowledge of original texts and comprehensive erudition. I cannot pretend to that here, as this genealogical work is contained within my broader study. But it has seemed important at least to begin such work and to profit from the insights offered about consulting using a pre-modern lens.

Tackling a genealogical review

My genealogical search has been contained by focusing predominantly on 'live' material, that is, the words of people carrying out advice-giving to those leading or managing the complex organisations of their day. This helped steer a course close to my discursive view of consulting and explore directly how notions of advice-giving and consulting may have been constituted. Focus on such material was, in the case of women, especially limiting. I am necessarily highly selective depending on accessible sources and choosing figures that seem to illuminate the aims of this genealogy.

Overwhelmingly, in the pre-modern, the 'organisations' in question are states, cities and large private landed estates. The first two immediately reflect my public sector interest. The latter for centuries represented the nearest to the private sector organisation seeking profits for its owner, but of course also enacted public services, such as the administration of justice, and were the focus of much political activity.

In looking for those who advised the leaders of these organisations, I am also searching for genuinely *external* advisers, rather than those directly beholden to or employed by the leader. Of course my view is informed by modern concepts and 'employee' is not a pre-modern concept, certainly not in (pre-)feudal times. However I distinguish between those directly paid and beholden to those who sought their advice, such as Elizabeth 1 of England's long-serving adviser Cecil, holding a paid post in her government (although his advice was often trenchantly independent nonetheless) and those remaining autonomous as advisers, often working for several people, but who may nonetheless have received payment for their services, such as Plato who advised Dion of Sicily. This is not a simple line to draw and some people worked in both capacities at different times, notably Machiavelli.

So I have worked with material in relation to *key figures*; to *key roles* I have identified; and, in the light of the importance of women advisers to my research, I sought material about and from *women*, both particular figures who were advisers or confidantes, and those in key roles such as queens consort.

Advice-giving in the ancient world

In the ancient civilisations of Egypt, Greece, Rome and China, numerous figures stand out but few have left their words behind, and those in many layered translation. After a brief overview, this section presents the words of three figures, indicating the scope of others who were advice-givers. The resonances from this time to our own are striking.

Rawson (1989) describes the scope of ancient advice-giving, such as the treatise Aristotle wrote for Alexander the Great and how the Greeks tried to persuade Roman rulers to use (Greek) philosophic advisers. She lists Areus of Alexandria advising Augustus, Dio Chrysostom advising Trajan and notes a tradition of the philosopher's letter of advice to a ruler, for example Cicero, 'himself powerless in politics, ... returned to the role of philosophic adviser ...'. (Rawson 1989:240). The interplay of issues of power and knowledge with values is visible here, along with how the provenance of ideas matters to their recipients: Rawson's observations regarding Greece and Rome parallel how the credibility of management consulting/knowledge from the USA, Europe or Asia is viewed.

In the first century BCE Gaius Maecenas was an intimate confidant and influential trusted adviser to Augustus, the first Roman emperor: he acted as the emperor's representative and chief negotiator (Kitsopoulos 2003). It is striking that the modern consultant to such a high profile leader would more likely be in the 'backroom' than visible to all, to circumvent conflicts of interest with other clients. Maecenas was differently positioned: a long-standing friend and confidant from Augustus' youth, working for the effective superpower of the day: securing other advisees was not important.

In ancient Egypt the chief adviser to Pharaoh was frequently a multi-talented individual who combined architect, soldier, patron of arts and religion and administrative roles with the ease of what we might term a 'renaissance man'. A prime example of this apparent polymathy was Senenmut, adviser to Pharaoh Hatshepsut, who as a female Pharaoh was herself highly unusual. The relics of her reign suggest his influence was resented and contemporaries assumed Senenmut had a further role as her unofficial consort and lover as well as being chief of public works and tutor to her daughter (Tyldesley 1998a). Similar advisers attached to male pharaohs, such as Imhotep with King Djoser, were not criticised but were often deified after death; some were powerful enough to estab-lish their own dynasty when the pharaoh's failed, as with Horemheb after Tutankhamun. Others were scribes (for example Amenhotep, with pharaoh Amenhotep III), the key profession of ancient Egypt which led to influence and position at court and in the priesthood, institutions with huge landed estates and building projects. Egyptian advisers were well known to the royal family, often through a family tradition of such roles and/or their children being raised alongside royal children

(Tyldesley 1998b). The importance of drawing on long-established networks is clear.

I now turn to three exemplars whose words we can access.

Mencius

Mencius or Meng K'o of 4th Century BCE according to tradition first learned from his mother, a sage in her own right (Everything2 2008). Adviser to Chinese Emperors, he valued his external adviser role and felt the need to keep separate from the king – he writes for example of how to avoid having to see the king. He tells the king never to listen directly to his counsellors when making decisions on the trustworthiness or guilt of one of his subjects, but rather see for himself and act accordingly. But he nonetheless emphasises the key role of advice:

> If a prince have not about his court ... worthy counsellors then, even if abroad there are no hostile states or other external calamities, his kingdom will generally come to ruin. (Legge 1895)

Mencius was much concerned with the good and the key role of the king in ensuring good government. However his view of advice suggests that even where there is no apparent need then it is still necessary. This may appear self-aggrandising, despite his espoused Confucian philosophy of humility and focus on the common good of all the people. Alternatively his view may stem from recognition of how competing factions arise when no external threats help the kingdom pull together; when such rivalries develop then 'counsellors' are needed.

Plato

Plato (1976) in his *'Republic'* wrote directly of his views regarding government and in his letters set out advice. In introducing *Republic*, Bambrough (*ibid*:xiii) highlights Plato's rejection of the 'unexamined life'– what we would term a lack of reflexivity. Plato's theory of forms assumes objectivity is crucial, but he blends personal issues and values with work for the public good:

> for Plato there is no inescapable distinction between knowledge and practice, between right conduct and self-fulfilment, or between the needs of the individual and the needs of society. (Plato 1976:xiv)

All this suggests many links to this inquiry about working with those managing organisations, especially those concerned with public service.

In *The Republic* Plato's words about the government of cities are relevant to the management of organisations today. Cities were the prime form of complex social organization with which leaders had to grapple and there were alternative models in existence. There were the competing discourses of Athenian democracy, Spartan totalitarianism, theocracy, tyranny etc. So in what follows, for 'cities' read 'organisations'.

I present excerpts from his dialogues in the *Republic* which express, so far as I can tell, his views about the process of advice-giving to rulers.[3]

Can anything be done as it is spoken, or is it nature that action should lay less hold of truth than speech, though not everyone thinks so? (1976:165)

This echoes for me both the criticism of the consultant that their words cut no ice in the real world, but also that to expect such direct connection between words and action is a chimera. This is also an early assertion of the primacy of words over action – the reverse of our culture today (Grant *et al.* 1998). He continues:

> **Reflection**
> *As a consultant, I think Plato's conclusion is self-evident. But for managers, their criticism of the visions we may paint, especially in management development work, of what they can aspire to, can be extreme. For example, a participant in a recent development workshop referred to 'platitudinous management speak' in dismissing all attempts to theorise and reflect on the experience of leading a public service.* (journal April 2002)

...do not compel me to show that what we have decided in our argument could in all respects be reproduced in experience. If we manage to discover how [to organise] in any close correspondence to our description, then you must allow that we have discovered that your commands could be realised. Will you not be content with that? I certainly should be.

He seems here to be arguing that the ideal (the description referred to) is unlikely ever to be wholly reproduced in reality and that if you can get even close then that is a decent result worth having. He is firm and direct in stating his view to the person in 'command'.

Plato's dialogue turns to change and sets out an interesting view:

> Then, next, apparently we must try to discover and demonstrate what evil practice in the cities of today prevents them from being organised in this [ideal] way, and what is the smallest change by which a city might arrive at this manner of [organising]. We shall hope to confine ourselves to a single change, or, if that is impossible, to two, or if that will not suffice, to changes as few in number, and small in their effect, as is possible.

This approach to change suggests that Plato both recognised issues of change (and not simply achieving stability), and saw the complexity of change very clearly and advises acting on levers for change, however small. In a sense this prefigures contemporary thinking about working with complex adaptive systems (see for example Shaw 1997). He is also approaching the problem of creating good management from a perspective of removing barriers rather than driving forward the vision, a facilitative rather than heroic approach.

Talking of the difficulty of communicating knowledge to others Plato says:

> Then what shall we do if this person is angry with us because we say that he believes but does not know and if he disputes the truth of our statement? Shall we be able to appease him and gently persuade him, without letting him know that he is barely sane? (1976:170)

Plato's confidence in his rightness alongside the contrasting intent to be 'gentle' with the person receiving advice is striking. He expresses clearly the strong emotions involved in the exchange, where he feels they are 'barely sane' but he still must 'appease'. He then discusses how he must acknowledge that the person 'knows something'. What he does

Reflection

This sums up some of the feelings I experience, at least in working with managers absolutely different in thinking from me, such as medical doctors, for many of whom any and all material from organisational theory seems to be impossible to countenance as valid. I 'know' that traditional science cannot answer the difficulties of managing change; medical doctors for their part 'know' that traditional science works for them and so want to apply this to organisations. They believe my approach is flawed, unproven and not rigorous, I believe their approach is too limited, too partial and not fit for the task. (journal entries 2002) not reconcile is how we (advisers) have such a solid view that what *we* know (and indeed *he* knows as he writes here) is 'truth' and what others know may for us be a matter of their belief, which Platonically speaking is a lesser power than that of knowledge.

While espousing ideas of change Plato always returns to the idea of universal truths. This assumes that some learning or ideas are transferable, some kinds of ultimate truth which we can offer in relation to government. His idea of the 'philosopher' is the adviser or consultant figure. However Plato's dialogue has Adeimantus comment about such people:

> .. most are very queer creatures if not rascally knaves, and the best of them seem ... to have achieved the result that they are useless to their country. (1976:179)

This is trenchant criticism that absolutely reflects much common parlance about management consultants! Plato explores how such people are almost never accepted as leaders, like the ship's navigator who is inevitably called 'star-gazer' and 'useless talker in the air' by sailors. This perhaps reflects something of the tension of knowledge and action, but also a tension between being the professional and the gaining of trust, given that one is always viewed as outside the organisation.

Plato comments on how the organisation sucks the person in, ending in corrupting their thinking. For the person trying to work with the public or 'the multitude' as he calls it: 'the fatal necessity is laid upon him of doing whatever they approve' (1976: 183). Here he acknowledges not only the pull of the 'client' but also the difficulty of holding your own views of what is right.

> **Reflection**
> *This absolutely connects with the problem of advising people who have little knowledge of the issues in question. For example, in one situation approval by someone who self-confessed to know little of education regulations threatened a learning programme's viability and so her declared aim of changing the nature of leadership in the organisation. Her control and grip on details of the consulting process undermined our sense of purpose, both for the project and for our own ends.* (Journal entries 2001–2002)

Levy (1956) sees Plato and Dion of Sicily 'hitting it off' right from their first meeting, triggering their shared, creative and prolific output of ideas about rulers and philosophy. However, this could not prevail under Dion's uncle, the actual ruler, and his *realpolitik*. When he imprisoned Dion, Plato wrote a series of letters to Dion's relatives and friends. He was imprisoned himself and once he escaped Sicily was unwilling to return, trying instead to influence from afar.

He writes in the 7th letter:

> if, while the government is being carried on methodically and in a right course, it asks advice about any details of policy, it is the part of a wise man to advise such people ...if [a person] seems likely to listen to advice about the things on which he consults me, I advise him with readiness, and do not content myself with giving him a merely perfunctory answer. (Plato 2006)

This is both careful writing to protect himself, but also expresses his belief in his right to judge those commissioning him: in the first place to decide if they are 'methodical' and 'in a right course'; and second to prejudge how far the person will act as a result. He discounts their right to decide not to act on the advice. He presumes his power to expect their action. He also implies working only in a situation already favourable to his ideas, in order to have impact, where people are 'likely to listen'. He is not framing advice as combating lack in others, but more in supporting positive work. Notably he links this to his own motivation: when he feels he will be listened to, he will offer a deeper, more developed response.

Zeno

This is 'live' material from an ancient adviser's letter of c. 277 CE to Antigonus of Macedonia, who pressed Zeno, a famous philosopher and adviser, to come to help him with his government. Zeno resisted going, primarily due to his advanced age. Here are the King's request and Zeno's response:

> *Antigonus*: "I think that in good fortune and glory I have the advantage of you; but in reason and education I am inferior to you, ... On which account I have thought it good to address you, and invite you to come to me, being convinced that you will not refuse what is asked of you. Endeavour, therefore, by all means to come to me, considering ... that you will not be the instructor of me alone, but of all the Macedonians together. For he who instructs the ruler of the Macedonians and who leads him in the path of virtue, evidently marshals all his subjects on the road to happiness."

Zeno: '…a noble nature, when it has received even a slight degree of training, and which also meets with those who will teach it abundantly, proceeds without difficulty to a perfect attainment of virtue. But I now find my bodily health impaired by old age, … on which account I am unable to come to you. But I send you some of those who have studied with me, who … are in no respect inferior to me, and in their bodily vigour are greatly my superiors.'

Antigonus sets out his and especially Zeno's accomplishments but is clear that he commands and expects Zeno to comply. He refers to the broader good that may come of advising a ruler, that one influences all the people, perhaps an attempt to persuade Zeno the project is worthwhile, or to emphasise his own power. Zeno explains his non-compliance, starting with rather a back-handed compliment to Antigonus about his 'noble nature' in relation to the 'abundant' teaching he himself could offer. This mirrors the start of the king's letter. He makes clear he cannot come and offers his protégés instead. Antigonus continued to press for Zeno himself to come, without success, influenced by Zeno's great reputation. He felt he could demand he come, persistently requiring the actual presence of the person most trusted to advise.

Early centuries in Europe

Advisers in the early centuries in Europe are dominated by monks or priests. These include: Alcuin, the confidant of Charlemagne; and in England Asser, adviser to King Alfred, William of Pagula with Edward III (Nederman 2001), John of Salisbury and Thomas Becket who advised Henry II. Women also appear, for example Abbess Hildegard of Bingen (see later section).

Crossley-Holland's medieval anthology (1984) offers letters extant from pre-conquest England – mostly of churchmen to each other or to kings. Alcuin, 'the leading scholar of his day' went to be a 'consultant' (Crossley-Holland's term) to King Charlemagne from 782. He was Charlemagne's Palace School headmaster, personal friend and taught his sons (Ritchie 2001). Below is the introduction of a long letter to the king of Northumbria, when the Vikings raided Lindisfarne in 793, arguing that the decline of standards in Northumbria led to the wrath of God via the Vikings:

…Alcuin the humble deacon sends greeting.

Mindful of your most sweet love, …I do not cease to warn you very often … either with words, when present, if God should grant it, or by letters when absent, by the inspiration of the divine spirit, and by the frequent iteration to pour forth in your ears, as we are citizens of the same country, the things known to belong to the welfare of an earthly kingdom and to the beatitude of an eternal kingdom; that the things often heard may be implanted in your mind for your good. For what is love in a friend, if it is silent on matters profitable to the friend? To what does a man owe fidelity, if not to his fatherland? To whom does he owe prosperity, if not to its citizens? We are fellow citizens ... Thus let not your kindness shrink from accepting benignly what my devotion is eager to offer for the welfare of our country. Do not think that I impute faults to you; but understand that I wish to avert penalties... (in Crossley-Holland 1984:185–186)

Interestingly he refers to connections between friends, to issues of trust and the broader public good as a rationale for intervening. Alcuin is keen to speak plainly but not to cause offence, and like Plato does not assume a lack in the king. He clearly believes in the power of repetition to get the message across. He also positions himself as equal to the king as fellow citizen. Here a dual approach of conventional humility yet sense of his own rightness is visible. He makes common cause with the king trying to build on the positive dimensions of their shared experience and values. While this may reflect the contemporary niceties of writing to a monarch and the moral certainties of a Christian, his words reflect mutual affection and close connection over time with the king. Alcuin was viewed as a leading adviser in Europe due to Charlemagne: the king would likely take his views seriously.

Another key early source is Asser's *Life of Alfred* (Crossley-Holland 1984). This excerpt shows the adviser in action as reported by himself. So we may assume he presents himself in what he thinks is the best light for an adviser to a king. It therefore illustrates how the process of advice-giving was construed at that time, albeit from churchman to monarch:

On a certain day we were both of us sitting in the king's chamber, talking on all kinds of subjects as usual, and it happened I read to him a quotation out of a certain book. While he was listening to it attentively with both ears and pondering it deeply with his inmost mind, he suddenly showed me a little book which he carried in his bosom ..., and thereupon bade me write the quotation in that book. ... Since I could find no blank space in that book wherein to write the quotation, it being all full of various matters, I delayed a little, chiefly that I might stir up the choice understanding of the king ... Upon his urging me to make haste and write it quickly, I said to him, 'are you willing that I should write [it] on some separate leaf? Perhaps we shall find one or more other such which will please you; and if that should happen, we shall be glad we have kept this by itself.' 'Your plan is good', said he. ... that same day I wrote in it, at his request, and as I had predicted, no less than three other quotations which pleased him. From that time we talked daily together ... (Crossley-Holland 1984:216)

The adviser encourages the habit of reflection and recording learning (as in the reflective diary of today's continuing professional development). The deliberateness of the adviser's actions and the carefully set scene of intimacy are noticeable. Equally Asser privileges the king – only action at his request is taken and explicitly sought. The adviser is also clear that he has more understanding or knowledge – and predicts the king's reactions. He is consciously aware of doing this; this awareness was not shared with the king. Again the certainty of the adviser is coupled with deference to the advisee.

The Renaissance

This period was one of turbulent change in Europe previously unimaginable, both socially and politically, for example the advent of the printing press,[4] 'discovering' the Americas, the rise of Protestantism. The end of the Hundred Years War in Europe and the rise of the Italian city republics with their patronage of arts and sciences liberated creativity, as well as triggering revived interest in classical times and achievements. Educated people looked to learn from the ancients but also to experience their world from new perspectives. However, we must view the 15th century in relation to the horrors of the 14th – the 'black death', long wars in Europe. In this context anyone suggesting change, outside of a monastery, was regarded with suspicion. This is a shadow perhaps still cast today on people like consultants, seen as harbingers of change.

Old Roman virtues, Greek philosophy and republican ideas all resurfaced. Advice-giving to leaders reflected this classical tradition until Machiavelli, who broke the mould of such advice. Following an exploration of his impact and approach, I turn to a more prosaic figure: the all-purpose helper of the courtier and his family in 16th century England, here exemplified by John Husee, 'Lord Lisle's man' (St Clare Byrne 1985); finally I briefly explore the role of the fool as adviser.

Niccolò Machiavelli: 'profiting from the experiences of others'

Machiavelli stands out as a figure for study. Not only was he acting as adviser and consultant to senior figures of his time but he was arguably the first to write uncompromisingly about the realities of working in organisations as he saw them. He has been much criticised over the centuries for writing and publishing what others knew but perhaps dared not say (the view of his recent biographer Michael White (2004) who tries to rehabilitate Machiavelli in modern eyes). His work has never to this day been out of print since first published, which makes his work key in the emergence of discourse about organisations and management. I explore here his specific words about advice-giving, especially regarding his own work when independently commissioned by others.

Machiavelli (2001) discusses the role of advice and advisers, focusing on those commissioning advice. Typically prior writers advised their prince to be transparent and ask for the truth at all times from all people, be approachable and affable to encourage this. Machiavelli sees this as a route to contempt: if everyone can say what they like to the prince, he will soon lose their respect and become an object of contempt. So from observing actual princes in action he advises: only listen to a few advisers, only consult them on topics you are interested in, that contempt is provoked by those who seem 'changeable, pusillanimous and irresolute'.

> A ruler, then, should never lack advice, but should have it when he wants it, not when others want to give it; rather he should discourage anyone from giving advice uninvited. Nevertheless, he should be very ready to seek information and opinions and listen patiently to candid views about matters that he raises. Indeed, if he learns that anyone is reticent for any reason, he should be angry. (2001:82)

He clearly acknowledges strong feelings such as trust and anger in the process of advice-giving. He is clear that getting good advice and good advisers is a function of the shrewdness of the ruler; it is a key necessity (2001:80), echoing the earlier views of Mencius. But like him Machiavelli may promote his own interests (Anglo 1971) in saying this, for he writes in the margin of his letter to his client Soderini in 1506:

> Do not advise anyone, or take advice from anyone, except in very general terms; everyone should act as his spirit moves him and audaciously. (2001:97)

He seems to conclude that no matter what policy you follow, follow it wholeheartedly and fully. He asserts that being seen to achieve results is the most important because that is all most people can access – your image and impression rather than what or who you actually are. He also places much importance on reading the times and acting in tune with them. These are current issues for managers and people who commission consulting: being *seen* to deliver is critical to the modern (managerial) government's performance management and media management strategies.

His views on the role of adviser in relation to his own experience of advice-giving, emerge in a letter to Francesco Vettori 1513, where he talks about securing work with the new Medici rulers of Florence following their overthrow of his previous patron, Soderini. He agonises about the *Prince* and whether to present it in person or send it, and how presenting it may help him secure some money, given his pressing needs:

> if my present condition persists for very long my poverty will make me despised... there is also my desire that these Medici rulers should begin to use me, even if they should start by making me roll a stone. [ie do something unimportant] If I did not then win them over, I should only have myself to blame. This work, if they should read it, will reveal that I have not been asleep or wasted my time during the fifteen years I have been engaged in studying statecraft. And anyone should very much want to be served by a man who is very knowledgeable through profiting from the experiences of others. (2001:93–95)

He is espousing the 'foot in the door' approach here, as well as a sense of the importance of perception in setting a price on his services, redolent of modern marketing. But also interestingly he is assuming his power in making the relationship face-to-face will seal the contract, regardless of the purposes of the ruler himself. Machiavelli was seen as convincing and persuasive in person by his contemporaries: after meeting him, Pope Clement VII, previously linked to his opponents, thenceforth used Machiavelli as adviser (White 2004). He also assumes a unitary view, of having the same purposes as the ruler – which may be valid for the time, but different from personal views expressed in his 'Discourses' (Crick 1970) about republicanism as a preferable form of government. He also sees his prior service as primarily 'study'. What would Soderini have called it?

Machiavelli was commissioned in 1521 by a Florentine council, following his years as unemployed writer, to resolve a dispute with the

Franciscan monks of Carpi. While he 'held the clergy in very low regard' Machiavelli 'was in no position to spurn the offer' (White 2004:2). The monks' leader felt Machiavelli was too low rank to deal with this issue and prevaricated. Machiavelli meanwhile sent his powerful friend, Guicciardini, letters criticising the monks. Guicciardini paid for despatch riders to arrive up to three times per day, which impressed the monks. Machiavelli asked Guicciardini to send one letter by a crossbowman in full livery on a lathered horse in the middle of a session with the monks. Machiavelli told them these were important letters regarding the Holy Roman Emperor and King of France. This impression management seems to have worked and is a striking early example of image manipulation.

Machiavelli's commission in 1520 to write the history of Florence is interesting for the complexity of its setting up. Those commissioning were the Studio Fiorentino and the university but the Medici (via Pope Leo X) were the funders. Machiavelli was asked to draft the contract for his work himself. He wrote that the contractor would do the history: 'from whatever time may seem to him most appropriate, and in whatsoever language – either Latin or Tuscan – may seem best to him.' (Letter to Francesco Nero 1520 in White 2004:233)

> **Reflection**
> *Shades of much of my work where if I want a contract or proper letter I have to draft it for the person commissioning to sign – I have four such outstanding at the time of writing!*

In writing the history he grapples with pleasing all involved yet being 'true':

> I shall continue to seek advice from myself, and I shall try to do my best to arrange it so that – telling the truth – no one will have anything to complain about. (White 2004:236 quoting letter to Guicciardini 1524)

The confidence of the consultant in both setting the boundaries of the contract and in 'seeking advice' from himself are notable here. This reflects the theme of certainty of their own views that we have repeatedly seen from the premodern advisers – and hence perhaps the space he took to determine a complex piece of work.

Machiavelli was not a lawyer (common training of the diplomat or adviser to kings) and had little experience on starting out other than 'a set of very useful contacts and a talent for networking' (White 2004:46).

He relies on his friends, the Vettori, to make links to Rome when he is out of work in 1514. The power of the Medici not to employ him is described in terms of their 'distrust' and that his views and theirs on issues like religion were at odds. Lorenzo Medici in 1516–17 would not use him – he already had his trusted advisers. Machiavelli turns down two rich permanent jobs in 1521 on the back of his 'consulting' commissions being by then more important to him. In his latter years Machiavelli was the leading light of the Rucellai group – a learning network where he acted as a mentor to younger men.

The position of Machiavelli in relation to people who commissioned him is contradictory and perhaps challenges the tradition of humility that went before. For example in his dedication of the *Prince* he writes:

> Nor I hope will it be considered presumptuous for a man of low and humble status to dare discuss and lay down the law about how princes should rule; ... to comprehend fully the nature of the people, one must be a prince, and to comprehend fully the nature of princes one must be an ordinary citizen. (White 2004:202)

John Husee: 'I do write your ladyship my mind ...'

'My Lord Lisle's man', John Husee worked for the Lisle family during the reign of Henry VIII in England. The Lisle Letters (see St Clare Byrne 1985) are a key primary source regarding Henry's court and its politics. Lord Lisle needed advice being a minor remaining relative of the preceding Yorkist/Plantagenet dynasty and Husee was his faithful 'man' over considerable years, corresponding regularly with all members of the family on a wide range of issues. He seems to have acted as a self-employed agent or life style adviser, doing everything from lobby government to organise the purchase of children's clothes. He organises the constant sending of gifts to people the Lisles feel they owe social obligation or with whom they want to connect – their relatives but also a broader social network. Husee seems to have also worked for the king or others of the king's retinue. He refused a position as the Lisle's full-time steward. He was based in London, in the centre of things, working out of the Red Lion Inn at Southwark – an early 'serviced office' space. St Clare Byrne believes he:

> knew, as well as anyone outside the circle of power could know, what was likely to happen, and could often see one move ahead so that a 'petitorie' epistle could arrive at the crucial moment. ...one of those young-old men who always profit from and learn by any

experience the first time it is encountered. As the years go by, his relations with both [Lady Lisle] and her husband become more personal, more affectionate and confidential; but he never takes advantage of the increasing intimacy to bate one jot of the respect due [the Lisles]. (1985:50)

The excerpts here show a glimpse of his role and how he carried it out. First in a letter from Husee to Lady Lisle he acts as human resource agency, gift adviser and refuses a permanent post for himself:

Pleaseth your ladyship to be advertised I have received your sundry letters. Answering first touching your gentlewoman, I am sorry she [pleaseth] your ladyship no better. Randall and I will do our best in procuring of such a one as your ladyship desireth, which will be hard to come by...

And as touching your monkey, of a truth madam, the Queen [Anne Boleyn] loveth no such beasts nor can scant abide the sight of them ...

Madam, I do humbly thank your ladyship for the offer of your stewardship, but surely it is no room for me, for I have no such knowledge or experience in that office... It is a room for some wise man being exercised and learned of continuance in the same, having great experiences ... And xx or xl marks were well bestowed on such one, being expert, for his year's wages. I do write your ladyship my mind in this behalf.. (Letter to Lady Lisle 21 July 1535 in St Clare Byrne 1985:109)

Here Husee shows a fascinating mix of blunt statements and modesty touching on the obsequious. He gives clear advice in strong terms and signals problems ahead for her ladyship – and possibly the escalating cost of securing a suitable maid. He also self deprecatingly refuses the post offered, interestingly using the metaphor of a 'room' as though he sees this as somehow joining the household in a way he feels he cannot or doesn't wish to do. He nonetheless immediately offers his advice on the pay for such a person and clearly signals it as reflecting a matter of knowledge and experience which he feels he does not have.

In a letter from Husee to Lord Lisle, he advises Lisle how to get his request actually read by the king following a first draft. He comments exactly as though briefing someone to influence a modern chief executive:

> But meanwhile I have drawn a letter to the king, which I do send your lordship herewith, so that if the contents thereof do like you may please your lordship to cause the same to be new written and fair penned, and written in as little space and as few lines as it conveniently may be, being legible, to the end that his Grace may read the same himself; and then your lordship to make up the same and send it to me with all speed. ... and in case your lordship do alter the said letter ... then to send me the copy thereof, to the end that if his Grace would reason anything therein, I might be prompt and prevented [forewarned] to make him a direct answer. And now that I have written your lordship my poor mind, it lieth in you to follow what best liketh you ... (Letter to Lord Lisle June 1536 in St Clare Byrne 1985:353–354)

This letter again emphasises the directness of his advice while keeping Lord Lisle as the one who decides – at least in the rhetoric of what he writes. He is careful to give reasons for his suggestions, painting a clear picture of the busy monarch and the need to consider him as reader. He also makes clear his own expert knowledge of this process. Husee writes to Lady Lisle in 1536, frustrated with the progress of matters at court:

> ... I have there followed and spent all time in vain, for I can there speed of nothing nor have any comfort ...; one thing assuring your ladyship, unless my lord procure new friends he shall do little good at their hands that he now taketh to be his friends, for here is nothing but everyone for himself. Madame, I am at my wits' end for payment of this money, for unless God help I see no remedy ... But in the meantime I will do the best I can. I assure your ladyship this matter grieveth me as much as anything that ever I had in hand ...
> (Letter to Lady Lisle 18 September 1536 in St Clare Byrne 1985:354)

Here we gain a sense of the dangers Husee is fronting for the Lisles and the emotions this entails for him. He again writes directly of what is needed and attempts to influence the lady so that she will in turn advise her husband to act and develop friends at court.

Fools and jesters

Turning to a different kind of adviser role, the jester or fool, which has
existed for centuries alongside rulers in almost every culture around
the world (Otto 2001), here I refer to Will Somers, jester to Henry VIII.

> But this Will Summers [sic] was of an easie nature, and tractable dis-
> position, who ... gained not only grace and favour from his Majesty,
> but a general love of the Nobility; for he was no carry-tale, nor whis-
> perer, nor flattering insinuater, to breed discord and dissension, but an
> honest plain down-right, that would speak home without halting, and
> tell the truth of purpose to shame the Devil; so that his plainness mixt
> with a kind of facetiousness, and tartness with pleasantness made him
> very acceptable into the companies of all men. (A Pleasant History of
> the Life and Death of Will Summers (1676) quoted in Otto 2001:233)

Otto points out how the jester was at the same time 'an isolated and
peripheral figure somehow detached from the intrigues of the court'
but also a trusted intimate. She comments that their trenchant criticism and pointed comments to the ruler were made possible by this
separation but also

> because of the trust that could exist between king and fool – part of
> the jester's role included that of confidant. And of course candor
> itself can be disarming, particularly when combined with the ten-
> dency among jesters to be true to themselves and hang the con-
> sequences. (Otto 2001:238)

Her view is that jesters could do this as fundamentally they were not
interested in power, they were not about to overthrow the king. They
were an established, different type of adviser that could use humour to
say the unsayable. Kets de Vries (1990) explores the jester role referring
explicitly to consultants. For him the jester is 'truthsayer' and a means
of keeping the leader in touch with reality.

> both underdog and culture hero, ... who provides order out of chaos
> by connecting the unexplainable to the familiar...the privileged critic,
> a paradoxical figure both depreciated and appreciated... the disinter-
> ested truthsayer who speaks frankly about how things really are.
> (1990:759)

The paradox of how people feel about the fool is expressed in positive
and negative images held at once. He asserts that the knowledge of the

fool is to make links obscure to others as well as to reflect reality. De Vries comments that insiders take risks in this role and so mostly outsiders do it: 'frequently taken on by a consultant' (1990:761), and especially 'the consultant in the role of the fool as catalyst (1990:765). So the fool or jester offers a different view of advice-giving as outside the power play of the patron, essentially an outsider role but one with catalysing potential through a capacity to simplify and reflect back reality to others. The assumption here of a 'truth' that can be 'said' is also striking.

Towards the modern: 17ᵗʰ and 18ᵗʰ centuries

Examples of the adviser we have seen so far, trusted and intimate with a range of experience and skills, continue into 17ᵗʰ and 18ᵗʰ centuries. Two examples illustrate this. In the 17ᵗʰ century, Père Joseph was the confidant and highly appreciated adviser to Cardinal Richelieu. Due to Père Joseph's extensive experience in diplomatic missions to many European courts, Richelieu when prime minister, invited him to come to the court as his consultant, saying:

> God designated you as his principal agent to guide me through all the high positions I had the honor to occupy, I beg you to come immediately and share with me the management of our current affairs. There are pressing issues, which I would neither assign to anyone else nor resolve without you. (quoted in Kitzopoulos 2003)

Here Richlieu shifts the ground from advice to 'sharing' the work and conveys his substantial admiration of Joseph. It is clear that this commission is including implementation as well as advice; they are to work together.

In the 18th century, Johann Wolfgang Goethe worked with Duke Carl August of Weimar. Goethe was a trained lawyer but also a poet, writer, and scientist in the 'renaissance man' mould of pre-modern advisers. Working closely with the Duke, he developed a strong relationship of trust and ended up as finance minister. Kitzopoulos (2003) comments on the contrast between Goethe and 'today's highly specialised management consultants'.

In addition the 17ᵗʰ and 18ᵗʰ centuries saw the rise of professions and the formation of key aspects of how we view the term 'profession' today. These developments are important for this genealogy given current debate on management and consulting as professions. The influence of humanist ideas in the development of the professions was important: the professional acts 'for the good of society as well as ... his and his family's interests' (O'Day 2000:28). Equally as professions developed, the tension between theory and practice was noted:

> be sure not to study much bookes of learning for they divert busnes take up the memory too much, and keepe one from more useful things. (Sir William Drake's journal 1631–42 quoted O'Day 2000:29)

O'Day comments that anti-professional feeling grew as professions were established. They were seen as a monopoly exploiting need. Knowledge was made a 'mystery', as the trades of medieval times were termed 'the mysteries'. There were assaults on professionals writing in Latin through 'vitriolic attacks' (2000:15): the negativity around professions with distinctive terminologies is not new. She goes on: 'They possessed the skill to offer advice in given areas of life, not to do anything..' (2000:25), here highlighting a distinction between talk and action. Their status derived from activity that was not manual and so not viewed as 'work' but as skill. Thus the professions were seen as offering 'skilled service ... in ways more highly esteemed socially than ... trades and crafts' (Holmes 1982:3) Increasingly such early professionals were 'keeping the wheel turning full circle...[and] patronised... increasingly their fellow professionals' (Holmes 1982:14). Holmes sees increasing wealth as the colonies expanded and Britain developed international trade fuelling this rise in professional people, who all used each others' services in a network of mutual benefit.

Women's roles: from confidantes and consorts to consultants

Looking to the premodern, in advising the leaders of the major organisations of the day, the forerunners to women consultants were the wives of male leaders. Typically the intimate relationship of the wife (or mistress) and her access to the details of what went on in the organisation – be it city, state or estate – mirrored the trusting relationship cultivated by the more visible adviser figure who was usually male. For every Machiavelli we can identify an Eleanor of Aquitaine, for every powerful Cardinal a queen consort with the king's ear.

Women have figured little in this review so far, partly since finding their words directly recorded in history is a relative rarity. I also decided to collect all references to women in one section to ask specifically what we can learn about women advisers of the pre-modern. This section reviews early figures, confidantes and consorts (chiefly queens and mistresses of kings), the salonnières of the 17th and 18th centuries and finally early management consultants.

Early figures

One of the earliest figures is Hildegard of Bingen (11th–12th centuries) who was so popular with leaders in Europe that she did four lecture tours: 'an unimaginable undertaking in the early Middle Ages, particularly for an ageing woman in poor health.' (Diehl and Donnelly 2002:58) She wrote to a patron:

> I am not accustomed to speak of the various elements in the lives of men and what their future will be. For poor little untaught feminine form that I am, I can know only those things that I am taught in a true vision. (Diehl and Donnelly 2002:58)

It was apparently a frequent device of hers to speak as unworthy and humble to avoid criticism and to be respected for humility – and interesting that here she names her position as a woman and as a passive vessel for 'true vision'. Her tone of humility thus contrasts with that of Alcuin, seen earlier, in its gendered nature, although both take the humble initial tone conventional for the time in addressing important personages and in enacting the identity of churchman or nun.

Christine de Pizan was born at the end of the 14th century and famously wrote her *Treasury of the City of Ladies* reviewing history from women's point of view. The Italian widow of a French courtier, she earned her living from writing and also wrote advising women on their roles (Leyser 1995). She was invited to England by Henry IV but never went. Her *Book of Deeds of Arms and Chivalry* of 1410 (Willard 1984), was very popular and unique in being written by a woman yet presenting substantial and pragmatic detail about how to pursue war – notably she advises not to do it without plenty of money and men to back you (Barker 2005). The book was one of the first Caxton printed such was demand.

Few other figures can be seen in these early centuries until we recognise the women who were the consorts, confidantes and mistresses of rulers.

Confidantes and consorts: 'I plainly tell you ...'

Most hidden, and yet perhaps most obvious, as female advisers in the pre-modern are women who had the king's ear and so influence their husbands, lovers, sons and brothers: consort queens and mistresses. This section will show how these women carried out the role of adviser principally through working on relationships; how they were nonetheless viewed as distant and Other; how they carried out a key role of intercession linked to the values of upholding the rights of the common person against sovereign power; how they struggled to be paid their due; and how they were (and some still are) often perceived negatively.

Consort queens are universally one of two types: the foreign princess or the home-grown. This distinction explains how different queens have been viewed in terms of their influence over kings. They nonetheless share key features: Leyser (1995) discusses foreign princesses:

> as foreigners .. a likely target for criticism. Perhaps this was part of the job ... [occupying] so distinctive a space as both consort and outsider ... [with] tasks only they could perform... [the] shield of the king, taking on their own shoulders some of the criticism of his handling of affairs (1995:84–86)

She expresses the paradox of being close and intimate to the king yet perpetually distant and never actually an insider. Eleanor of Castile was loved by the populace and Edward I of England but at the same time 'in certain circles, resented and reviled both as a foreigner and as a spendthrift.' (Leyser 1995:84–85) However the view that it was part of the job to be foreign and distant created problems for the home-grown consort. Women in this position seem to come in for more, and more unwarranted, criticism than foreign consorts; for example Elizabeth Woodville, English queen to Edward IV, was heavily criticised for promoting her relatives and for extravagance. However she had one of the smallest, most solvent households of any queen and her relatives did not earn more than those of other queens (Crawford 1994), nor did she promote as many as others did, such as Eleanor of Provence (queen to Henry III) with her Savoyard friends and relatives (Howell 1998).

Exploring the interesting space occupied by queens consort suggests it may both prefigure and construct the resentment of close trusted advisers in general. One cannot criticise the king so the queen is criticised for her influence, as one of his 'evil counsellors'. I will refer to several very different queens to develop this exploration.

Some of the earliest consorts whom we know had influence are from ancient Egypt: Nefertari, wife of Ramses II, and Nefertiti, wife of Ahkenaten. It is possible that their influence is known due to the ripples it caused at the time, since neither of them were pharaoh's sister (and so above criticism) nor a foreign princess, and so must have been Egyptian. Working out their parentage has in fact occupied numerous Egyptologists to this day (Tyldesley 1998a). For Nefertiti, her apparent influence has led to assertions that she led Ahkenaten into his religious revolution of monotheistic sun worship. A tomb inscription about her shows an early example of the key queenly role of intercession for others with the king: 'may she grant the entrance of favour ... and a happy recollection in the presence of the king' (Tyldesley 1998b:81). Her influence also features on a statuette inscription: 'one trusted of the king ... great in his lifetime' (Tyldesley 1998b:151) This reminds us that a queen only had influence so long as the king existed – however the king could of course be husband or son of the queen.

Howell (1998), only biographer of Eleanor of Provence, comments that contemporary chroniclers like Matthew Paris wrote of real queens differently from the typical mode of allegory with the Virgin and intercession linked to humility. Paris described Blanche of Castile, Eleanor's mother, as 'sexu femina, concilio mascula' [in sex female, in advice male] (1998:260) making the issue of gender explicit. Queens in 11th and early 12th century Europe were active in governing with the king, for example Matilda with William the Conqueror. They were not servile and were simply an alternative to the legalistic power of the king – interceding more personally for individuals. This feature extended to other royal women not just the queen. Equally there was 'a mass of male intercessors' (1998:258) so again the women simply stand out by their rarity relatively.

Philippa of Hainault and her intercession for the burghers of Calais shows the king can choose to listen or not: if he does there is no loss of face and no precedent is set – the argument has to be made again in the future. This view of the person receiving advice suggests it does not show weakness to use advice. Philippa intervened strongly yet was 'at the same time ... humble and pregnant'. (Leyser 1995:86) The source of her power remains unclear – that of queen or of symbolic woman-in-a-vulnerable-state. All her extant letters are written on behalf of others, pleading a cause, such as to release from prison, welfare of a ward, extortion of more fines than proper and so on. Similarly Leyser (1995) compares queens with Mary as queen of heaven and intercessor, and with Esther in the Old Testament 'at one and the same time wise counsellor to her king and abject suppliant' (1995:85).

Princess Joan, widow of the Black Prince and her daughter-in-law Anne of Bohemia intervened in the fate of John Wyclif, the religious reformer, despite the orthodoxy of King Richard II (Crawford 1994:17). To challenge the king on matters of religion was a major undertaking and demonstrates their strength and certainty. The important aspect of queenly intercession or mediation is taking up the cause of the ordinary (not royal) person, someone with less power. Londoners expressed this public expectation in their Bill to Queen Anne in 1382, they wished her to 'assume ... the role of mediatrix between your most illustrious prince [and ourselves]' (Leyser 1995:86) as her predecessors had done. Anne subsequently acquired a reputation as mediator with the king (Crawford 1994).

English queens were entitled to 'queen's gold', a tax collected on certain legal transactions and due to the queen. With it she could acquire and dispose of estates, in addition to her dower lands. Until the late 19th century only the queen, as a married woman, could thus hold and dispose of property. However much extant correspondence of queens from 12th to

> **Reflection**
> *Shades of clients paying us when they are 'not too busy' as one emailed to us after a piece of work was complete! Extracting payment can seem a full-time occupation on some pieces of work.*

16th century concerns problems in accessing and retaining this money and land, even for very powerful women such as Eleanor of Aquitaine or Margaret of Anjou (Crawford 1994). These resources were their right but seem to have come at the end of other priorities for the king or his ministers. Clearly this reflects something of the marginality of the queen's power, yet the awareness and determination of queens that this is a key right, as well as the reluctance of men to pay them. I shall now turn to the actual words of queens consort, taken from their letters, to explore their advice-giving and related roles.

Matilda, queen of Henry I of England, was highly educated and caring of ordinary people – she built St Giles Hospital and roads and bridges in the Lea Valley. Henry appointed her regent in his absences and so clearly trusted her. Chronicler Robert of Gloucester praised her influence: 'the goodness she did to England cannot be here written nor by any man understood.'(quoted in Crawford 1994:21) Her letters are the earliest English queen's letters extant and seem to have been dictated by her. She writes here to Anselm, Archbishop of Canterbury, in exile due to a breakdown in relations in the previous reign, still not resolved. Matilda was close to Anselm who had helped achieve her marriage. She writes about how she is trying to influence the king:

I am encouraged to hope [for your return] from the confidence which I have in the prayers of good men, and from the good will which, by skilfully investigating, I find to be in the heart of my lord [i.e. the king]. His mind is better disposed towards you than many men think; and, I favouring it, and suggesting wherever I can, he will become yet more courteous and reconciled to you.' (Letter from Matilda wife to Henry I to Anselm Archbishop of Canterbury c.1103 in Crawford 1994:22)

She gives a picture of subtle indirect influence; she recognises her skill in both questioning and suggesting, yet is clear that her favour alone has some influence with the king. Her daughter, Empress Matilda coincidentally had a similar mission in her turn. She writes to Thomas Becket to try to broker peace between him and Henry II:

my lord Pope sent to me, enjoining me, ... to interfere to renew peace and concord between you and the king, my son... You, as you well know, have asked the same thing from me; wherefore, with the more goodwill, for the honour of God and the Holy church, I have begun and carefully treated of that affair. But it seems a very hard thing to the king ... seeing he so loved and honoured you ... believing he might trust you rather than any other; and ... he declares that you have ... roused his whole kingdom against him; nor was it your fault that you did not disinherit him by main force [in other words he nearly did!] .... One thing I plainly tell you, that you cannot recover the king's favour, except by great humility and most evident moderation. (Letter from Empress Matilda to Thomas Becket 1185 in Crawford 1994:28–29)

The Empress speaks bluntly and makes clear her multiple roles and loyalties. She emphasises taking great care and talks of the trust connecting advisers to the king. She sets out reasons for the enmity and impresses on Thomas how close he came to destroying the king – implying that this would have been in no one's best interests. She is clear in her advice: 'I plainly tell you'. It is noteworthy that both queens are influencing to mend relationships between the major power centres of the day: church and sovereign, at the request of the men involved, including the Pope himself.

Eleanor of Provence writes regarding her task in Henry III's absence of raising money for his defence of Gascony:

...all the earls and barons of your kingdom, who are able to cross the sea, will come to you in Gascony, with all their power; but from the other laymen ... we do not think that we can obtain any help of your use, unless you write to your lieutenants in England firmly your great charters of liberties, and let this be distinctly perceived by your letters to each sheriff... and publicly proclaimed ...since by this means they would be more strongly animated cheerfully to grant you aid ... we shall hold a conference ... about the aforesaid aid and we supplicate your lordship that you will write us your good pleasure concerning these affairs with utmost haste. For you will find us prepared and devoted according to our power to solicit the aforesaid aid for your use and to do and procure all other things ... which can contribute to your convenience and the increase of your honour. (Letter from Eleanor to Henry III 13 February 1254 in Crawford 1994:74)

Eleanor is stating her advice unequivocally: 'we do not think', 'distinctly perceived', 'we shall hold', 'utmost haste'. She is spelling out how people feel about what he has asked her to do and its consequences. At the same time she keeps the deference of the adviser and consort in the final lines.

Katherine of Aragon wrote letters as regent during war with Scotland when Henry VIII was in France at the Field of Cloth of Gold in 1513. Here writing to Wolsey she makes clear she wants to amend a decision about a noble French hostage. She points out the inconvenience; she will house him in the Tower:

Here is none that is good for it [guarding the Duke] but my lord Mountjoy, who now goes to Calais [i.e. to join Henry] as chief captain of 500 men. And for this cause and also that I am not so well accompanied as were convenient for his keeping here, it is thought to me and my council that it should be better the said duke be, as soon as he comes, conveyed to the Tower; especially the Scots being so busy as they now be and I looking for my departing every hour, it should be a great incumbrance to me ... I pray you shew this to the king ... Letter from Katherine to Wolsey 1513 (Crawford 1994:172)

Katherine writes in delicate and careful understatements. She distances and qualifies her views: 'not so well', 'it is thought', 'it should be better'. She bolsters her position by making clear both she and her council think this. She talks of the Scots as 'busy' which plays down the dangers of the war and the coming battle (which was the famous victory of Flodden). Yet she conveys clearly what she will not accept ('great incumbrance') given what else the king is asking her to manage. She asks Wolsey to show this to the king, perhaps to make clear that she is not complaining to the king himself but would like him to know with what she has to contend.

Philip of Spain, consort to Mary Tudor, presents a marked contrast to these queens. Kamen, his biographer (1997) comments that Philip had no power to intercede in Mary's executions of Protestants – he worked indirectly, his chaplain preaching against this. He also is known habitually to have referred matters to the queen, staying 'detached from affairs' (Kamen 1997:62). This differs from the intercessive role of consort queens and their involvement on behalf of the king in matters of state. Unlike foreign queens who were often unpopular, Philip seems to have been popular, except for his Spanish retinue. This may be another example of criticism of followers to avoid criticism of the king – Philip was king of Spain in his own right and thus seen as much more powerful than a consort queen. This probably influenced his decision not to be (seen as) a major influence on Mary and so upset the power balance in England. Philip's approach makes clear the woman consort has a different approach to the role, by expectation of others as well as in how she can act.

Alongside the consort queens, it is important to note the similar role of influential mistresses. The names of these women are numerous and many are attributed with substantial influence, such as Madame de Pompadour, Madame de Montespan in France. Two examples are noteworthy here for their acknowledged and more public advisory roles. Diane de Poitiers, the long-established mistress of Henri II in 16th century France was much older than him and acquired such influence that letters of state were signed in the joint made-up name of 'HenriDiane'. Her intelligence was considerable and like other advisers she was also in charge of the royal children's education (Kent 2004).

The second example concerns George I who came to England with two women in his 'inner German court' (Beattie 1967): Fraulein von der Schulenberg, later Duchess of Kendal, who it is widely thought was married to the king, and Sophie-Charlotte von Kielmannsegge, thought to have been his half sister, being the daughter of his father's mistress. Both were assumed his mistresses at the time of their arrival with him, perceived as close to George and so influential they were cultivated by courtiers and politicians. The Duchess was more influential especially in later in the reign. The king always dined with her. Ministers took to 'mention[ing]' to the duchess things they wanted the king to agree: for example Stanhope writes to Sunderland in 1719:

> I have mentioned to the dutchess [sic] ... and she has promised and judges it most proper to open it herself first to the king. (Quoted in Beattie 1967:241–242)

She became progressively more important politically once the Walpole administration was established after 1722. She was however seen as actively profiting from her close position as favourite, receiving payments from those she assisted. The French king Louis XV wrote to his ambassador in 1724:

> There is no room to doubt that the duchess of Kendal, having a great ascendancy over the King of Great Britain, and maintaining a strict union with his ministers, must materially influence their principal resolutions. You will neglect nothing to acquire a share of her confidence, from a conviction that nothing can be more conducive to my interests. (Quoted in Beattie 1967:247)

Here she is clearly seen as critically influential – how far this was perception or reality is a moot point for Beattie. He sees her as a linking person primarily, a conduit, especially for 'delicate subjects' – this may be his own (gendered) view. Walpole said (reported in Lady Cowper's diary) that she was 'in effect, as much Queen of England as any ever was' (Beattie 1967:248).

Brown (1999) considers the intimate confidante in exploring the roles and influence of Elizabeth I's ladies of the Privy Chamber. Until Mary Tudor and Elizabeth these roles did not exist. Posts in the Privy Chamber were held by men senior in the kingdom and able to companion the king, for example being near in age. So Elizabeth especially was largely breaking new ground. She 'forbade her women to participate in politics' and to concentrate on personal tasks and service. This prohibition suggests political involvement was occurring and she may have been covering herself and the women. Her women 'had an important role in the critical management of access [to Elizabeth]' (1999:132) and 'as barometers of her moods' (Mears 2005:68). Brown emphasises the constancy of these women around Elizabeth (in 44 years only 28 women held 16 positions) and their 'elaborate network of influence and political interconnection based primarily on [direct] kinship relations' (Brown 1999:132) to the Queen rather than connections through their husbands. In this way public and private realms were inseparable for the queen. The women's influence is private but others acknowledged it: Sir Robert Sidney's agent, Whyte, describes Sidney's aunts' role in the Privy Chamber. Lady Huntingdon for example offered advice about approaching the Queen.

> [she] is resolute not to deliver your leter to the Queen till there be cawse ... and yf need be she will thoroughly deale with the Queen about yt.
>
> Letter from Whyte (quoted Mears 2005:133)

This closeness and intimacy with the Queen enabled the women to benefit their own networks/relatives through procuring helpful god-parents, advantageous marriages and so on. Similar trust networks with her formal, visible, male 'counsellors' are reported, with a blurring between Elizabeth seeking advice or it being offered unsolicited in 'an ongoing process' (Mears 2005:50). Along with the close relationships discussed above, Mears comments that both female and male advisers to Elizabeth held 'a shared perception of political issues' (2005:57) and that their own trusted networks, not wholly coterminous with hers, contributed to what they did. Importantly the controversial nature of women's involvement in policy persisted and affected Queen Anne and Sarah Churchill, her intimate, over a hundred years later (Mears 2005).

We can see then that consorts and confidantes hold an intimate place in the history of advice-giving. They may epitomise the trusted adviser who can speak out strongly, yet they are dependent on the monarch and must defer to his/her power. They are concerned with emotions and rela-tionships as well as with policy. They have taken an intermediary role, often on behalf of those with less power and for whom it would be dif-ficult to reach the king. They have been the subject of resentment and unpopularity, in effect absorbing criticism that may otherwise be directed at the monarch. To some extent this is seen as their role, especially the foreign queen as the perennial outsider. In addition, the gains, whether monetary or otherwise, of the consorts and advisers as a result of their positions feature in what is written about them and in what they say, much as the fees of modern consultants are subject to comment.

Salonnières

In discussing the professionals of the 17th and 18th centuries earlier, effectively I describe the activities of men. But in this period a new arena developed for women[5] – a space between the public and private spheres. Salon hostesses from early 18th century onwards presided over groups of (mostly) men active in both arts and sciences and Enlightenment thought generally. Such women, usually of independent wealth, wielded much influence as their confidantes and advisers, albeit in a subtle, nuanced form. Women shone as *salonnières* and their role as 'intermediaries' explains why women hosted the salons so well (Davison 2002).

They were viewed as possessing tact and discretion to bring out the best in their circle, encouraging others to shine, rather than attracting attention to themselves. In contrast Landes (1928 in Franko 2004) comments that despite this positive role 'women, especially salonnières, were accused repeatedly of artifice and authorship of stylised discursive practices in conflict with nature.' Thus this new space for women remained contested and for some represented an unacceptable shift for women.

The material presented here comes from the letters of salonnières or their guests' letters or memoirs. Firstly the multi-faceted service of Madame de LaFayette for the Duchesse de Savoie is remarked on:

> She watches everything, thinks of everything, combines, visits, talks, writes, sends counsels, procures advice, baffles intrigues, is always in the breach, and renders more service by her single efforts than all the envoys avowed or secret whom the Duchesse keeps in France. (M. de Lescure writing on Madame de LaFayette quoted Mason 2001 [1891])

Nor is the value of these services unrecognised:

> Have I told you that Mme. de Savoie has sent a hundred ells of the finest velvet ... to Mme. de La Fayette, and a hundred ells of satin to line it, and two days ago her portrait, surrounded with diamonds, which is worth three hundred louis? (Mme. de Sevigné to her daughter in Mason 2001 [1891])

Mademoiselle de Lespinasse's (1732–1776) salon was a forum for criticising prospective published articles. Many *'philosophes'* relied upon such assistance: for example Voltaire was coached by Madame du Chatelet (Lewis 1992). Mlle de Lespinasse wrote:

> [I] shall never be on my guard against you; I shall never suspect you. ... I will let you see the trouble, the agitation of my soul, and I shall

not blush to seem to you weak and inconsistent. ... I do not seek to please you; I do not wish to usurp your esteem. (Letter of Julie de Lespinasse to the Comte de Guibert in Grimm 1815:400–405)

She was friend and confidential adviser to D'Alembert (1717–1783) who knew a number of salonnières: he comments on the emotion of the process for Mme Geoffrin:

The passion of *giving*, which was an absolute necessity to her seemed born with her, and tormented her, if I may say so, even from her earliest years.
Memoir of Jean d'Alembert (Grimm 1815: 400–405 original emphasis)

These excerpts express the emotion, complex relationships and multiple functions of the women of the salons. Their capacity to influence leading thinkers is clear, although these people were mostly not directly leading what we might see as organisations, as with other pre-modern advisers considered here. Nonetheless, as a kind of borderland space, the salons offer an insight into the role of influential women and their quasi-invisible advice to male opinion formers of the day.

Early women management consultants

The most notable women in early management consulting are Mary Follett and Lillian Gilbreth. They worked in the early decades of the 20th century (although Gilbreth wrote extensively till her death in 1972). Their work has been obscure in the history of management and of consulting until recently and provides a fitting end to the female thread of this genealogy.

For Lillian, her husband Frank, who died in 1924, was viewed as the main thinker in their collaboration of 12 books although Lillian went on to write or co-write another 14 books. Of her book in 1947 with Alice Cook, Lyndall Urwick, early English management consultant, comments: 'the first book that has ever been published which has made a management consultant seem really human, so I have great sympathy with it' (Urwick 1950). Gilbreth was concerned with human aspects of organisation, unlike her husband who focused on time and motion within scientific management (Diehl and Donnelly 2002).

Follett, a single woman who died in 1933, simply had no such access to publish her work in her lifetime. While Mary Follett is typically viewed as a wealthy Boston woman, Joan Tonn's authoritative biography (2004) shows a less obvious story: her family relying on the

charity of wealthy relatives; her education achieved through the interest of early teachers. Her work in the poor areas of Boston followed
study of political economy and democracy; it provided practical appli-
cation of her ideas and management experience. Here she met and
impressed businessmen with her thinking to the point where they
sought her advice. Tonn comments:

> the brilliance of her analysis is due precisely to the fact that [she]
> was a woman ... in[.] the role of 'political outsider' ... she used her
> own experience ... to understand the value of informal sources of
> power... (Tonn 2004:90–91)

Again the female outsider draws on informal power and her own
resources to influence established male arenas, as did the consorts and
salonnières.

Graham (1991) and Tonn (2004) have recently promoted her ideas,
although Lyndall Urwick attempted this in the 1940s. In 1927 Follett
arranged a visit to England through Urwick who worked for Rowntrees
in York.[6] Her practice was to meet key figures and discuss their business
issues in a 'masterclass' setting rather than to undertake specific work
within organisations:

> I shall like also, as you both suggest, to speak to some employers
> in London. Having met so many of our own business men for dis-
> cussion, this would be very interesting to me. I don't mean more so
> than meeting your executives. [this last sentence was obviously
> added later into space at the end of the line]

> I have always been paid for my [input]. We need not, however,
> discuss the amount. Whatever seems right to you, or is possible
> for you, I shall be very glad to accept. I expect to learn so much
> that you may think I ought to pay you! (Letter to Lyndall Urwick
> 28 June 1926)

This letter is at once business-like, careful and assertive but also playful
and even flirtatious. She is careful to state her own interests but not to
offend the reader in England. She sets out her position on payment
which is both assertive and equivocal. Not a comment a man of that
time would write perhaps. For Follett payment mattered in the light of
her personal circumstances and she repeats this later to Urwick when
revising some of her papers hoping to get them published: 'If I have

the trouble of revising [them] I should like to make a little money out of them.' (Letter from Mary Follett 24 July 1927)

Follett's English visit went well and she comments self deprecatingly about her impact on men notably senior in contemporary new technologies:

> Mr John Lee, head of Telephone system of England and Sir Geoffrey Clarke, head of Telegraph Cable construction Co, ...have both (poor misguided things) expressed a wish to meet me! (op. cit.)

Reflection

Follett's words strike a chord in a discussion group (June 2005): someone says 'that's me!' and another comments: '[the] profound etiquette of it. Laying down the terms of the exchange in a tough but deeply courteous way. We don't trust those conventions at all, we don't have them, it strikes me how little is explicit, a cipher language'

Another sees issues of payment and the commercial process as gendered:

' ... a lot of wrestling with the notion of our worth, financially, and being prepared to charge anything like what the big five charge, and absolutely not wishing to do that, coming to articulate a quite clear position that if you are working for the public or voluntary sector it is unethical to charge them shedloads of money – the opposite of the male model of get as much as you can.' (discussion group participant June 2005)

It is hard to escape the sense that Follett's gender and the rare sight of a woman in business played a key part both in her popularity and her subsequent drop into obscurity. Her contribution in terms of democratic approaches to work and the notion of 'power with' rather than 'power-over' is still being recognised (Tonn 2004).

Conclusions

This chapter has explored predominantly extant text from pre-modern figures and roles, advisers or consultants to the leaders of their day in a necessarily selective, but discursively focused review. The advice-giving we see reflects significant tensions:

- *Humble but sure of their advice*: advisers conformed to the conventions of a humble approach in addressing powerful people in writing; but still express their own uncompromising points of view. Whatever the advice, when it comes it is extremely clear. Advisers are certain of their view and conscious of the act of expressing it.

- *Intimate yet 'other'*: pre-modern advisers have close, often emotional relationships with those they advise, for example as wife, relative or friend working over long periods together; but at the same time are often in the explicit role of 'other' and so distant, as foreigner, woman, person of the church, someone of a lower class.
- *Autonomous yet dependent*: advisers have their own reasons to act, their own views, but are only involved so long as the key person is in power: the mistress disappears once the king is dead, the ousting of a prince can mean his adviser is imprisoned as Plato and Machiavelli found. Their livelihood depends on the favour of the powerful, despite contractual rights – as the queens found.
- *Powerful yet marginal*: advisers' influence is clear; they are often highly sought after; yet they are often marginal figures with little apparent power: the salonnières, the foreign consort, the fool. They work in informal power networks, connecting people and ideas, as the salonnières and Mary Follett did. Their power lies in their lack of rivalry for the advisee's position. Their hold on their financial due is also precarious – and resented.
- *Trust* from the person commissioning the adviser exists alongside *distrust* of them by others: arguably the greater the first the greater the second. The power in this process reflects the importance of the adviser to deflect criticism from the leader and enable him/her to act. The reputation of advice-givers is important – the powerful want the best person. This tension produces for the adviser both respect and contempt together.
- *Ethics/values and 'realpolitik'*: means and ends, personal gain and common good are all recurring themes. The importance of intercession by queens for commoners and the resentment of advisers seen as exploiting the monarch for their own wealth express this tension. Plato and Machiavelli especially contrast here since Plato (and other classically inspired advisers) emphasises the 'good' and 'justice' and Machiavelli is concerned entirely with the leader staying in power. But even Machiavelli is concerned with social stability and the common good, holding strong personal views on the desirability of republicanism.
- *Supporting strong people*: advice-giving helps the powerful develop, consolidate or extend their power. For example Plato is explicit about not remedying weakness and his motivation to develop capable people. Advice is not about helping the weak compete with the

strong. Queenly intercession confronts the strong with the weak and is identified with the 'feminine'.

Thus a number of discourses of advice-giving emerge:

- *Trust* : the powerful image of the 'trusted adviser' where the relationship between leader and adviser is key and intimate, often cemented by kinship or other reciprocal ties
- *Certainty* : advisers' sense of being right whoever they are addressing
- *Impression management* : the use of rhetoric or other powers to convince the listener (this can include 'magic' or occult attribution of the powers of the adviser by others)
- The *Other* : reflected in negative images and stories about 'grasping', greedy or simply foreign advisers

The importance of *relationships* stands out. Intimacy is a strong theme for advice-giving by both men and women. Women especially advise from a position in the private sphere, such as wife or mistress, or in a borderland position such as churchwomen or salonnières (for churchmen their roles were more public, career positions in the social mainstream). Women advising in the public sphere focus strongly on *mutual gains* or *the public good* but this is an aspiration that is often explicit for both men and women. We can also see that advice-giving involved *heterogeneous work* involving many small, hidden tasks/processes especially making or repairing links between people. Within this work *feelings* are freely expressed and permeate the texts reviewed. The use and fostering of *dense reciprocal networks,* which enable the advice-giving work is also striking.

We must also note some historical specificities, differences or shifts, that suggest care in drawing conclusions for management consulting today.

- The context of *strong social ties* such as those forged through feudalism, kinship and religion affected individuals enormously in the pre-modern. It may be hard to understand their force although family and friends still hold sway for many and ties with co-religionists are vivid

> **Reflection**
> *This reminds me of the closeness over decades of some of the women in my network and the sense of community that some of us have, for example as people with a shared work history or politics.*

currently in relation to Islamic communities in the UK feeling strong bonds to those in difficulty in Afghanistan or Pakistan.

- Advice-giving in the pre-modern aimed for *stability rather creating change*. It is hard to identify when this shifted, but it is linked to the growth of empire and of capitalism. An argument can also be made that today's focus on change is merely rhetorical, that we continue to seek order and stability, the powerful still want to retain their control.

- *Adviser or mediator?* The role of intercession with those in power seems very different from anything we do today. On the other hand, the public sector consultant raising the concerns of the public, of the service user, in a managerialist context, or voicing staff concerns to the most senior people, may possibly inherit this ancient process.

- *From adviser to expert?* Although the adviser is certain of his/her advice they are not claiming expertise – mostly they make common cause with those being advised, as Alcuin did. But the shift to more 'expert' approaches can be traced after the Renaissance and in the rise of the professions. For example Machiavelli asserts his (empirical) know-ledge and expertise, Husee claims he does not have the right know-ledge to be steward. However, people commissioning 'experts' expected them to (be able to) do tasks rather than simply say what had to be done, whereas later the rise of professions privileged the expert adviser over the craftsman 'doer'.

Importantly however, this genealogical exploration reflects concepts important in relation to gender and work, especially that of 'separate spheres' (Padavic and Reskin 2002:22) and assumptions of the 'feminine' as proper to the intimate and private realm. It casts advice-giving in terms we might characterise as 'feminine', for example the priority to mutual relationships and feelings, the patient and detailed 'back-stage' work. Women advisers in the intimate, domestic realm only gradually emerge into the public arena. This evolving shift for women is visible in the review, yet still continues. Modern debates about women in the labour force keep this public/private dichotomy alive. Arguably the intimate realm gives women power, in a Foucauldian sense, as they enact their relationships with others. Overall we can also see a gradual shift away from 'feminine' concepts in how advice-giving has been constructed, perceived and carried out, with the emphasis on trust and relationships at the core of the process.

3
Images of Consulting: What Currently Shapes How We See Consulting and How It Works?

Introduction

Exploring the terrain of management consulting must include asking how contemporary writers conceptualise management and organisational consulting, especially given its multifarious nature, as Weiss tartly describes:

> We [consultants] are an amalgam, a farrago, a gallimaufry of people who claim an umbrella title while actually performing in areas ranging from coaching to expert witness, from organizational diagnosis to sales training, and from technology implementation to compensation practices. (And from long-term, highly regarded practitioners to short-term hucksters peddling the latest magic bullet. Welcome to an unregulated profession, warts and all.) ...so little in common that you're hard pressed to find another word that embraces them short of "humanity". (Weiss 2003:14)

This chapter will explore six images that we can see commonly portrayed in writing and research about consulting. Consulting is explored, researched and conceptualised in two distinct literatures which I term the 'mainstream' and 'critical management'. The 'mainstream' is concerned overwhelmingly with functional aspects of consulting and how to improve its effectiveness in relation to management. This assumes the legitimacy of management and its knowledge base.[1] In contrast 'critical management' writers question management legitimacy and knowledge as part of their project to expose structural power at work and change power relations (see for example contributions in Clark and Fincham, 2002).

A broad sweep through the extensive mainstream literature about consulting identifies the following genres of work:

- *auto-biographical* work by well-known consultants, such as Peter Block (2000)
- reviews of consulting *approaches and methods* such as Czerniawska and May (2004), Lippitt and Lippitt (1986), Maister *et al.* (2000), McLachlin (1999), Neumann *et al.* (1997), Schein (2002)
- *'how to'* books on being a more effective consultant, such as Ashford (1998), Czerniawska and Toppin (2005), Greiner and Metzger (1983), Senge *et al.* (1994), Williams and Woodward (1994)
- *industry reviews* focusing on size and shape of the (corporate) market, trends and developments for (large) consulting firms, such as Czerniawska (2002a), Kubr (2002)
- relevant *research studies*, of which there are few, such as Battersby (1984), Esprit Consulting (1992), Fullerton and West (1992), Ram (2000)

The key positions of the 'mainstream' literature are to explore how to make consulting more effective; to consider, theorise or research approaches to working with management/organisations; and to present the experience of consultants for others to draw from. These writers take the management task at face value and investigate how through consulting it can be more effectively prosecuted, how management knowledge can be developed. Implicitly their perspective assumes the interests of profit and capital – mostly not explicitly. This work is overwhelmingly American, and primarily based in male consultants' experience of working in the private sector. Much of this work dates from the early 1980s, at the start of the huge growth in consulting of the last part of the twentieth century. The 'critical management' strand developed partly in response to this growth and its implications, but also as a result of seeing consulting as part of the so-called 'knowledge society', which attracted critical attention as this discourse and the 'new' technologies themselves grew so quickly (Alvesson 1993). As the 1990s continued, groups of writers and researchers (notably Tim Clark, Graeme Salaman, Robin Fincham and Andrew Sturdy in the UK and Lars Engwall, Matthias Kipping and Andreas Werr in Scandinavia) published a stream of work, taking a 'critical management' view of consulting and consultants, along with others such as Czarniawska and Mazza (2003); Clegg *et al.* (2004).

Clark and Fincham (2002) see these two bodies of literature as *phases* of research and writing about consulting, which both continue in parallel. The *organisation development* phase is about the 'change agent' and Clark and Fincham find it problematic that often consultants themselves are writing, from an 'inside' perspective. The *critical perspective* starts from the 1980s with critical management academic researchers and commentators who view writing by insiders as a weakness. This is an 'outside in' perspective that questions the value of management consulting; it is not about success in consulting or improving practice, but about broader socio-political issues, power and rhetoric, and how practice, claims of success and the knowledge base interact. Consulting is studied in relation to and alongside a critique of management theory in general, questioning in whose interests consultants act and management knowledge is developed and applied, and with what effects. Such research concerns the (mostly) explicit exposure of power and ideology at work. Clark and Fincham (2002) comment that:

> From its birth as an institution ... managerial identity was linked with the first consultancy products, ... like Scientific Management ... management and management consultancy have evolved together and are mutually defining institutional systems. (2002:11)

Similarly Kipping argues that 'consultancies are ultimately dependent on the evolution of management' (2002:29). More recently this view of consulting history has been challenged (Czerniawska 2004; McKenna 2001) as a more complex process connected to situated factors such as the role of accounting firms in a particular economy.[2]

My work suggests however that both 'mainstream' and 'critical management' writing and research share common concepts of consulting. Particular images

> **Reflection**
> *This reflects my own experience when thinking about the shifts in requirements of managers in the public sector in the last 20 years which in turn dictated my focus in consulting. This has primarily been about the driver of increasing managerialism and its impact on consulting; for example, management programmes for professionals to take over from administrators in the late 1980s; waves of work on business planning and 'quality' in the public sector in the early 1990s following the policies of Conservative governments; and the emphasis on leadership from the mid 1990s. And now in the 2000s a new emphasis on contracting & commissioning.*

of consulting occur repeatedly in both bodies of work so reflecting, creating and powerfully propagating *discourses* of consulting.

The six images that I have identified are[3]:

1. consulting as an *economic transaction*
2. consulting as a *service*
3. the enduring image of the *advice-giver*
4. consulting as a *'knowledge industry'*
5. consulting as a *profession*
6. consulting as *performance and rhetoric*

I interrogate these images drawing on both sets of writers, and on additional (meagre) material on women in consulting. I join my conclusions to the findings of Chapter 2 to identify defining discourses of consulting in Chapter 4 that we may expect to frame the consulting interactions presented in Part II.

Consulting as an economic transaction

Probably the first thing in our minds in relation to consulting, whatever our stance, is that it is about money. Being a commercial transaction entails enormous assumptions. We are imbued with established notions of the 'client' (despite the rather chequered nature of this term, meaning both subservient claimant, person in one's thrall, appreciated customer and service recipient!). We assume 'contracts' give power to the person paying the bill and that 'projects' are set up, costed, managed, completed and evaluated (Sadler 2001). We reify the process of commercial transaction and the resulting commodification of work, partly in response to the intangible nature of consulting as a service.

The growth of consulting and its economic impact, including on the public sector (Czerniawska 2004) is well charted (Kipping and Engwall 2002; Kubr 2002). For Kipping and Engwall, however, research does not explain why managers keep buying consulting. They see a poor understanding of the commercial interaction process and its 'successive adaptations' as the parties interact. They comment that *trust* is therefore key (2002:8). Collaboration through interaction is part of all commercial processes, which are highly situated and socially constructed. Parker (2002) warns that ignoring this 'decontextualise[s] a social practice' and that an overarching word like market (or economic), 'tells us rather little about how specific markets are constructed and performed.' (2002:185). He comments that:

> ...there is no one immutable market form. Markets are socially con-
> structed sets of rules that provide legitimacy to certain transactions
> ... there are minimal similarities in terms of sellers and buyers, but
> there are also substantial differences – who can buy and who can sell,
> what can be bought and what can be sold, how the parties establish
> some mechanism of exchange and expectations of information, ... the
> degree of formalization or professionalization, ... moral constraints,
> the commonly expected time horizons, and (perhaps most impor-
> tantly) definitions of success or failure. (2002:185)

Parker is arguing for a highly contextualised and differentiated view
of the economic process, for example distinguishing small scale public
sector consulting from large scale private sector consulting, underlining how differently we may then see interactions and how power
operates. I offer some examples of differences in Table 3.1. Given the
heterogeneity of consulting this situated-ness seems fundamental but
is not highlighted in the contemporary literature.

   Seeing consulting first and foremost as a commercial transaction
presages other images: the nature of services, the importance of
interaction and of trust, dimensions of power in a situated process,
what animates the manager to buy and what it is that the consultant
sells.

Consulting as a service

In investigating consulting, it makes sense to start from studies of
service industries and firms, especially so-called professional, less tangible services. Clark and Salaman (1998a) refer to seminal work by Berry,
Lovelock and others in the 1980s to identify key differentiating characteristics for services as compared to manufactured products, such as
intangibility, interaction, heterogeneity, perishability. These are important features of consulting too. Clark and Salaman take the view that
the very nature of services creates opportunities for consultants to
'construct a reality which persuades clients that they have purchased a
valuable and high quality service' (1998a:18). They stress that the
intangibility of services means those commissioning cannot work out
in advance the quality of the service. So they 'will tend to view consultancies as perfectly substitutable', that is, they cannot differentiate

Table 3.1   Differences in the commercial process

Issue	Large scale, private firm consulting	Small scale public sector consulting
Relationship	Large organisation to large organisation relationship/contract	Many kinds of relationship/contract 1 to 1, 1 to small or large organisation(s), small group/team to organisation(s) – large or small
Who's involved	The sellers and the doers may be/are usually different people	Sellers and doers are the same
Money	Large sums of money and large corporate profits involved	Much smaller sums of money involved – individuals aim to earn a comfortable living
Approach to knowledge	Proprietary knowledge and models in use by the consultants	An eclectic *'bricolage'* approach to using knowledge and experience
Buying process	Formal procurement processes and project management approach	Occasional formal procurement, but more often only a brief discussion via personal contact. Rarely a formal project management process
Nature of the contract	Hiring a major consultancy can be a statement about the organisation, or expectations of kudos, of benefits, desperation but also routine buying as in IT, 'headhunting'	Hiring is less a 'big deal', more routine business, with some exceptions. But routine contracts for the hirer can be major for the consultant in size/time/fee
Approach of those who commission work	The 'client' discourse is strong and those commissioning hope to tightly manage the 'grasping' and 'unreliable' consultant. There is a rhetoric of trust and partnership	Similar approach. Consultants may feel it's a 'sledgehammer to crack a nut' – they resist this approach, as organisation to organisation not between individuals. Trust and co-operation is preferred

Table 3.1   Differences in the commercial process – *continued*

Issue	Large scale, private firm consulting	Small scale public sector consulting
Consultant response	Consultants must be seen to deliver what is promised as much money and credibility rides on it for all – danger of slide into impression management when things get tricky	Similar, but more room for manoeuvre and emerging issues
Image	Stereotype of the sharp suited, young brash (male) MBA, the pushy sell-in	Relative invisibility. More women involved
Power	Viewed with major market power – especially given the audit function and how consulting developed from accounting (Tisdall 1982; Czerniawska 2003)	Power not attributed – a 'pair of hands' or quick way to get something done – but constructing power in relations and processes

high from low quality, being 'able neither to sample nor test a service prior to purchase' (1998a: 20–21). This reading of the impact of intangibility scrutinises only the consultant's position and betrays an assumption that 'quality' is there to be discovered rather than constructed in the process; that responsibility for 'quality' lies with the consultant alone. Effectively they (and those commissioning) treat the service as a tangible good, something my work challenges.

> **Reflection**
>
> *Conversely in my experience people commissioning are becoming more and more aware of this issue and increasingly impose buying procedures which help them sample what they are buying: the production of detailed proposals, testing consultants' skills through presentations and – often several sets of – discussions before they contract. Occasionally they reap the benefit of this effort and thinking on the part of consultants to help them with their issue and then do not buy, resourcing the project internally after all, or simply do not go ahead, as their initial brief was flawed or impractical.*

Confusingly Clark and Salaman (1998a) do later refer to interaction within services:

> the quality of a management consultancy service is determined during enactment/consumption .. the outcome ... is highly dependent upon the quality of the interaction between client and consultant. (1998a:22)

While 'collaboration, or interaction, between the two parties is both the central and consistent feature of a consultancy service' and key in the choice process, they argue consultancies must

> **Reflection**
> *This seems to describe a lot of the endless discussion and talk between consultants about how to tackle (interesting word when I mean 'work with') a person commissioning work.*

therefore be 'systems of persuasion' (here citing Alvesson 1993). Consultants make themselves indispensable through a process of 'translation' (quoting Callon and Latour 1981): 'all the negotiations, intrigues, calculations, acts of persuasion and violence thanks to which an actor or force takes ... authority to speak or act' (1998a:23).

Thus Clark and Salaman's commitment to processes and interaction remains contradictory.

> **Reflection**
> *One client was so keen to control the process that she, ironically enough, brought in another consultant to help her 'hold the line' on 'the service need' in her organisation during protracted pre- and post-contract discussions. My team named him the 'pet' consultant! Were we therefore 'wild' or at least 'undomesticated'? (is this what 'critical' means for us?) This illustrates perhaps the anxieties underlying her actions and the proliferation of advisers for the modern manager.*

> each transaction between client and consultant is unique ...each assignment represents a new start ... a service supplier has a high degree of discretion ...they are not constrained by a straitjacket... are free to tinker with, adjust and customise ... (Clark and Salaman 1998a)

The impact of endless 'new starts' on the consultant, the pressure this produces is not explored; nor the two-way nature of interaction or 'tinkering'. The person commissioning changes things too. Clark and Salaman (1998a) constantly refer to interaction but not to all those that participate, nor how actors constrain each other in the process of interacting. This is interesting since initially those commissioning mostly define the situation and the consultant responds. They also fail to note that the intangible and unknown-till-delivered nature of consulting also allows those commissioning to 'move the goal-posts': this is an emergent process with all the actors involved in shaping it. How this works is what needs exploring.

Ambiguities or 'achievement'?

There is some agreement across the two strands of literature about the difficulties in measuring or seeing achievements and so the inherent ambiguities of consulting. The issue of (lack of) proof has already been raised in terms of the intangibility of the service and how clients can assess it in advance. The critical writers emphasise the contested claims for consulting and its impact.

In a key mainstream text, Greiner and Metzger (1983) discuss 'effectiveness' and make assumptions about the consultant knowing more than the client, commenting that appointing consultants may be read as a sign of defeat. They discuss the importance of 'collecting solutions' and 'simplifying complexity' for the client. Consultants 'sell recommendations'. This is a discourse of transaction and commodification, reifying concepts such as 'effectiveness' and taking a deficiency view of the client.

In reviewing the question of results, Wildavsky's work on policy advisers (1979) in the public sector is enlightening. He discusses public agencies escaping negative evaluation, through:

> making what one can do into what one is supposed to accomplish, or choosing capable clients who are already accomplished, [both] are means of constructing a benevolent environment. (1979:6)

This shifts the view of consulting from remedying deficiency to building on strength. Wildavsky assumes working with capable clients is duplicitous and undesirable, whereas perhaps it is the only process that is possible; 'deficiency' is of course a social construct too.

He further argues that 'problem finding' is a key part of the problem solving process as only things that *can* be attempted are really seen as problems to *be* attempted. So he sees data collection, reviewing findings or analysing situations as partly about uncovering new problems to be tackled – as much as about solving already recognised problems. 'There is a difference between problems as presented, and as transmuted through the search for answers.' (1979:354) We may conclude that consulting only works if the problem being tackled is constructed to enable success. But also that it is inevitable in this work to raise further questions rather than to provide answers, or other visible outputs. With these ideas in view the terrain of 'achievement' is full of fog for commentators and intensifies the ambiguity and intangibility of consulting as a service.

Alvesson (1993) considers ambiguity within 'knowledge-intensive' work. He points out that even if people commissioning are happy with a piece of work, equivalent experts may not have been. He is explicit about the difficulties here for management consulting:

> To separate out any consequences of 'expert knowledge' from the placebo effect in, for example, management consulting is not just empirically very complicated, but also theoretically misleading. The belief and expectations of the client are a necessary, indeed a crucial component for success. (1993:1006)

However, he does not explore how beliefs and expectations are formed, nor how they affect constructs of 'success'. Fincham (1999b:344) reports that consultants provide methodologies, structure and background 'rather than direction and leadership'. He implies a limited technical utility, but not a transforming impact and sees the process as at best an exchange, with consultants learning as much as the client. Later (2000a) he comments that for consultants the issue has been:

> 'the *legitimisation* of consultancy skills. ... to convince managerial clients of the worth of the advice being sold to them. Consultants exploit managerial areas of high uncertainty, ... there can be no concrete demonstration of managerial problems in such areas having been solved.'(2000a:6 his emphasis)

Fincham and Evans (1998) comment also that:

> in the complex and challenging world that consultants' managerial clients inhabit there is reassurance to be gained ... [consultants] supply not only a measure of enthusiasm and inspiration for the

managerial crusade, but also the mechanisms and how-to procedures ... (1998:51).

From all this we can conclude the critical literature concedes some exchange, some practical utility in consulting services, but sees this inherently as a reassurance process, an intervention into something essentially uncertain and not amenable to 'results'.

Fincham (2000b) goes further in considering the issue of failure in consulting and how consultants visibly allude to failure. Fincham points out that the test of what is failure is constructed, drawing comparisons with magic, and he asserts 'when magic succeeds the shaman gets the credit, and when magic fails the followers get the blame.' Here his analogy breaks down, since often the point of engaging consultants is to blame them for failure and to take credit yourself for any successes. Fincham sees a mix of faith and belief, as in magic, may account for the paradox of managerial ambivalence about consultants yet their increasing use of them: 'while doubting the powers of individual con-sultants, managers may still entertain rationalistic beliefs that solutions to their problems exist somewhere.' (2000b:188)

The 'advice industry'

The trusted adviser acts variously as a mirror, a sounding board, a con-fessor, a mentor, and even at times the jester or fool. (Maister *et al.* 2000:37)

Agreeing that advice is the key component of consulting, Fincham and Evans (1998) comment, from a critical perspective, that:

the key difficulty for [consultants] is that of legitimising their advice ... [their] ideas and practices ..need to be inherently persuasive. (1998:52)

Bloomfield and Vurdubakis feel that 'the very notion of 'advice' pre-supposes and requires a kind of (knowledge) deficiency or 'ignorance' on the part of the recipient' (2002:115). This assumes a 'knowledge' is possible and sets up a particular power relation between consul-tants and those commissioning them. The resulting problematic 'otherness' of consultants is charted by Kipping and Armbruster (2002). Pellegrinelli (2002) also struggles to reconcile the importance of closeness with apparent requirements for objective independence.

Harvey (2005) discusses the consultant caught in 'no man's land'. All this involves the related issues of trust, interaction and the linked notion of 'partnership'.

Trust

Maister *et al.* (2000) add 'trust-based' to the common typology of product- based, needs-based or relationship-based views of consulting. They argue trust-based work requires both deeper personal relation-ships and the broadest business focus in working with the client. They describe 'trusted advisers' at length:

> a predilection to focus on the client, rather than themselves. [with]
>
> - enough self-confidence to listen without prejudging
> - enough curiosity to inquire without supposing an answer
> - a willingness to see the client as co-equal in a joint journey
> - enough ego strength to subordinate their own ego.
>
> Trusted advisers focus on the client as an individual, not as a person fulfilling a role. [they] believe that success in client relationships is tied to the accumulation of quality experiences. As a result, they seek out (rather than avoid) client-contact experiences and take personal risks with clients rather than avoid risks. (Maister *et al.* 2000:40)

They articulate a trust gap between clients and consultants:

> ... we must work (continuously) to convince others that we truly are worthy of their trust. As a starting position, they think we are less trustworthy than we think we are; and we have our doubts about their trustworthiness. There is work to be done! (2000:41)

The overwhelming emphasis on trust, and the concept of client-consultant relationship as personal connection, produces a complex process of interaction focused on the client's issues. Salacuse however assumes advice is simply part of an organised process towards a clear end point:

> Advising someone is a *process* – a progressive movement toward an end. ... a course of action that will help a client solve a problem. The advisor organizes and manages the advising process (Salacuse, 2000:7 his emphasis)

In reviewing Peter Block's book 'Flawless Consulting' Griffin (2001) comments:

> The effectiveness of ...advice rests on the twin pillars of credibility and authenticity. If one pillar is weaker than the other, effectiveness suffers. The consultant is therefore challenged to build both credibility and authenticity in [client] relationships.

Authenticity is Block's key concept for consulting, which he sees as a critical developable skill. 'Credibility', 'authenticity' and 'effectiveness' are reified and not interrogated for what they may mean in terms of the consulting process.

The mainstream literature frequently emphasises an ethical dimension, such as trust of the client, remaining authentic, for example to your own values (Block 2000), or adhering to codes of practice of professional associations. Block discusses values and acknowledges a 'shadow side' to consulting where perhaps values and integrity are stretched. Others conclude a more ethical approach is required from consultants (Poulfelt and Paynee 1994; van Es 2002). McLachlin (1999) asserts that a central notion of consultant integrity is putting the client's needs first. He elides the needs and interests of the client – which may not be the same. He quotes Harrison, who reports:

> I have always had my own agendas ...The idea of value-free consulting has no meaning for me. I endeavour to give clients what they and I contract for, but I have often had a covert agenda as well, and I have not always been open about my larger goals and motives out of fear of losing the work. At times, I have felt some shame over having an agenda different from that of my clients. (1995:174 cited McLachlin 1999:395)

Harrison experienced shame and fear in holding to his values in doing consulting and McLachlin supports his covert strategy, commenting:

> ...reputation is almost everything in consulting This means that it is worth doing almost anything to establish and maintain one's reputation for integrity and competence. (1999:400)

This shows the power of the discourse of the 'client as king' (Sturdy 1998) and its interweaving with the subjectivity of the consultant to produce the 'trusted adviser'.

On the other hand, Wildavsky's (1979) consideration of policy analysts in the public sector acknowledges that clients may insist on specific solutions; analysts can only refuse these if they can afford to walk away; and anyway the client may find analysts who identify with their values. He concludes that what we must consider is how analysts' values enter into the making of policy. This emphasis on values seems important, especially to 'critical consulting'. The question is raised: how far there can be a critical, ethical stance in doing consulting within the overwhelming discourse of the 'client' and their 'trusted adviser'.

Interaction and exchange

Block emphasises that what happens between the consultant and the client(s) is what matters. He sees the authenticity of that interaction as critical to its success, although he does not make this explicit and seems to privilege 'being' authentic in some essentialist form over describing any actual process.

> the consultant is as much a learner as any client. We in fact are often more changed by our consultation than the client, and this is as it should be. ... In the end it is our authenticity, the way we manage ourselves, and our connection to our clients, that is our methodology, our marketing strategy, and the fruit of our labour. The fact that we show up with a briefcase, a resume, and a conceptual framework is more a function of habit than necessity. It will be enough if we simply show up. And that is the heart of the matter. Block (2000:342)

Critical writers also identify interaction as key. For Alvesson 'talk and conversation is a crucial part of the work day. ...knowledge workers are often language workers' (1993:1007–1008). Fincham (1999b) reports that people see consulting as exchange, that consultants learn as much from them as they from consultants. Sturdy (1997b) presents consultancy as 'an interactive and dialectical process founded on both consultants' and clients' self-defeating concerns to secure a sense of identity and control.' He acknowledges the importance of broader social/political conditions and of capital in the interactive process: '...crucial for an understanding of the process of consultancy, its associated anxieties and, in particular, the fragile and often conflictual nature of client-consultant relations.' His analysis seems more connected than that of Block, or other critical writers, to the notion of shifting and mutually shaping interactions, consistent with 'high modernity' where identity is fragile (Giddens, 1991). He does not assume the consultant controls the interaction and emphasises dynamic processes rather than static typologies of relationships.

The interrelation of 'client' and consultant is typically seen as pivotal: explicitly and implicitly connected to the nature, process and power dynamic of consulting and its knowledge. However, Marsh (1992) and Fullerton and West (1992) suggest the consultant overstates the importance of relationships. Fullerton and West assume the entities must interact: the consultant's job is to 'bridge the gap' and to 'enter the client system'. 'We' must join 'them'. They suggest clients want both process and content roles from consultants and the ability to move between them, drawing on 'congruent values'.

Williams and Woodward (1994) define criteria for 'client orientation' as:

- 'Does the client actually feel helped?'
- 'Are the goals realised without the consultant breaking recognised ethical codes?'
- Are clients helped to bring about change in ways 'which avoid *unnecessary* conflict, resistance to change, human and financial costs?' [their emphasis]
- 'Does the consultant cope successfully with new (and perhaps unexpected) demands from clients?' (1994:50)

These criteria present major concerns for the 'critical consultant', trying to develop positive interaction and relationships, yet wishing to challenge both existing 'codes', their recognition and their validity. How from a critical perspective can we determine the necessity or otherwise of conflict and resistance? (Always assuming we have any control over these) Is it appropriate only to take the client's perspective? Similarly, according to whom will success be agreed? If these issues are not addressed, or even seen, there is no critical challenge to clients or prevailing values. Fincham (1999a) sees the client as rival: 'the first that the consultant has to challenge'. Making a challenge may on occasion help in getting work, but also may be disastrous. In contrast Czarniawska and Mazza highlight the lack of a right to assert one's own will in relation to a client: 'a consultant cannot decide that, for the good of humanity, the client had better perish'(2003:275). They see the discourse of transaction as dominant in the relationship on the part of the client and effectively rule out space for 'critical consulting':

> [consultants] abdicate control over their time. ... consultants must not have their own objectives: their role consists of internalising those of the client. (2003:274)

Clark and Fincham (2002) highlight the shifting nature of the client/ consultant relationship. They comment how research seems either to show consultants as all-powerful or as insecure and dependent. And that both aspects are seen, either in different stages of a piece of work or at the same time. They conclude that dependence is a consistent element in the relationship, commenting:

> ...perhaps because consultant expertise consists of a more uncertain set of methods that a relatively intense and intimate client relationship has come about. This kind of expertise above all requires interpretation – to discover whether knowledge is needed in the first place (whether indeed the client has a problem), how to apply knowledge, how to be sure anything has changed – all factors that underpin a complex, multi-layered client relationship. (2002: 10–11)

Clark and Salaman (1998a) however conclude that while both parties seek to exploit and manipulate impressions, interaction is about negotiation and is 'not a one-sided process'. But still they return to the issue of intangibility: that consultants influence the entire arena of the interaction through images and are 'dominant'.

Alvesson and Johansson (2002) emphasise the interaction and its effects, especially the impact of the person commissioning:

> ...the willingness and capacity of clients to resist consultant-driven discourses on management change projects ... is far from insignificant. ...The position of consultants is always to some extent an outcome of clients' intentions, resources and moves. ... less something fixed than emerging in the interaction. (2002:244)

This raises the interesting question of how far a consultant's subjectivity is the result of those who commission her/him?

Case (2002) notes the 'ritual demands of the interaction... the imme-diate imperative to maintain face' and comments on the effort it takes to keep this stable situation in place:

> this mundane stability has to be worked at, collaboratively manu-factured. This kind of interaction ritual requires *moment-by-moment mutual* monitoring and management. (2002:102 my emphasis)

The unremitting and mutual nature of this maintenance is striking – Case was a participant drawn into helping the consultant's process along, despite his research role.[4]

Fincham (1999b) also sees that managers and their power are part of how consulting works in practice:

> The seemingly inexhaustible managerial appetite for consultant advice should not be taken as a substitute for the political will of managers ... they had ways of talking that subtly reduced the methods and techniques of outside experts to what they themselves were doing anyway.

McLachlin (1999) suggests strong prior links with closer, trusted rela-tionships as more the norm than managers might acknowledge. Schein (2002) sees the key element is the helper needing to enter the relation-ship and give up the power position of remaining aloof. The helper is:

> dependent on the client for accurate information and feelings ... The ultimate challenge ...to be influenced, to change their precon-ceived views of what the client tells them, to be helped. ... consulta-tion means to provide help, and to provide help one must be willing to be helped.' (2002:27)

This suggests a mutual interactive process. Fincham comments sim-ilarly that, contrary to much literature about the 'expert', consultants:

> in terms of their own subjectivity, ... tend to be uncomfortable with overly dominant or 'professional' images of themselves ... prefer to see clients as partners in some joint endeavour... (2002:197)

This is about the close relation between the process of the transaction, the process of the relationship and the consequent work. Fincham con-tinually compares the rational and the ritual aspects of consulting:

the tangible contribution of apparently rational processes, within a constructed dialogue and 'repertoire of performances'.

Partnership

> partnership is itself a rhetoric .. a personalised emphasis that helps stabilise an essentially market-driven exchange. ... for the consultant [it] ...means...a position of trust ...not being forced to bid for work (Fincham, 2002:197)

Fincham identifies narrative themes in his work, of which 'the client as a partner with the consultant' (1999a:4) is key to considering power and relationships in the 'advice industry'. He defines partnership as 'a generalised type of relation bound by indeterminate commitments and reciprocal responsibilities and favours.' (1999a:8) He sees partnership narrative as a realistic strategy for consultants as many managers will either want to partner this glamorous person, or will resist consultants having any monopoly on knowledge. He feels however consultants cannot simply build self-serving identities as 'the consultant-client relation is not a fixed reality, but rather is reflexively constructed out of the images both sides hold of each other.' (1999a:9) He sees partnership as a 'credible but malleable' concept that consultants can both apply to many different situations and use in one dynamic situation to cover a range of issues. 'Partnership' helps 'construct a *multi-layered* relationship' (his emphasis), open-ended and providing:

> less need to compete for jobs. Thus consultants become the confidantes of management, entrusted with work that arises naturally in the context of the relationship. (1999a:9)

Fincham rightly sees this as contradicting not only the market assumptions of much mainstream literature but also the vaunted selling point of consultants as cross-organisational. However he perhaps confuses *long-term* work with organisations (of which several pieces may run concurrently) with *full-time* involvement in one. He concludes the partnership approach is probably an aspiration for stability. Crucially he sees 'the idea of partnership is not a step down from a professional strategy, but a step up from employee status.' (1999a:12) He comments:

> If consultants are to be seen as partners (*and not paid employees*) they have to at least partly take over the problem, and be seen to

> be working with the client not working for them. (ibid:10, my emphasis)

This puts partnership into a structural category, inevitably placing the consultant as a 'lower' in the situation, compared to the manager as an 'upper' (Chambers, 1997), especially if status is an explicit issue. While this sums up issues in my own work, both in long term relationships and the specific trickiness of handling a one-off commission, where people may view me as a hired pair of hands, it also highlights a dilemma:

> Whatever the route to rapport and credibility, if [consultants] re-defined the problem they were arrogant, if they didn't they were not telling the client anything new. The answer was to finesse the dilemma within the layered relations of the partnership. Building a personal relation with the client cushioned the blow .. 'working together through the problem' was itself the only lasting basis for partnership. (Fincham, 1999a:13)

Exchange seems key to Fincham and 'not depicting the consultant-client relation as a set of fixed dependencies.' He sees tensions but nothing to prevent co-operation; what is important are the competing knowledges of manager and consultant.

Trust and partnership both privilege closeness of relationship in advice-giving as an interactive process and challenge the assumption (and apparent objectivity) of consulting as about knowledge and professionalism, the focus of the next two sections.

The 'knowledge industry'

Mainstream economic analyses of consulting largely attribute its growth to the development of the 'knowledge economy' and 'knowledge work' (Czerniawska 2004; Kipping and Engwall 2002). But how far can consulting be seen as a knowledge industry and what may that mean for consulting processes?

Writers in both mainstream and critical strands assume the knowledge/expertise of the consultant and its centrality. For example, Williams and Woodward (1994) put 'Expert' as the number one attribute in the centre of their skills model, saying : 'a consultant's expertise ... makes him or her attractive to a client in need.' (1994:46) Expert knowledge and skills are the 'given', minimum requirement for them, as in all the literature they reviewed. The question of how far consulting carries and creates management knowledge also forms a key strand of critical management inquiry (see especially Kipping and Engwall 2002). Heller acerbically sums up the critical management debates:

> A major theme ... is the under-utilisation or misuse of knowledge. ... Is this the academic, the font of epistemology, prevented from having adequate access to management, or is she unmotivated to share her wisdom? Is the consultant-guru spreading insubstantial or misleading information for personal benefit? Is the client-manager over credulous, easily taken in by rhetoric and perhaps a little naïve, or is he cunning, self-serving and determined to use the consultant-guru to fight his own corner, or does his conscience on behalf of shareholders make him seek whatever advice is easily available? Or, perhaps, there is no substantial knowledge base to communicate and share?' (Heller 2002:270)

But first, what is knowledge in this context? Scarbrough (1995) sees knowledge as something typically shared rather than transferred: that is, the seller continues to partake of what s/he has sold. Also the acquisition of knowledge depends on the possession of certain kinds of prior knowledge and the production of knowledge generally involves 'bootstrapping', that is, using existing knowledge as a platform for innovation. Scarbrough's approach suggests how a consultant's knowledge remains current, how interaction with a client may develop and affirm consultant knowledge and how consultants' accumulated knowledge may help keep the knowledge base productive. He emphasises that 'knowledge-based transactions depend on social and cultural processes of communication ... as much as upon economic processes of exchange.' (Scarbrough 1995:999). This suggests processes of interaction produce knowledge, rather than it existing independently.

Alternatively, we can draw on post-structuralist thought for insights about the problematics of consulting and knowledge. Best and Kellner's (1991) discussion concludes meaning is never complete but infinite and ever-changing. The endlessly changing *curriculum vitae* of the consultant echoes this. The consultant re-does it for each piece of work, constructing each time new meanings for their experience and knowledge. It also echoes the reflexivity and related anxiety that Giddens (1991) identifies – that no knowledge is secure in the modern world.

Consultant knowledge in action

Fincham in his identification of consultant 'narrative types' sums up the 'real knowledge' narrative as: 'the problem is re-shaped around the consultant's own knowledge' (1999a:10). He connects this to the consultant simultaneously expanding the issue (and so the fee – see later 'peddling pejoratives' section) and telling the client what the problem 'really' is. His work suggests that 'in the final analysis there is no claim to be the originator of best practice.' (1999a:11)

Fincham and Evans distinguish consultants from gurus, in that consultants:

> may be dependent on personal influence and persuasion, but they have to produce solutions that 'work' in particular contexts. Theirs is a more specialised and differentiated kind of expertise; consultants are the archetypal 'knowledge worker'... (1998:52)

But they also find that, despite the standard process models the big firms use, 'consultants' need for flexibility also emerged clearly... adapting methods and tailoring work, getting away from totally rationalistic models, becoming 'more nuanced and forgiving"(*ibid*:59). Werr's research also suggests consultant knowledge is dynamic:

> The more experience a consultant had the less important methods and tools were said to be. Growing experience also allowed larger deviations from the method. Only when the method was really mastered, could it be departed from. (1998:19)

The managers he interviewed confirmed the knowledge role of consultants as 'important sources of knowledge to their client organisations... expected to continuously provide state of the art business knowledge.' (2002:92) For him that knowledge clearly went 'beyond the mastery of impression management or knowledge of the latest management fads and fashions' (2002:101) and emphasised the importance of 'translation' of knowledge from situation to situation. Crucini (2002) echoes this, emphasising the dynamic mix of skills and know-how in consulting. Describing 'knowledge arenas' and personal networks, Faust (2002) similarly sees management knowledge 'emerg[ing] from overlapping networks of consultants, managers, management trainers, academics, and representatives of intermediary organisations.' (2002:156)

Fincham (1999b) questions the basis of consultant knowledge referring to Schein's medical model of 'supposedly' joint diagnosis, but agrees only partly with critics who say there is no professional know-ledge base: 'the very act of consulting an external expert implies an inadequacy in the client's own understanding' (1999b:338); they accept there is a knowledge to be gained. Fincham's research identified 'competing claims to expert knowledge', rather than no attribution of knowledge to the consultant, redolent of what Alvesson later terms 'knowledge-claims-intensive' work (2004:225).

More pragmatically Clark and Salaman (1998a) point out clients may not understand what their expert advisers say. This is an interesting

---

Reflection

This dilemma was encapsulated in a consulting assignment where approval by a client who self-confessed to know little of the issue at hand is nonetheless built into the process. The client's lack of knowledge became fatal to the endeavour, to change the nature of leadership in the organisation away from a transactional style. Her control and (lack of) grip on details of the process undermined the consultant team's sense of purpose, both of the work and of our own aims. Here the client resisted the transfer of knowledge of the consultants, limiting how it could be deployed, and mirroring the exact issue she wanted consultants to address.

---

dilemma and for specialist service providers a well-known problem (Marsh 1996), which may mean that the client judges consultants based on symbolic outputs and explains why a client may not feel the consul-tant *has* knowledge – it is simply impossible to conceive of what they themselves do not know.

This re-emphasises the role of people commissioning work. Consult-ing is an interaction, but the client is nevertheless paying for a service. Kipping and Armbruster's work (2002) charts the long history of this problem of 'otherness' as they term it and how hard it is for either con-sultants or clients to overcome. Kipping and Engwall conclude in their study of the knowledge dimension of consulting that consultants 'face an uphill struggle when it comes to putting [their] knowledge into practice .. [it is a] constant challenge' (2002:14).

The knowledge intensive firm or worker

Alvesson takes a more structural approach in discussing the idea of the 'knowledge intensive firm, organisation and/or worker' or KIFOW (1993). His ideas resonate with issues in consulting and he refers to management consultants specifically. He questions 'common-sense' view of the KIFOW, stemming from the generalised sense of economic movement from manufacturing to services to knowledge-based economies, examining what is meant by knowledge. He is concerned with the symbolic value of knowledge to individuals and to organisations, which may drive these shifts: 'to define knowledge in a non-abstract and non-sweeping way seems to be extremely difficult. Knowledge easily becomes everything and nothing.' (1993:1000) He suggests that while knowledge or core competence is still vital, it is more to do with social recognition as an expert, or knowledge about how to act in an 'expert-like' way. This underlines the persuasive or rhetorical element and the implicit dimension of interaction and discursive practice for KIFOWs: 'being perceived as an expert is then more crucial than being one.' (1993:1004) Similarly for Clark:

> **Reflection**
> *In the process of winning and starting work on a large contract, a consultant colleague, with whom I had not worked before, was attributed expert status by the commissioning group (possibly since she had recently left academia and had written at least one well-received text book). She behaved as an expert with them, referring to her book and acknowledging their plaudits by talking at length about senior people she had worked with. She always talked about being an 'insider' in relation to the sector concerned, which they clearly liked. With us, her colleagues, she acted in the opposite way. She asserted knowledge where she had none, or no more than others, and rode rough-shod over our decision processes; our opinion of her sank to the point where we parted company. The commissioning group was horrified at this major loss as they saw it. They wanted a visibly accomplished team on the work and pressurised us to add another such person to our team. This despite our track record by then of delivering to the brief and on time without her input. We felt under intense scrutiny throughout as a result.*

> a core feature of consultancy work is impression management. In this sense, consultants are systems of persuasion seeking to convince clients of their authority and expertise. Being perceived as knowledgeable is more important than being knowledgeable. (1996:95)

Alvesson identifies three key elements that seem significantly ambiguous for KIFOWs: their claimed core product or knowledge; what they are actually doing in 'working with 'knowledge' compared to behaving in ways that are loosely connected to this quality' (1993:1007); and thirdly the results of their work and 'its mythical meaning... clarity and order are not the best words for providing accounts of [their] work and contributions' (1993:1007).

But others must recognise your KIFOW status – so being seen to have the right clients leads to mutual confirmation of having the knowledge sought and indicates they are the sort that knows the right knowledge when they see it. Alvesson comments that:

> only insiders can by definition evaluate who is very knowledgeable. ...[k]nowledge does not exist in a vacuum ... ready to be sold and distributed ... As a socially constructed phenomenon it is in a sense interaction, dependent on recognition – without [this] 'knowledge' is, for all practical matters, nothing. (1993:1007–1008)

This has echoes of how we may conceptualise power/knowledge in a Foucauldian sense as enacted but notably power is missing from these discussions of knowledge. Alvesson concludes by emphasising KIFOWs as 'systems of persuasion' and knowledge work as 'symbolic action' (1993:1011).

Kieser (2002) claims consultants 'mystify' to enhance the image of their knowledge, using 'theoretical mock-ups' (he suggests 'chaos theory'), and emphasising intuition.[5] Similarly Clark and Greatbatch (2002) describe how management gurus portray stories and observations from the 'frontline', linking them together in an analysis, 'constantly referencing managers and organisations'. The authors see this as gurus' attempt to justify their rather 'ordinary' research and 'elevate' their material as special and beyond their audience's capabilities – who could just as easily do similar visits themselves. Clark and Greatbatch clearly see such stories as banal anecdotes rather than 'knowledge', thus going against ideas of 'story' as an archetypal and valuable source of knowledge (Gabriel 2004). Perhaps the simplest response to this debate is not only to form new concepts of the knowledge in question, but to distinguish carefully between the getting of consulting work and the doing of it, and the roles of 'knowledge' in both. Too often writers seem to conflate the two.

Knowledge and uncertainty

More critically, Legge (2002) comments that:

> Most commentators, however, whether explicitly or not, appear to equate knowledge workers with those that create uncertainty ... to

achieve competitive advantage via innovation in a post-Fordist world of disorganised capitalism. (2002:76)

With a social constructionist perspective of knowledge, she explores the linked concepts of networks, permeable boundaries, the learning organisation and environmental interconnectedness – this is how knowledge workers' work is currently 'dressed up' if they are consultants. Similarly, Kieser concludes that 'infecting managers with uncertainty' about the sufficiency of their knowledge generates demand for consulting (2002:216). Puzzlingly then managers who are uncertain of their knowledge turn for help to the very group, consultants, about whose knowledge it seems they are not convinced. The explanation is seen to lie in the power of consultant rhetoric.

> **Reflection**
> *A voluntary sector organisation in commissioning work through a tendering process repeatedly emphasised their need for the consultants' work to legitimise the conclusion they had reluctantly reached – to wind up the organisation. 'You are the experts here' was their phrase which filled me with trepidation – how could I be the expert on their 15 year old position in 3 days work? But we did reach that view quite easily and tried to start a new process to continue the work more positively through other means and new partners.*

Salaman (2002), however, points out that the flawed knowledge argument assumes we accept 'proper' truth/knowledge can exist. To argue about quality of knowledge misses the point of consultants' actual power in the world. He argues for examining the thinking process that automatically says consulting is non-truth because it is not coming from a scientific source. For him this approach betrays untenable underlying assumptions about the rationality of organisations and of managers as decision makers. He lays bare the ideological nature of much commentary on management and consulting: if we know that irrationality in organisations is normal, why are we so amazed that consulting is the same? He feels this confusion is misdirecting inquiry on management consulting into unhelpful areas, concluding that academics may be pre-occupied with the dodgy status of consultants' knowledge precisely because they are concerned about their own for some of the very same reasons (see also Czerniawska 2002b).

Insecurity and marginal role

Sturdy (1997a) challenges the prevailing critical view that the insecure manager seeks help from consultants to cope with the changing world:

> such a view of insecurity is partial. It highlights dependence and underplays the related preoccupation with securing a sense of identity and control over others and the environment. (1997a: 392)

He locates this in social and economic structures, seeing managerial anxiety as 'a condition and consequence of those structures and their inherent tensions and contradictions.'(1997a:397) So managers satisfice on capitalist priorities of profit, while pursuing their own agendas for promotion or more interesting work, that is, for their own concerns of identity. Kieser (2002) sees the consultant as simply part of the organisation's environment like any other – certainly this rings true in terms of the (in)attention a project may get! For him the management consultant attempts to get the organisation 'to reconstruct parts of itself' – a difficult 'game', like learning to play chess well it is beyond simply knowing the rules. He concludes that 'consultants have to develop strategies for a game whose rules they hardly know' and achieve this either through 'brute force' in imposing solutions, or in contrast through consultation, where the organisation 'talks to itself' or the consultant 'stir[s] up the organisation.' (2002:217)

Jackall (1988) considers consultants in relation to internal management structures, seeing them in dependent relations, the 'benign parasite'. The internal power game is key: 'the circulation of ideas at or near the top' creates the demand for managerial advice. He sees the nature of large organisations as almost in the premodern, medieval world, 'unstable pyramids of fealty and alliance' where those in power constantly intrigue and 'group and regroup the work of subordinates'. Fincham summarises the point:

> consultants are a main supply of ideas; ... they are feeding a political process, and consultants and managers alike are locked into a relation of supply and demand. (2000b:176)

Here consultancy is seen as a 'by-product' of the corporate world. Similarly for public sector consulting, the pull of the 'modernisation' discourse from the UK government produces demand for consulting activity. For Fincham, consulting comprises 'a market relation between different managerial groupings... a kind of parallel management ...' (1999b:347)

Clark (1995) comments how unfair it is to criticise consultants for not having codified expertise, since their operating arena of management has none either. Fincham also notes 'the inherent *uncertainty* of the management task' (1999b: 341 his emphasis) as accounting for consulting as reassurance, with attractive, outside answers.

> **Reflection**
>
> *This reflects my own experience of how especially senior managers seem to assume there is an answer to management issues, there is definitive expertise or magic out there; they don't support the uncertainty view. And despite the understanding Fincham identifies yet the distance I feel...*

The belief that consultants can work the necessary magic is part of the process of shoring up managerial self-esteem; by displacing their anxieties outwards onto the figure of the ... consultant, managers are seeking to stabilise their position, while consultants ... act as the focus of this projection. (Fincham 2000b:177)

> **Reflection**
>
> *This contrasts with my experience of using 'whole systems' approaches, to involve groups at all levels in the organisation and external stakeholders such as the public. Here managers can regard the consultant almost as a traitor – since the method creates more uncertainty for the manager, including about their role and how to behave. In two cases management teams simply did not know what to do faced with a roomful of staff and others working competently on an array of key topics, and in one case the chief executive figure made sure that action plans people made were subsequently quashed.*

We need new ways to conceptualise knowledge work and knowledge in consulting, in order to escape the cul-de-sac of seeing consulting as wholly about rhetoric and impression management. For example, Deleuze and Guattari's concept of 'rhizomatic'[6] thought suggests consulting 'knowledge' makes unseen and unpredictable connections across organisations and sectors. Or, following Fincham, we could '[see] knowledge not as a possessed entity, but as the product of a system of social activity' (2000a:4). Such ideas challenge the debates about knowledge and the notion of 'professionalism' that often underlies them.

Consulting as a profession?

Fincham looks at knowledge work, 'not as a new grouping of occupations, but as a means of claiming occupational status' (2000a:2), a dynamic perspective contrasting with the stress professionals typically place on the intrinsic qualities of their work. For Fincham professionalism is more about strategies for power and social power/knowledge formation. While management consulting is seen as the 'archetype' of knowledge work, he criticises the tendency, even of critical observers, to react to an (often consultant developed) rhetoric of everyone's job becoming a 'knowledge' job, living in the 'knowledge era' and so on.

The question of professionalism is thus raised and the debate about how far consulting is a profession links strongly to issues of knowledge, of power and society at large. How knowledge links to the question of claiming professional status is contested by critical writers, and unexplored by the mainstream. The traditional view promulgated by professions themselves, emphasises the: 'central role of science and knowledge, autonomy, the solving of problems vital to society, affective neutrality and altruistic service to clients' (Alvesson 1993:999). In relation to this definition, management consultants may seem less concerned with society and their connection to the client may not involve affective neutrality, as we saw in considering the 'advice industry'. Perhaps the adviser or consultant can be distinguished from the professional in this way. But a 'critical consultant' *is* concerned with society.

Alvesson and Johansson conclude: "Professionalism' is best seen as a resource on which management consultants can draw selectively in their claims for authority, status and credibility.' (2002:228) They discuss the 'mingling' of professional and anti-professional approaches by consultants and conclude that political imperatives in consulting work often require professional practice, or the appearance of it, to be listened to and ensure legitimacy. So for Alvesson and Johansson, asserting management consulting is a profession helps hide its non-professional aspects. Yet these are what clients may want, that is, a scapegoat or 'hatchet' person. They conclude that increasing professionalism, as a strategy, could hinder consulting work. Alvesson later comments more strongly: 'the centrality of political awareness and subordination to power structures [for consultants] runs directly against most claims of professionalism building on objectivity, neutrality and autonomy' (2004:114).The objective professional is thus incompatible with the trusted adviser.

The limit of a professionalizing strategy for consultants is noted by Fincham (2000a), who sees consulting 'marked by weak professional-isation and no really serious attempts at collective mobility.' (2000a:7) Kubr similarly (2002), a mainstream writer, charts and comments pos-itively on the rise of management consulting, but finds limited cer-tification, membership of professional bodies etc. This contrasts with views of consulting as an emerging 'young profession' (Czerniawska 2003), and may instead link to the very old traditions of individual advice-giving.

Lippitt and Lippitt (1986) present the consulting process in set phases, such as 'diagnosis', 'intervention', redolent of a clinical model with sick client, a disempowering though prevalent metaphor in the main-stream. This deficit model of the client makes them a consumer, rather than an empowered actor, emphasising their 'needs' for 'help' and 'sup-port' by the consultant as 'change agent'. Their view of the profes-sional role reflects Giddens' (1991) picture of the professions and people's dependence on the 'expert systems' of 'high modernity'.

Fincham sees consultants not as professionals but: 'knowledge workers operating within a set of structural constraints ...[with] dependent status ... a kind of benign parasite, a supply corps feeding managers with ... ideas ...' (1999a:12) For him, the structural links to client organ-isations, their nature and environments are 'partly an antidote to rhe-torics of persuasion and other action-based accounts of consultancy.' (*ibid*) His final points are telling: that while consultants have no know-ledge monopoly, they are: 'probably ... the best at selling advice ... only consultants [compared to professionals] are in the long-term busi-ness of commodifying their knowledge and they tell the best story.' (1999a:13) So Fincham (2000a) sees professionalism 'as a strategy that distance[s] [consultants] from clients'. Consultants want 'a layered and multi-faceted relation built around something much more complicit and inclusive than a professional diagnosis.' (2000a:8) This telling phrase echoes the closeness and trust explored earlier. Fincham sees this approach as pragmatic since consultants 'seemed well aware that managers were unlikely to grant them a monopoly of knowledge.' (in

---

Reflection

This strongly reflects my own declared interest in connection and dis-tance. I started with concerns about distance and lack of connection, so privileging closeness in the client relationship and assuming this was vital, so not taking up a discourse of the professional.

contrast to, say, a lawyer) He contrasts the implicitly individualist occupational strategies of 'knowledge' workers with collectivist professional strategies. Often too the 'client' is not an individual, as usually assumed by the professional image. He comments that smaller firms or sole practitioners are more likely to use the professional route as a means of legitimacy. Fincham feels most consultants prefer 'partnership': 'stressing how much, much closer to clients they are [than professionals].' (1999a:8)

Consulting as performance and rhetoric

The use of concepts of impression management, 'systems of persuasion', performance, dramaturgy and magic to understand consulting processes have all been mentioned earlier, but deserve a thorough focus, especially in order to explore the relationship between consulting and management. Clark and Salaman (1998a) emphasise that intangibility means consultants stress:

> **Reflection**
> *For example in the case of the voluntary sector organisation which my colleague and I recommended should be wound up, the presentation of our final report was staged carefully by the board of trustees at their AGM with great attention paid to ensuring a good number of its members were present as well as funding bodies, in order to ensure a legitimated end to the organisation heralded by our presentation and thus manage any later criticism of the outcome.*

> the art of impression management (i.e. the manipulation and regulation of images relating to client perceptions of the service delivered) (1998a:19)

This 'enabl[es] consultants to take command of the process' (1998a:21) through 'systems of persuasion'.[7] These concepts also link to a pejorative discourse about consulting, also seen and heard in popular culture, which I examine in this section.

Performance

Performance as a feature of consulting suffuses the literature. McLachlin (1999) comments that in 'today's climate ... a consultant has to hit the ground running because clients want immediate knowledge and experience' and expect to see it. Grey quotes a respondent talking about their consulting firm requiring its auditors to be enthusiastic. 'yes, we will tell someone to seem enthusiastic because clients don't want to pay for someone to stand around looking fed-up' (1994:487). Being fed up and standing around are assumed to represent not performing, but 'enthusiasm' is doing things, being in action (Grey does not discuss the emotional labour implied here). Consultants are judged on this (pressure of) performance – having to *act* in a certain way regardless of how you feel or whether it helps your work. This links directly to Foucault's notion of 'dressage' (Jackson and Carter 1998). Fincham and Evans (1998) refer to the '*spectacular* results demanded of the outside expert' (my emphasis). The notion of a spectacle is vivid: it has to be seen, has an audience, and produces pressure on the performer. But performance is also interactive:

> a successful performance is the result of a triadic collusion between author, actor and audience .. the process is not one of interpreting followed by expressing, but a commingling of the two (Mangham, 1990:107)

Bloomfield and Vurdubakis (2002) in exploring how the assumed advice 'deficit' is identified or constructed, like others, debate the nature of the 'knowledge' work that may be going on and conclude it is *performed*: 'a carefully choreographed sequence of stages'.

Reflection

This reminds me of how I feel in doing, say, a training session many times over; each is effectively rehearsal for the next and so is not spontaneous but scripted. For example the questions people ask on recruitment programmes recur and recur. Equally after a number of years working in the public sector in management development, there are also stories that recur and recur, for example about the habitual poor performer and how to handle them. This emphasises for me the cumulative nature of consultant 'knowledge'. 'Choreography' also resonates with elements of how I experience the careful staging of bidding processes, workshops or the presenting of a report.

Clark and Salaman (1998a) draw on Goffman's view of actors as a series of selves including playwright and (critical) audience of others' performances – but they ignore the performance of people commissioning consulting. They discuss the concept of 'backstage', where the audience is excluded, where things can be prepared, concealed etc.

This helps the performer as 'all performances involve [the] risk' of the audience seeing a glimpse of the backstage. They conclude that:

> ...successful consultancy work is the successful management of risk, promise and opportunity within a particularly highly demanding situation which carries the potential of total and public failure or acclaim. (1998a:28)

For consultants such exposure and vulnerability is a critical issue especially at the outset with a new client, but also a constant pressure. Clark and Salaman acknowledge this double-edged nature of performance but performance is little explored in terms of actual events within consulting work.

In the search to explain the influence of consultants, Fincham (1999a) draws parallels to 'obscure but potent kinds of influence' such as shamans or witchdoctors alongside the dramaturgical metaphor of performance by the consultant to persuade the client. Live performance is key as the emotional and the magical are fused in the marginal figure of the consultant:

> ...consultant knowledge resembles magic – the achievement of rationalist ends (profit, cost cutting) by decidedly non-rational means, the parallels between consultant techniques and magical formulae, and ... accounting for failure features in both magical practice and consultancy. (1999a:3)

His ideas of consulting as akin to magic, positioned between religion and science, and which 'seeks profane ends by sacred means ... based on belief and faith ... impervious to reason and correction.' (2000b: 175) builds on Cleverley (1971). His work portrays the consultant as shaman, sorcerer or medicine man: 'when religions decay and lose the allegiance of the culture, sorcerers ... flourish' (1971:57). Managers 'seek help chiefly from sorcerers who have developed their own medicines to ensure salvation through profit. They call them consultants.' (1971:59) This 'sorcerer' is often competing with professional knowledge holders such as accountants and can be termed 'the independent wise person'.

> Most bosses will assume that outside specialists command more powerful medicine than their own subordinates, for no other reason than that they are from outside. ...Their vague and ill-defined sense

of something missing is an infallible indicator that a magico-religious principle is involved. (1971:60–61)

For Cleverley 'foreign magic is mysterious and therefore more powerful than the domestic variety.' (1971:70) This analysis echoes the 'otherness' of the premodern advisers and is also highlighted by Kipping and Armbruster (2002). While the tradition of the shaman and of magic is honoured in many parts of the world, the 'foreign' notions of 'witch doctor' signify the opposite for this intended audience and link to a pejorative view of consulting and consultants.

Peddling pejoratives

We are perhaps inured to the general media and press presenting negative and mocking images of consultants, as in this early example:

> Of all the businesses, by far, consultancy's the most bizarre.
> For to the penetrating eye, there's no apparent reason why,
> With no more assets than a pen, this group of personable men
> Can sell to clients more than twice the same ridiculous advice,
> Or find, in such a rich profusion, problems to fit their own solution.'
> (Bernie Ramsbottom, Financial Times, 11 April 1981; quoted in Canback 1998)

But throughout my reading of the research and writing on consulting I was struck by the way in which academic writers have felt able to comment with impunity in highly pejorative terms on consulting and on consultants. The question is not only whether this may be justified, but also how far this is legitimate 'critical management'.[8] Alvesson and Johansson (2002) comment on the 'peculiar' lack of 'neutral' texts on management consulting. While questioning just how neutral any text can be, we must also query whether pejorative work constitutes genuine critique, and what may motivate it. Alvesson and Johansson suspect it stems from a lack of empirical work detailing what goes on – existing work is based on images and perception rather than 'in-depth studies of assignments and relations'. It is precisely this lack that I hope to begin to fill.

Clark and Fincham refer to the 'shallow, faddish, greedy consultant-as-prostitute' versus 'inward-looking, academic bookworm' – hardly an even-handed set of terms and the former distinctly gender-inflected (2002:230). But they do acknowledge the problem raised:

> Texts of management consulting can hardly claim to stand outside the fight for recognition, legitimacy and the right to speak with

authority. ...[but we acknowledge] worries about using consultants as the Other [and] academics as the superior interpreter of what goes on in the management world (2002:230)

This tension permeates the current critical management literature about consulting where writers lack reflexivity in relation to their own quasi-consultant status and contestable relation to relevant knowledge.

Clark and Fincham (2002) also refer to the 'popular journalistic criticism' of management consultants which is endemic, portraying negative images, citing overpayment, uselessness, consultants as hard to control, extending their work needlessly and so on (Fincham and Clark 2003).

Clark and Salaman (1998a) suggest experts intentionally jargonise to obscure their meaning. Alvesson also comments in rather cynical tone: 'Less important than having knowledge is to appear to have knowledge, or other qualities different from the mortals'. (1993:1012) Fincham and Evans (1998) write extremely cynically about consulting firms with their mystique of the grand database, their promotion of the importance of out-of-sector examples which only they can access.

> **Reflection**
> *In contrast my experience suggests it is hard enough to communicate when you are trying to be clear!*

Fincham especially uses pejorative terms such as: 'the specific ideas that consultants *peddle*..' [my emphasis] and 'consultancies with many mouths to feed', evocative of a mother with dependent children (1999a). Every specialism in management has a consulting equivalent with specialist knowledge, 'which substitutes for it', implying the consultant is not real or equivalent, betraying his fundamentally negative, rather than critical cast. In this piece (1999a) Fincham explores a range of 'narrative types' he sees consultants speaking. He sums up a narrative of 'real knowledge' as: 'the problem is re-shaped around the consultant's own knowledge' such that the consultant simultaneously expands the issue and the fee. He further sinks into pejoratives: '...vague, shifting terms, such as facilitator, catalyst, guide and mentor, ... consultants tend to shy away from direct and unequivocal terms, like leadership.' (1999a:9) He does not explore the notion of leadership in the marginal position of consultant, nor his assumption that 'leadership' is a 'direct and unequivocal' concept. A cursory review of leadership debates and literature refutes this. On the other hand, 'facilitation' comprises a set of fairly well recognised skills developed in a substantial literature. His term 'shifting' importantly implies a dynamic process although he rather invites the reader to infer 'shifty'. Fincham consistently uses negative language: 'simple anecdotal evidence', managers are 'wide open' to persuasion – this despite his acknowledgement of the 'scornful humour' at work here (1999b); and consultants who may be there 'long enough to be found out'(2000b).

Sturdy focuses on the managers consultants work with:

> [managers'] ambivalence or equivocality towards new management ideas or initiatives. ... criticism, scepticism and/or cynicism ...at ideas in management texts, but also towards consultants and the ideas they promote. (1997b:525)

He surveys the reasons for criticism of consultants – such as life cycles of ideas, over-identification with transient ideas, managers not commissioning the work who try to limit its impact and divert it from their area of responsibility. But also people commissioning who may feel under threat and so resist, criticise, or downplay the role of consultants to bolster their own. He, uniquely, comments about the difficulty facing the consultant 'of maintaining a sense of being a 'rational expert' faced with the fear and resistance of client middle-managers.' (1997b:530)

Clearly not only managers and the general public are at best conflicted about and at worst totally denigrating of consultants, but many academics see them as fair game too, despite the limited empirical evidence other than in relation to the biggest firms in the most lucrative settings. The rhetoric of consulting begins to be matched by the rhetoric of its critics.

Change, symbolism and rhetoric

Fincham and Evans see consultants exploiting the fears that accompany a narrative of permanent change: a 'threatening environment in which outside expertise becomes the business's only salvation.' (1998: 60–61) They comment that the 'change culture that consultants perpetually try to propound' (*ibid*:55) produces even more reliance on consulting

> **Reflection**
> *Equally those commissioning often seem to want instant, fast 'magic' and if someone else will do it, why do it themselves...In one local authority department the senior management team wanted their team managers changed to fit the 'modern' world as they saw it, but weren't prepared to change themselves.*

and reinforces its influence. For them consultants play on managers' fear of change and the potential predicaments they face. They see this as a persistent 'stick and carrot' narrative that creates more business for the consultant. We should note that managers also talk in these terms, using the change discourse as a resource for their own projects – and who can say where this discourse began? Case (2002) reflects on this 'hyperbole' of change and asks in relation to management consultants: 'Who better positioned or more practised not only to take advantage of the apprehension, frustration and fear of client organisations but also to cultivate them?' (2002:94)

Fincham and Evans conclude however that despite the strengths of consultant persuasion there is no hegemony over the client – consultants are too marginal for that. 'There is little permanent in the consultant's world' (1998:61). Sturdy (1997b) also concludes that 'consultancy is resisted and subject to competitive forces', that the emphasis on 'systems of persuasion' may overplay consultants' power. He emphasises the structural dimensions:

> the pursuit of control founded on capitalist social and economic relations and parallel existential insecurities is self-defeating for it denies both structural conflicts and dilemmas and the interdependence and impermanence of the social world. (1997b:533)

Alvesson and Johansson (2002) discuss their consultant type: 'agents of anxiety and suppliers of security', who trade off the discourse of constant change and the search for novelty. They feel this gives consultants power referring to Foucault's notion of disciplinary power where the subject is formed through the setting of standards that people desire to meet:

> Consultancy projects are affected by consultants' claims and strategies, but also by clients. They are affected by structural conditions and management discourses defining what is normal, rational, progressive and leading edge, thereby providing input for the constitution of consultants as well as clients. (2002:243–244)

Fincham comments on how those inside the organisation see consultants: 'creatures of senior management,... posing as unbiased outsiders, [to] ...add a gloss of rationality to expedient and unpalatable decisions..' (1999a:2) He sees rhetoric as 'the most fundamental technique of persuasion' meeting 'managerial needs for reassurance'

(1999a: 3) and linked to the development of fashions in management,
rhetorical constructs which com-
modify knowledge. Consultancy
brochures give 'a long list of named
terrors ... hyped and exaggerated in
every possible way.' (1999a:6) The
assumption that change is constant,
ever faster and bigger than we have
known, is not challenged. He makes
the case that this assumption helps
consultants keep ahead of managers,
who always 'come back with a new
problem or a new angle'. The image
of consulting as rhetoric privileges

> **Reflection**
> *This analysis does feel right in
> some ways – though more as a
> pressure on me than some-
> thing I create. One of my fre-
> quent colleagues is always
> keen for us to be on to 'the
> next big thing' for the public
> sector and we discuss this fre-
> quently in our development
> network – where is the new
> frontline for public services
> going to be?*

the getting of work over the actual doing of work once secured. Fincham
concludes that:

> As long as consultants remain masters of the marketplace their
> input will always be in demand, though mastery of the wider picture
> assumes a capacity to provide a constant turnover of ideas. (1999a:7)

Alvesson (1993) turns to the view of organisations as rhetoric, which
consultants help 'conform to the institutionalised expectations of their
environments.' A key part of this is they are: 'broadly recognised as carriers of advanced knowledge ... highly visible and sanctioned in terms
of knowledge and expertise...' (1993:1004) The use of 'professionals' is
thus symbolic, announcing the well-run organisation does this sort of
thing. Legge (2002) refers to Alvesson's view that knowledge intensive
firms are also ambiguity intensive and so rhetoric must be their core.
The question not explored is how can a person live this ambiguity? In
particular, how can a solo practitioner live this?

Jackall (1988) emphasises the symbiotic nature of managers' and
consultants' mutual symbolic work:

> managers' use of certain kinds of expertise, namely that generated by
> management consultants ... themselves virtuosos in symbolic mani-
> pulation, aptly illustrates their peculiar symbolic skills (1988:137)

Clark and Salaman argue this symbolic work is equally about managers'
identities: 'a central, critical, heroic, almost mystical role.' (1998b:155)

Fincham sees rhetoric embedded in both the culture and practices of consulting, 'in the structures imposed by the relationship with the client.' and 'the consultant's ambivalent position as outsider.' (1999a:4) He warns that approaching the study of consulting through a focus on rhetoric risks the trap of rhetoric, that of assuming things are real rather than intentions. For Alvesson, it risks the trap of dualism: falsely posing rhetoric against 'reality':

> The constructedness of reality and the reality of construction, the realness of symbols and the symbolic character of reality, should be borne in mind – especially perhaps when the knowledge-intensive is studied. (Alvesson 2004:84)

Women in consulting

The major debates and key images set out in this chapter do not take account of gender in terms of women's experience. Arguably they derive from a 'masculine' view of organisations and management. If we take modern consulting as beginning in the late 19th century or early 20th century (Canback 1998) then women take time to make an appearance and remain a minority, especially in major firms (Meriläinen *et al.* 2004). Similarly there is a paucity of academic material focused on or including women in consulting.[9] This section reviews what there is and contrasts it with the mass of foregoing material.

An early study (Gealy *et al.* 1979) uncovered few gender-based differences in consultants' experience and approach, although women felt 'more restricted' by male than female clients. Berry later concluded that barriers to access and progression were worse if a woman 'had the bad luck to run into a client who does not want his professional counsel from a female' (1996:34). Waclawski *et al.* (1995) report on the motivation of women organisation development consultants: the women are concerned with the position of women in organisation development and the need for learning, both for themselves and for new women entering the field. Their motivators embrace power, change, helping others, making a difference through consulting work.

Three auto-biographical studies present very different material, drawn from personal reflection recounting women's approaches to their own consulting practice.[10] Harris (1995) identifies a paradox of being 'central and local' in consulting work. She writes of her 'rage' at this and her feelings at being judged as over- or under-competent, usually by men. She also describes her views of her worth in relation to her earnings.

Similarly, three women, writing as 'spirit hawk collective' (1995) present a reflective, practice-based account of how their impact as consultants stems from their presence as much as what they do. They analyse linked elements of feeling, reflection, voice and nurturance. They do not examine these in terms of gendered assumptions about women and nurturance, or women and emotionality.

Thirdly Kaplan (1995) presents a qualitative study of women consultants who are entrepreneurs in their own right. She identifies four themes: women's work, their journey, the context of their oppression as women, their relationships. She feels that the overall story is of 'women becoming whole. ... The women embody, not just talk about, systems thinking.' (1995:58) Her respondents are concerned with empowering others; they want to be 'role models for doing work with integrity and collaboration' and are 'not happy if they are not making a difference.' (*ibid*:63) These ideas resonate with Waclawski *et al.* (1995). Kaplan's work also notes how women are constrained in a patriarchal system.

More recently Rehman and Frisby (2000) focus on self-employed women consultants in the Canadian leisure sector and explore self-employment as either liberational or marginalising. They conclude this is too simple a dichotomy: both perceptions hold for their respondents. The personal situations of the women, their social contexts, gender relations at large and the nature of the work itself all influence them. They find women speak at length about autonomy and control in their work, about rejection and emotional investment. They are surprised that women talk spontaneously about money and the economics of their work.

It is striking how similar are the two frameworks offered for considering the experience of women consultants and how these firmly place women in the broader social context – see Table 3.2. The four elements in each contrast starkly with images and issues in the foregoing discussion of the mainstream and critical management literatures. Their strongest link is to the image of the 'advice industry' which

Table 3.2 Frameworks about women as consultants

Author:	Rehman & Frisby 2000	Kaplan 1995
Key issues for women consultants	Social context Personal situation Broader gender relations Nature of the work	Relationships Individual journey Oppression The work

emphasised trust, relationships, being intimate yet 'Other', as with the pre-modern advisers.

Both frameworks situate women in a gendered terrain, noting its impact in concert with the other issues.

Conclusions

The images of consulting explored feature in both mainstream and critical management literature. They have substantial power in affecting how we consider consulting. This section summarises how I see this terrain and how it affects the rest of this book.

Seeing consulting as a *commercial transaction* itself raises other key images: the nature of services, the importance of interaction and of trust, power in a situated process, what animates the manager to buy and what it is that the consultant sells. Professionalism, knowledge and performance are all implicated in the commercial framing of consulting.

The image of consulting as a *service* emphasises heterogeneity and ambiguity, providing space for notions of both the 'trusted adviser', the 'objective professional', for impression management and magic. It raises different assumptions of the 'client'. The intangibility of service also produces the discourse of the 'project' to construct manageability and measurability. The image of the tangible commodity haunts the literature on consulting in opposition to the image of consulting as a co-constructed service process.

The *'advice industry'* discussion challenges how far there can be a critical, ethical stance in doing consulting within the overwhelming discourse of the 'client' and their 'trusted adviser'. This close mutual process raises the interesting question of how far a consultant's subjectivity is the result of those who commission her/him; and that the close, trusted relationship may be more the norm than clients wish to acknowledge. Trust and partnership both privilege closeness in advice-giving and challenge the apparent objectivity of consulting as about knowledge and professionalism, the work of the external 'other'. Yet the discussion of interaction is confused and privileges assumptions of the dyad. It proposes either client or consultant power dominates; that 'achievement' and success are tangible rather than fleeting, ephemeral or about raising new questions through advice-giving; it skates over the role of values, expectations, beliefs. *Partnership* is viewed more structurally, as about exchange and rhetoric not mutuality. The approach to advice assumes a deficient client and thus a definite knowledge base. Fundamentally the 'advice industry' image claims a process bias but speaks in essentialist terms of authenticity and credibility, without exploring how trust is enacted between participants. While values and ethics are raised, the client is still king: what then can constitute 'critical consulting'?

Consulting viewed as a *knowledge industry* is riven with contradiction: managers uncertain of their own knowledge turn for help to the very group, consultants, about whose knowledge they are least convinced. The explanation is seen to lie in the linked rational and ritual aspects of consulting: the tangible contribution of apparently rational processes, within a constructed dialogue or rhetoric and 'repertoire of performances'. We need new ways to conceptualise knowledge work and consulting as using knowledge, for example exploring the cumulative nature of knowledge.

Seeing consulting as a *profession* added little clarity. Management consultants are viewed as less concerned with societal goals; their connection to the client is mostly not the espoused affective neutrality of the professional acting for some common or societal good. We can conclude consultants are largely constrained into professional practice, or the appearance of it, to ensure legitimacy and be heard. The objective professional is thus largely incompatible with the trusted adviser: 'the tension between the knowledgeable, autonomous expert versus the client-centred, adaptable service worker.' (Alvesson 2004:216). This contrasts with views of consulting as a 'young profession' but reinforces links to very old traditions of advice-giving and questions of the role of affect and values.

Consulting as *rhetoric and performance* represents a double-edged problem: exposure and vulnerability are critical issues at the outset with a new client, and performance a constant pressure. Both consultant and those commissioning shape performances although this is little acknowledged. However performance is barely explored in terms of actual events within consulting work. Equally performance implies impression management, rhetoric and ritual by consultants, widely interpreted in pejorative terms such as 'sorcerer'. Considering rhetoric points to a paradox for consulting as simultaneously about reassurance *and* anxiety creation in the face of the 'permanent change' discourse. How to live this 'ambiguity-intensive' work is not explored, although we should avoid the false dualism of rhetoric and 'reality'.

The little material available about *women in consulting* contrasts starkly with the rest of the chapter. It focuses on the situation for individual women, on women's differing roles and lives, but also on societal issues

Table 3.3 Dimensions of consulting from research and writing

Dimension of consulting	'Mainstream' assumptions	'Critical management' contribution	Key question for the 'critical consultant'
Overall mode	**prescriptive** – 'models' of practice and knowledge, the adviser	**challenging** – notions of 'knowledge', a social constructionist stance	*How to co-create for progressive social change?*
Key concepts	**effectiveness** – about how to improve practice 'professionalism' managing the client relationship	**'systems of persuasion'** – symbols and 'rhetorical narratives' to persuade managers	*How to be credible and challenging while bringing knowledge & expertise to bear?*
Consulting relationship	**'professionalised'** – an objective approach but also **'trusted adviser'** closer to the client	**'performance'** and **'impression management'** – relationship and interaction shifting, emerging, manipulative – but also exchange & partnership with 'active client'	*How to develop and work in dynamic but mutual relations?*
Structural stance	assumes **unitary** goals of consultant and client in the capitalist world	sees consulting as a **by-product** of the corporate capitalist world, it supports/feeds off capital	*How can consulting be a means to change/challenge power relations?*
Link to management	assumes a (shared) **knowledge-base** of consulting and of management, neither of which is problematised	sees management and consulting as **mutually defining** and constituting each other, knowledge-base is problematised	*How to live with and yet challenge the connection to management?*
How practice is situated	In the **organisation** or firm, linked to its goals and concerns for **effectiveness, change and success** (profit)	Driven by consultants selling **reassurance** and relying on **rhetoric to meet individual managers'** goals and concerns	*How to 'deliver' for those commissioning work while keeping a concern for society & goals of social justice?*

of gender, their aspirations beyond themselves, their needs from their consulting work and the strong feelings it evokes. They seem to view this work through completely different lenses, although the images of the commercial process and consulting as a service are still vivid. The paradox of being at once powerful yet marginal is especially noteworthy in relation to the adviser role.

This chapter has moved some way from the definition in the Introduction of consulting as 'advising', but key dimensions have crystallised, summarised in Table 3.3 together with the questions that arise for what 'critical consulting' must address. While the mainstream literature privileges the 'client', providing an overwhelmingly consumerist view of the process, the critical literature privileges the consultant, but with a negative spin and many openly cynical, pejorative and judgmental statements, often unhelpfully conflating 'gurus' with consultants. There is little work searching out the emergent processes of relating between consultants and managers as they happen, and none exploring this as a gendered process. Much work produced by consultants is criticised simply because they produce it and are assumed to intend self-promotion and self-justification. On the other hand, work researched by academics on the outside, looking in, relies overwhelmingly on reportage from interviews, not direct observation of interactions. The view of the critical management research seems to be that consultants 'would do that, wouldn't they?' and that mainstream writers, especially consultants, 'would say that, wouldn't they?'

4
Consulting as a Discursive Practice

Introduction

This chapter draws together the insights from both the genealogical review in Chapter 2 and the review of contemporary images of consulting in Chapter 3 to conceptualise consulting as a discursive practice.

> Discourse is a practice not just of representing the world, but of signifying the world, constituting and constructing the world in meaning …[it] helps construct social relationships. (Fairclough 1992:64)

As a result I identify continuing and competing discourses of consulting, such as the 'trusted adviser', the 'objective professional', the 'client is king' and consulting as commodity. I also signal key emerging issues that will be considered further in discourse analysis of my autoethnographic material on consulting interactions in Part 2, such as the visible shift from pre-modern 'feminine' approaches to current discourses drawing on a 'masculine' perspective of organisations.

Learning from the genealogy: 'feminine' discourses of advice-giving

The genealogy offers a different view on the notion of advice-giving to organisational leaders. It raises key issues of means and ends – rarely explicitly raised in contemporary writing and research. It offers a picture of advice-giving processes and their origins, away from specified expert knowledge or professional power. We see discourses of advice-giving involving:

- *Trust* and the persistent image of the 'trusted adviser' where the relationship between leader and adviser is intimate, often cemented by kinship or other reciprocal ties

- *Certainty* and advisers' sense of being right, having something to say and saying it directly
- *Humility* and deferring to the person being advised
- *The 'Other'* with negative images and stories about advisers as 'grasping' or greedy or simply foreign
- *Impression management*, that is, the use of rhetoric or other powers to convince the listener (including 'magic' or occult attribution of the powers of the adviser)

Apparent differences in the pre-modern from viewing present-day consulting include:

- The context of strong *social ties* such as those forged through feudalism, kinship and religion which is much less universal in 21st century industrialised countries
- Aiming explicitly for *stability* rather than creating change
- The important role of *intercession* with those in power
- A *shift* from adviser to expert post Renaissance
- A shift from expert do-er to expert adviser with the rise of the *professions*
- A shift from *visible to invisible* advisers

The genealogical exploration also raises concepts important in relation to women advisers, especially assumptions of women operating in the intimate and private realm. Several discursive and extra-discursive practices, which we might term 'feminine', are visible in pre-modern advice-giving:

- The importance of *relationships* with intimacy and emotion strong themes for both male and female advisers
- Explicit aspiration to *mutual* gain or the public good, again for both men and women, which are identified with the feminine (Miller 1976)
- *Supporting* or nurturing the *strong* rather than viewing the advisee as deficient
- The use and fostering of *dense reciprocal social networks* which enable the getting and doing of advice-giving work
- That advice-giving involved *heterogeneous work* involving many small tasks/processes especially making or repairing links between people

Overall it is possible to see a shift from 'feminine' to 'masculine' in how advice-giving has been constructed, perceived and carried out, with an emphasis on trust and relationships at the core of the process. The notion of women as advisers, confidantes or consultants explored in Chapter 2 reflects gendered boundaries: women in the intimate private arena of the body and emotions; men operating more in the rational 'outside world' of work and public life – although the earlier we look, the more men work in both arenas. The question is raised: how far are these issues still reverberating today for women and men in consulting? My empirical work will take this up and I return to the contested question of the 'feminine' in Chapter 9.

Discourses of consulting from contemporary ('masculine') images

Contemporary material about consulting shows that it is a highly heterogeneous phenomenon, in common with other intangible services producing ambiguity and so emphasising discourses of *advice*, *trust* and the credibility of the *'professional'*.[1] The service nature of consulting also privileges the *'client as king'*, reifying the client-consultant relationship and its importance. The intangibility of a service produces too the discourse of the commodity or *'project'* and assumptions of its substance and manageability. Importantly consulting is an economic process: the assumptions of the powerful 'client'[2] and the 'contract' in the process of commercial transaction are pervasive and frame how consulting is seen. Alongside the growth of consulting and its economic impact, comes the discourse of the *'knowledge intensive'* industry as critical to success in the new economy.

The most fundamental concerns about consulting have been raised, including the nature and extent of 'knowledge work' within consulting, the relation of consulting to management as a whole and questions of power between 'clients' and consultants. The critical management writers emphasise the complicity of mainstream writers, often consultants themselves, in the project to legitimise consulting and so bolster their own position. The mainstream is seen as making tendentious claims to knowledge and expertise in a business which is all about impression management and rhetorical claims. While the mainstream sees the 'client' as economically powerful and the focus of the consultant's attention, most critical writers take the opposite view: the powerful consultant exploits the ambiguities and intangibility of their service. The critical writers also see consulting crucially as interaction: they discuss the centrality of interaction to the consulting process and the issues of connection, distance, partnership and performance that result.

Critical work expresses a discourse of consulting as *rhetoric*: about impression management, performance, dramaturgy and magic. Consulting as a 'system of persuasion' is the dominant perspective. Consulting is thus seen as a *prop to management* and the progress of capital, at best symbiotic and at worst parasitic in its relationship with managers, who above all crave certainty and personal kudos in an uncertain and competitive world.

> A recurring picture of the consulting client in the critical literature is one of the insecure and anguished manager faced with a nearly impossible task ... [They need] predictability and control, [and] increased social and personal esteem. Both ... can be fulfilled by management consultants, without the application of any functional management knowledge. (Werr 2002:93)

The limited contemporary material about women in consulting reviewed in Chapter 3 links strongly to the discourse of trust but raised different images of power. It strongly echoed the issues of the pre-modern advisers – being intimate yet 'Other', of marginal, heterogeneous work, of dense networks and relationships, mutual gain and public good, and supporting others' power. It suggests the existence of alternative 'realities' or 'underprivileged' discourses (Grant *et al.* 1998:12) in contrast to the dominant images of consulting drawing overwhelmingly on the work of men and focused on male consultants within a problematic framing of the 'neutral' organisation (Acker 1990).

Contested issues and competing discourses of consulting

The age-old experience of advice-giving intriguingly illuminates our picture of the modern consultant. A Foucauldian 'genealogical' review of advice-giving to organisational leaders provides a more grounded historical perspective to consider present-day discourses of consulting. Drawing on the words of advisers in the pre-modern helps see different discourses, both those that continue such as trust, and a 'feminine' cast to advice-giving which is much less visible in contemporary literature.

We can see that while contemporary literature emphasises consulting as interaction, most privilege 'client' or 'consultant' or their 'relationship' or 'contract' as entities in themselves. Equally while critical management literature does emphasise the role of talk and language, and discusses power, the notion of consulting as *discursive practice* is surprisingly absent; most research does not refer to concepts of discourse.[3] Deetz (1998) draws on notions of discourse in how consultants are managed in his study of a consulting firm i.e. not in how consulting is done. Whittle (2006) uses discourse as a concept to interrogate paradoxes she found in the work of management consultants. Uniquely Clegg *et al.* (2004) have made a case for consulting as a discursive practice, asserting that consultants are positioned to introduce 'noise' into a system and create positive change through 'disruption of dominant orders'. Sturdy *et al.* (2004) marshalled a trenchant critique of this case as an apolitical view of management and power. The inability of either set of authors to reconcile the pragmatic agency implied in the former with the solidly structural cast of the latter sums up the impasse in current critical thought on consulting.

Importantly, the notion of discourse helps see consulting within the context not only of management and organisation but also in society at large, now and at other points in history. Competing and evolving discourses form and are formed by consulting processes and the action of individuals as well as by other forces. Seeing consulting as a discursive practice helps locate issues of power and knowledge within situated interaction using a Foucauldian lens and offers explanatory resources for the contradictions raised and discussed in Chapter 3. For example, Hackley (2000) reformulated his approach to the study of an advertising agency in discursive terms. While 'connotations of the word 'management' tend to privilege the conscious, the explicit, the directive, the cognitive and the causative', using discourse analysis produced 'an alternative understanding of management in terms of the discursive, the tacit, and the psycho-sociological' (Hackley 2000:253) which raised issues of silencing and power. Thus discourse may offer a way to attempt a new formulation of what is going on in consulting as a plurivocal 'struggle for discursive dominance' (Grant *et al.* 1998:8).

'Discourse is about the production of knowledge through language … all practices have a discursive aspect.' (Hall 1997:44). If consulting is a practice, is a form of knowledge work, then consulting is a discursive practice. Hall helpfully shows how discourse shapes and constrains action and defines discourse as:

> a group of statements which provide a language for talking about – a way of representing the knowledge about – a particular topic at a particular historical moment (1997:44).

Discourse bridges the separation of what we say from what we do, which links strongly to critiques of consulting as simply about impression management. This bridging in turn helps show how discourse shapes and constrains action, 'ruling in' certain ways of talking about a topic and just as clearly 'ruling out' or restricting others. Hall highlights the situated, historical dimension of discourse and its effects, which Foucault holds up to inquiry through his genealogical approach. For me then consulting is primarily a discursive practice 'through which realities are enacted. Indeed, what else do consultants do if they don't talk, listen, read and write? (Clegg *et al.* 2004:36)

Thus the learning about consulting in Part I identifies a series of discourses alive within the current consulting arena. These include:

- 'client is king'
- the 'trusted adviser'[4]
- the 'objective professional'
- 'permanent change'
- 'knowledge work'
- 'deficit model' of client
- 'partnership'
- consulting as commodity: 'project', 'contract'
- consulting as rhetoric, performance and magic – generally a pejorative discourse

The genealogical lens suggests some continuing threads in discourses of advice-giving: specifically the 'trusted adviser' and the negative discourses of performance, rhetoric and magic. It also highlights some strands not reflected in the contemporary literature, such as the paradox of certainty and humility.

What is helpful in exploring discourses is to make transparent how they compete and interconnect. My view of these dynamics follows.

The 'trusted adviser' and the 'objective professional'

These are the two discourses clearest throughout contemporary research and writing where they also rather overlap and are not always clearly delineated. The debate on professionalism emphasises the importance of distance rather than the closeness of the trusted adviser. Trust is however an ubiquitous issue, emerging throughout contemporary research and writing as a key idea; it is an equally strong theme in the genealogy. Tracking back into the pre-modern to trace the discursive formation of these persistent contemporary ideas shows a shift post-Renaissance from traditional adviser or confidante to the expert. The new expert believed in their knowledge and experience to advise others and to act. Another shift begins to occur with the rise of professions: from expert who does concrete tasks to expert professional for whom talk and writing are the key activities.

These two discourses of the consultant also paint pictures of the person, the role and so connect to my concerns with identity. The characterisation of the two can also be seen to reflect the poles of rational/emotional and so a link to 'masculine' and 'feminine' binaries. It is noteworthy that the contemporary literature does not discuss these issues; discussions of gender or of emotion in consulting processes are hardly present except in the sparse woman-centred material. The assumption of the neutral professional is widespread and the emotional labour of consulting not explored despite the emphasis on trust, authenticity, performance and interaction. The assumed dominance of the objective professional can be seen as contradicting the 'client is king' discourse, while the trusted adviser will swallow this discourse whole.

'Permanent change' and 'knowledge work'

These are two discourses ubiquitous in management theory and practice more generally (see for example Sorge and Witteloostuijn 2004), but which have particular resonance for the study of consulting. A modernist worldview concerning continuous change for organisations is a key discourse in the mainstream consulting literature. While this is a contested position,[5] some critical management writers believe the consultant draws on 'deep rooted modernist beliefs about the inevitability of change' (Fincham and Evans 1998) to achieve their persuasion of managers. The paradox that arises concerns the shifting requirements of any knowledge base in the face of permanent change. The notion of consulting as 'knowledge work' is another key mainstream discourse, positing that survival in the face of this change requires a knowledge focus. Critical writers take this up and conclude that revised definitions of knowledge as rhetoric and impression management enable consultants to square the circle.

The changing and contested nature of 'knowledge' also puts a spoke into the discourse of the 'objective professional' – for where is the professional without her recognised body of knowledge? Crucial here is what is seen to 'work' in the 'real' world, argue Dent and Whitehead (2002). They assert this produces a tension in the professional – between 'what works' and their personal value position but:

there is no uncontested ideological position to which [we] might retreat ... we are each left to our own devices as we attempt to navigate our way through new, unmapped globalised territories of professional identity. (2002:5)

They comment on the emptiness of this necessity for individuals who are constrained to live it and note the dualisms it produces such as instability replacing stability. The consultant perhaps lives this tension one step ahead of the manager, struggling to reassure while experiencing this internal turbulence. Alvesson sees this as producing 'knowledge-*claims* intensiveness' rather than knowledge intensiveness (2004), thus returning to a theme of rhetoric.

The genealogy in contrast showed the primacy for advice-givers of helping produce *stability*. Again discourse is the helpful concept allowing us to characterise 'permanent change' as a discourse that enables the stability of the powerful to remain unchanged. The competing discourses may then be supporting the powerful or producing change – which opens a space for an idea of what the critical consultant may do.

The 'deficit model' and 'partnership'

The concept of the 'client-consultant relationship' is found throughout contemporary research and writing. Two key forms of this are visible and seem to compete as discourses. Bloomfield and Vurdubakis point out that 'the very notion of 'advice' presupposes and requires a kind of (knowledge) deficiency or 'ignorance' on the part of the recipient' (2002:115). This puts the consultant in the position of expert, feeding a discourse of deficient 'client' – and arguably undermining the 'client is king' discourse. In the mainstream literature deficiency is taken for granted and often posed in terms of a medical model of diagnosis and prescription. This in turn not only sets up particular kinds of interaction but also assumes 'knowledge' is possible. The result is a particular process of dependence between consultants and those who commission them. Interestingly premodern sources favour supporting the powerful or the person who would best use advice, not using a 'deficit' discourse. When professions developed, although criticised for mystifying their knowledge, there is little sense they saw 'clients' as lacking; their networks, as for earlier advisers, involved mutual and reciprocal relations.

The contemporary discourse of relationship as 'partnership' suggests this more mutual and collaborative notion, which may not be compatible with the discourse of deficit, based on the discursive resource of 'expert'. Partnership implies a side-by-side approach of consultant with those commissioning. But this too can produce either its own rhetoric where the consultant is really in control, or conversely a situation where those commissioning treat consultants as simply pairs of hands. The reification of the singular 'relationship' in contemporary writing suggests that exploring competing discourses here is important. In order to remain alert to this issue I avoid the term 'relationship' from now on, preferring *interaction* or *processes*.

Both these discourses contrast with the paradox of certainty with humility seen in the premodern adviser. The sure adviser worked knowingly with the powerful to support them; the humble adviser acknowledged the power of the advisee when offering their strong views, and often mediated for those less powerful. The questions for the study are: how far this paradox continues, how does it affect consulting interaction and does it support the critique of consulting as propping up the managerial agenda, far from any notion of 'critical consulting'?

Whose power is it anyway? Commodified transactions and consultant rhetoric

The overwhelming use of the term 'client' in the contemporary literature has sensitised me to its discursive power. 'Client' seems to be shorthand in almost all cases for a discourse of *'the client is king'*; this draws on established views of a commercial transaction and locates consulting firmly within this economic frame. Linked to this a discourse of *commodification* has grown up to express (and influence) consulting processes, using genres such as the 'project'. These are also attempts to make tangible the intangible processes and interaction involved. The opposite of attempting to produce tangibility is the discourse of consulting as *rhetoric, impression, performance and magic*. This discourse challenges the notion that 'clients' 'manage' their 'projects' with consultants and paints a picture of the powerful consultant deploying her 'systems of persuasion', creating the right impression through polished performance and even drawing on (traditions of) the magical. Power is thus seen as either/or, with 'client' or consultant. In this book I challenge this: I privilege the (inter)active and avoid language which presumes particular power positions. I use the term 'people who commission' instead of 'client' and 'consulting work' not project. In this way I try to keep a process focus throughout and make issues of power more transparent, created in interaction. In this I hold to Foucault's genealogical approach of exploring *activity* rather than labelling *identities*. For example, examining premodern advice-giving activities, such as intercession with the powerful, may illuminate more than judging who has more power, those commissioning or those consulting.

Negative discourse and 'critical consulting'?

Existing perspectives also offer little space for a 'critical consulting' discourse, that is one which attempts to combat the perverse managerialism of public sector organisations while supporting public service values, such as equity and accountability, and striving for more progressive outcomes, both for people at work and crucially for the people and communities they serve. Questions of values, of ends and means, of mutual gain and the public good were raised in the genealogy. While the archetypal discourse of the adviser as 'Other' also featured in Chapter 3, the contemporary material focuses either on (implicit) assumptions of supporting corporate capital or on the pejorative in terms of consultants working for self-profit or to reassure managers, hardly raising questions of values at all. The paradox of competing discourses of trust and 'other-ness' is present now as in the pre-modern.

Where has exploring the terrain of consulting taken us?

The issues raised in Part I not only provided an intriguing backdrop for my research, but echoed the concerns with which I set out: the role of (my) knowledge; distance and closeness to people commissioning work; how to achieve the work, especially in an ethical way and in a critical spirit. The material reviewed in Chapters 2 and 3 has emphasised how much these issues are live for others doing this work, in the past and in how others today see consulting.

The closeness attributed to the adviser, especially the discourse of trust, echoes my concern about notions of distance. The critical voice which questions the source of legitimacy for advice links to my doubts about knowledge or value. The answers on offer in the mainstream take the route of developing personal 'authenticity' with all its problematic assumptions of an essential self. They require acceptance that legitimacy must rest on a deficit model of the 'client' and assumptions about a pre-existing body of knowledge. The certainty of the pre-modern adviser contrasts with the contemporary discourse of the 'client is king'. More fundamentally, discussions of the 'adviser' focus on concepts of role rather than on the processes involved. The emphasis on the 'trusted adviser' connects to the themes of self and of emotion within consulting processes, little explored in the consulting literature.

Studying contemporary work sharpens the challenge to explore the notion of 'critical' consulting, which seems otherwise to be effectively ruled out, but for which there are traces in the premodern material. It also raises the intriguing question of a shift from premodern advice-giving with a 'feminine' character to contemporary consulting built on 'masculine' perspectives of organisation.

The work in Part I also put renewed emphasis on the importance of my focus on actual interactions in the consulting process, in order better to explore the issues of knowledge, power, advice, ambiguity, emergent processes and identities within the commercial transaction. There is a major gap in terms of contemporary empirical work on the *doing* of consulting, specifically taking an 'inside' view as consultant, and a critical one. Research on consulting should 'recognise and incorporate the mutually constituting dialectical, structural and existential nature of the consultancy process.' (Sturdy 1997b:532) Existing work predominantly uses interviews to explore consulting work retrospectively. It is hardly concerned with the public sector, with small pieces of work or solo consultants. Research also typically focuses on the getting of consulting work, rather than the doing of it. Research approaches do not open up interaction sufficiently.[6] Sturdy (2002) makes my point: 'Consultant-client encounters ... have yet to be subjected fully to scrutiny, critical or otherwise' (2002:134).[7] Ram (2000) suggests a process focus in his study of entrepreneurship in small consulting firms: '[qualitative research should] focus on explicating the dynamics and social processes involved ... (2000:658). For him social relations between consultants are also key, 'inextricably linked' to interactions with those commissioning work (Ram 2000:660). Gammelsoeter (2002) proposes 'the study of the interaction between consultants and organisational actors specifically takes into account that the actors have to answer to both inner and outer contexts' (2002:225), endorsing the importance of the broader social/political context. 'Insider' research (Coghlan 2001) by women is therefore potentially important given their relative absence in the consulting literature and the apparently 'feminine' character of premodern advice-giving. For all these reasons I focus on the practice of women consultants through studying their interaction and stories of their work in Part II.

Part II

Discourse Analysis of Consulting Interactions

5
Researching Consulting Interactions: From Process Ontology to Critical Discourse Analysis

Introduction

I aimed to grasp what is between people in the consulting process. The work in Part I led me to explore what is actually going on in the consulting process: how far is it constructing and constructed by these discourses? And what else might be going on?

> ... repertoires of conduct are activated that are not bounded by the enclosure formed by the human skin... [they] are rather ... webs of tension across a space that accord human beings capacities and powers to the extent that they catch them up in hybrid assemblages of knowledges, instruments, vocabularies, systems of judgement and technical artefacts.' (Rose 1996:322)

Rose's idea of webs across a space expresses well the processes which catch us up in the 'hybrid assemblages' of consulting work. Focusing on actual interactions and viewing consulting primarily as a discursive practice enabled me to explore issues of knowledge, power, advice, ambiguity, emergent processes and identities as well as the commercial transaction. My studying the processes of consulting through *discourse analysis* helped me see what discursive resources were drawn on.

This chapter explains how I approached this research and the choices I made. I first discuss the theoretical base framing my inquiry. Some readers may be especially interested in applying critical discourse analysis in their own research and I would encourage them especially to dive with me into my discovery of a *process-based* ontological approach, its connection to discourse and to discourse analysis. Others more concerned with consulting practice may want at this point to skip to the later sections of this chapter which explain more about using Critical Discourse Analysis (CDA), in order better to get to grips with the material in Chapters 6 and 7.

In developing my approach I drew on Denzin and Lincoln's (1998) succinct summation of the research process:

> the gendered, multi-culturally situated researcher approaches the world with a set of ideas, a framework (ontology) that specifies a set of questions (epistemology) that are then examined (methodology, analysis) in specific ways. That is, empirical material bearing on the question are collected and then analysed and written about. (1998:23)

They characterise such research as 'bricolage ... a pieced-together, close-knit set of practices that provide solutions to a problem in a concrete situation' (1998:3). The bricoleur 'works with his/her hands and uses devious means compared to the craftsman ... is practical and gets the job done.' (1998:3) This chapter also gives a flavour of this practical process, particularly my autoethnographic approach that provided the corpus of material on consulting interactions, which I analyse using CDA in Chapters 6 and 7.

Reflection

The notion of bricolage sounds exactly like consulting work. We bring all sorts of material and people to bear and have to get a job done no matter what.

A process based approach

Adopting *process ontology* (Rescher 1996; Chia 1997a, 1997b; Nayak 2008) as a worldview is a fundamental shift from the dominant paradigm (of *substance* ontology) for work, life and research in the Western world. The process approach not only reflects what was emphasised about consulting in Part 1 but also connects to work on gender as a performed effect (Butler 1999). It therefore joins feminist and post-structuralist approaches to the construction of meaning and takes a predominantly Foucauldian view of the nature of discourse as *enacted* in power relations. A process approach helped me manage the 'theoretical pendulum' (Putnam and Cooren 2004:329) to bridge the micro issues of interaction and macro issues of power and policy; to deal with assumptions about agency and the subject in exploring consultant identity in relation to structure and organisations. I was concerned fundamentally with consulting *processes*, such as emerging relations between a variety of actors, and the ways these co-constructed knowing and power, and the 'becoming' of subjectivities in interaction. I view these micro-processes within broader socio-political processes, and as contributing to these.

A process based approach draws on thinking originating with Heraclitus of Ephesus who emphasised 'the primacy of a changeable and emergent world', in contrast to other Greek philosophy that 'insisted upon the permanent and unchangeable nature of reality' (Chia 1997a: 71). Augustinian thought similarly sees the individual 'stand[ing] in the river of time, where it must learn to understand that its past no longer exists and that its future has not yet begun,' (Bohmer 1999). Later Descartes' view of the self as a thinking being, a fixed point of certainty amid all doubt, separate from its natural and social surroundings (Turnbull 1999) helped privilege the opposite, substance ontology through a dualistic view of a world made up of entities. These competing concepts of certainty and mutability have swung to and fro in philosophic writing. Rescher concludes 'time, process, change and historicity [are] among the fundamental categories for understanding the real' and talks of 'the fundamentality of transformative processes' (1996:41). For Rescher 'the self ...is a mega-process ... our sense of self is the glimmering insight of part into the whole' (1996:108).

Reflection
Some of my themes in consulting are about time, history and change. My concerns also stem from issues of identity and Rescher's work encourages me to draw on self to explore consulting as a whole. (Journal 2001)

Process thinkers conceptualise 'self [as] ... not really a 'thing' of some sort but a centre of action' (1996:111). Similarly, Butler draws on Nietzsche to conclude in her ontology of gender that 'the 'doer' is invariably constructed in and through the deed' (1999:181). For Butler the metaphysics of substance are 'artificial philosophical means by which simplicity, order and identity are effectively instituted' (1999:27), based on a view – to her, illusory – that grammar and its subject/object entities reflect reality. So the process view of the world spoke to me strongly; it reflected what I was learning about consulting and my starting questions.

Critics of a process based worldview consider it fails to account for the impact of social structures and their power (Fleetwood 2005), such as patriarchy, and assumes that organisation is entirely composed of discourse, thus 'downgrading' the extra-discursive (Fairclough 2005). Such critiques are answered to some extent through broader discourse theory (Wilmott 2005).[1] Bhaskar and Laclau point out that action is:

> something that is entirely inherent to discourse. The notion of discourse could, if you prefer, be replaced by that of practice (Bhaskar and Laclau 2002:81, cited in Wilmott 2005:754)

Wilmott tackles issues of social structure, taking the view that structure can only be seen through what people actually do. Discourse theory proposes that there is a real world, but everything we do in relation to it is discursively constructed, including key concepts such as 'structure'. The critics nonetheless see agency privileged over structure by process ontology. I see this as an over-simplification occasioned by the conflation of 'process' with 'event' or agency (Fairclough 2005) alongside the centring of the human subject. Process ontology sees flux and change as underlying *all* of reality and not simply in relation to human agency. Structures are especially at issue here, the 'socially real' of critical realism. Process ontology sees the socially real as brought into being by an array of discursive and extra-discursive *processes*. For example a piece of consulting work is partly discursively framed and reproduced by actors, partly framed by processes of the production, transporting, selling and buying of goods (such as brochures, reports, presentation materials, venues and food) and labour (for example of consultants, their contacts and people commissioning the work), partly framed by discursive and extra-discursive notions of value(s) and so on. Without these myriad processes no piece of consulting work can exist; it does not pre-exist these processes except as an idea or discursive resource based on centuries of such processes. Similarly Putnam and Cooren (2004) recognise

> discourse as shaped by 'something else', for instance, ideologies, power, or political struggles... organizational discourse reveals structures of domination and control, but [studies] fail to address how these dominant or marginal groups come into being in the first place and to what extent memory traces of past interactions serve as texts in which organizing occurs. (2004:325)

The relative stability of some assemblages of processes as accepted social practice is in part an evolutionary process (as acknowledged by

Fairclough 2005).[2] The process theorists also emphasise Whitehead's idea of *immanence* whereby

> each organisational outcome or effect always already incorporates and hence implicates the 'weight' or 'traces' of its genealogical past. Accordingly the past is immanent in the present. (Chia 1997a:697)

This supports my genealogical work to develop a more broadly grounded view of consulting processes.

> we should begin by assuming that all we have are actions and interactions. ... [how do] some kinds of interaction become recursive and appear to 'succeed' in stabilizing and reproducing themselves, generating patterned effects such as organizations, whilst others disappear completely. (Chia 1996:53)

Consultants and consulting are similarly the patterned effects of recursive interactions.

For Chia (1997a), *language* is implicated in process ontology. The privileging of states, not processes, in the dominant paradigm promotes *nouns* rather than verbs – nouns that we rapidly reify to take on a life of their own. Law (1994) talks of a 'sociology of verbs', not of nouns, so re-emphasising processes, action and interaction framed by language.

Thus the linked notions of *discourse* and *discursive practices* emerged as critical to taking a process approach in examining consulting in action. They offered a productive theoretical base for my study of consulting interaction and my concerns with social processes, and especially human (gendered) subjectivities. Not only do they retain focus on power effects, but they offer helpful methodology, through *discourse analysis,* that can focus on human interaction and its critical deconstruction, rather than simply describing what happens. *Critical discourse analysis* further enabled me to consider discursive processes beyond the text itself and the power struggles they entail.

Studying discourse and discursive practices

Construing consulting as a discursive practice emerged from the work in Part 1. Writers on discourse emphasise its ambiguity: 'disparate and fragmented ... a plurivocal project' (Grant *et al.* 2004:2). Its multi-disciplinarity as a concept both undermines its credibility while also adding explanatory strength (Grant *et al.* 1998). Pritchard *et al.* (2004) emphasise Foucault's approach: what discourse *does* in creating power relations is more important than defining its meaning. So working with concepts of discourse must embrace power and its analysis. Wood and Kroger (2000) sum up discourse and practice: to see 'talk as action' despite our cultural bias to 'privilege action and ... downgrade talk'. (2000:5) They comment that, ironically, while we say actions 'speak' louder than words, the verb is still about talk!

So discourse produces things – is *constitutive* – it has 'power outcomes or effects' producing a 'truth' which aims to invalidate other views. Also 'discourses 'hook' into normative ideas and common-sense notions...' (Carabine 2001:269), thus playing a role in ideological struggle. Fairclough (1989) also emphasises power and the social process:

> what people have in their heads and draw upon when they produce or interpret texts... [is] socially generated ...socially transmitted and ... unequally distributed (1989:24).

He is explicit about the levels of struggle within discourse:

> ...any given piece of discourse may simultaneously be part of a situational struggle, an institutional struggle, and a societal struggle (including class struggle) ... struggle at the situational level is over power in discourse, struggle at the other levels may also be over power behind discourse. (Fairclough 1989:70)

Interestingly, most writers on consulting neither refer to concepts of discourse, nor to Foucauldian ideas of power, knowledge and discourse, as noted in Chapter 4. Uniquely, Clegg *et al.* (2004) do define consulting as discursive. They see 'consulting as discursive practice is the art of negotiating tensions and exploring spaces in between existing order and potential chaos' (2004:38). Their view is trenchantly criticised by Sturdy *et al.* (2004) for neither acknowledging nor challenging power relations within discursive practices. No studies take a thorough-going discourse-analytic approach to consulting work; some draw on the concept of discourse to inform their theoretical position and/or sense-making.[3] My exploration of consulting processes using a discourse analytic methodology predominantly on 'live' interactive material gathered through autoethnographic study is thus an entirely novel approach to researching consulting, but:

> if we wish to understand social events, we need to look directly at those events as they unfold, not at retrospective reports or second-hand data. ...experience [is] fundamentally constituted in discourse... (Wood and Kroger 2000:28)

Discourse analysis as methodology

This approach to the study of organisations and management has been growing enormously.[4] Discourse analysis (DA) comes from the critical social sciences tradition and helps bridge the micro with broader social levels. Taylor (2001a) suggests discourse analysis is 'the close study of language in use... looking for patterns'. This simple approach masks more complex issues: the situated use of language is not simply about transmission or transparently reflecting experience, but 'the site where meanings are created and changed ... an important means for *doing* things' (2001a:7 her emphasis). Similarly Wood and Kroger (2000) emphasise that DA explores 'what people are doing or not doing, how they are doing it, and how it is connected to other things they are doing' (2000:136). Wilmott (2005) differentiates DA from other qualitative methods and argues that discourse analysis is not concerned with actors' meanings but with how language is key to our constructing phenomena and our social world (2005:773). DA writers explicitly include multi-media and hybrid 'texts', oral, written, aesthetic and electronic (Fairclough *et al.* 2004, Grant *et al.* 2004). For discourse analysts events and the experience they generate are discursive in nature; interaction is discursive practice. Robillard (1997) sees interaction as 'the site of personal integration or fragmentation, security, power and powerlessness, anger, patience, memory and context relevance' (1997: 262), echoing many of my starting issues.

Taylor (2001a) identifies four approaches to DA:

1. language itself;
2. the 'activity of language use' that is, language as a process, looking for patterns;
3. the patterns around use of language in a particular topic or activity, such as an occupation like consulting;
4. patterns within much larger contexts, for example in society, culture.

The latter concerns values, consequences and social effects – 'the discursive' and the 'extra-discursive'. My study focused on analysis of local interaction within broader discourses of consulting, managerialism and the not-for-profit setting. It illuminates discourses of consulting, situated not only in a particular interaction 'but within a particular social and cultural context' (Taylor 2001a:8), that of women working in small-scale consulting for the not-for-profit sector. A focus on language itself would be a much more technically linguistic enterprise. However this aspect is part of my work as 'social meanings are grammatically encoded'; for example the passive voice denies agency. Thus 'the focus is on the *social* functions of the linguistic features.' (Wood and Kroger 2000:23 my emphasis)

In focusing on language as a process: 'the language user is ...understood as *constrained* by the interactive context' (Taylor 2001a:9 her emphasis); the interaction as it occurs shapes each contribution. Thus 'the meaning of an utterance is in the very next utterance', that is, how the listener constructed it and what they did in response shows meaning far more than what the speaker may say it means (Wood and Kroger 2000:109). This underlines the primacy of process and is visible in my material, where interaction not only between 'client' and consultant but between consultants demonstrates these constraints.

So talk produces action and language reflects and reproduces processes of power. My process-based approach meant that I used DA to examine how language affects the emergent process within an interaction. I did not follow textual elements, such as metaphor, across a number of different interactions. Also I looked at exchanges, not at isolated quotations – even in the reflective material stories were told with others in interaction. Additionally, I was 'working within the conceptual framework of those studied' (Silverman 1993 cited Taylor 2001a). My frame of reference was that of myself and my colleagues; I brought our mutual work into the inquiry. While this raises questions of my/our self awareness, some discourse analysts suggest 'bring[ing] the experience of the original interaction to the interpretation' (Taylor 2001a:18).

Hence my discussions with colleagues about our interactions formed new processes of sensemaking, where they could conduct discourse analysis themselves. Indeed I used DA as a distancing device to help me achieve the reflexivity I needed in the process of autoethnography. My highly charged work became bits of text and DA helped me consider what I could understand about the moment of the interaction or reflection.

Critical Discourse Analysis (CDA)

From the many approaches to discourse analysis (Wetherall *et al.* 2001), I chose Critical Discourse Analysis (Fairclough 1989, 2001, 2003, Fairclough and Hardy 1997). CDA's attraction lies in its clear framing within broad social and political processes, which Norman Fairclough has strengthened in developing his notion of CDA over the years. From seeing these broad processes as an outer layer offering context to the centred deconstructive analysis, he now sees the social and political as *framing* the entire question being posed before any analysis occurs. His explicit link between situated interaction and broad context is especially relevant, given my emphasis on interaction, my interest in 'critical consulting' for social change and the locus of my consulting work in the public policy sphere. For Hardy and Phillips (2004) CDA 'tempers' the determinism of discourse they read in Foucault and importantly suggests spaces for action: that attracted me. CDA offered the possibility to begin from issues of power (van Dijk 1993) and to explore specific 'micro' interactions of consulting within this framing. This section sets out the key features of CDA and its use.

Taylor (2001b) describes CDA as 'study of the refractive aspects of language' intending to link linguistic work with social change theory. For Hardy and Phillips, CDA 'explores how discursive activity structures the social space in which actors act, how it privileges some actors at the expense of others' (2004:304). For van Dijk it 'is primarily interested and motivated by pressing social issues' (1993:252). For Fairclough (2001):

> it aims to show non-obvious ways in which language is involved in social relations of power and domination, and in ideology. ...a resource ... for researching change in contemporary social life... [CDA] does not begin with texts and interactions; it begins with the issues... (2001:229)

My issues revolve around consulting to public/community bodies: how can this consulting be 'critical', how can it make a difference to the public good, and avoid the criticisms levelled at consultants in general? What role do consultants play in relation to the growth of managerialism in the public sector? More broadly how do consulting processes contribute to a masculine hegemony of work? CDA helped me explore how these issues affected the interactions within consulting but also

how these issues were 'refracted' through the stories and interaction
I studied.

> ...establishing what space there is for politics in processes ...is, to a
> large degree, establishing what sort of communicative interaction
> takes place. (Fairclough 2001:251)

Fairclough explicitly links his approach to social struggle: 'language itself is a *stake* in social struggle as well as a *site* of social struggle' (1989:88 his emphasis). Importantly for my work and its concerns with identity, he also links discourse to particular subject positions that a discourse type effects on people who 'operate within it', positions they are 'constrained

> **Reflection**
> *As a consultant I say things about how I work, how I behave, what I believe, especially in a proposal, which I then am constrained to act out in some way. Similarly for someone commissioning work, their brief holds them to a course of action which may be constraining – in the National Government work the person commissioning stated she wanted a list of competences; this constrained her and us in doing the work and 'competences' represented a contested term. In the Voluntary Sector work the required 'literature review' came to dominate the work despite the agreement to develop a series of events as well.*

to occupy'. (Fairclough 1989:102) This suggests positions such as 'consultant', 'client', 'compliant consultant', 'client-who-knows-what-they-want', 'expert-consultant-who-is-being-disregarded','consultant-who-is-trusted-colleague' etc, which are visible in my material. He concludes from this, similarly to Foucault, that 'there is a sense ... in which the speaker or writer is a product of her words' (Fairclough 1989:103)

Wood and Kroger (2000) welcome CDA's 'qualitative and detailed empirical work'. Hirst (2003) sees CDA as helping uncover hidden or unconscious discursive devices in order to 'generate multiple representations which may in turn inspire or provoke social change.' (2003:section 4.6) All this matched well with my aims.

Applying CDA

In his early work (1989) Fairclough describes three stages of CDA: *description*, *interpretation* and *explanation*. Later (Fairclough 2001) he emphasises prior consideration of the broader issues at stake. In all presentations of his methodology, however, the key stages of the analysis revolve around:

1. *description* – the actual text, its words and how it is constructed
2. *interpretation* – the relationship between the text and interaction, what is going on, with whom, in what relations and what is the role of language
3. *explanation* – the relationship between the interaction and the social context or the social analysis of interaction

The aim is to connect the micro-text with the broader social context. What is going on socially is at least in part what is going on in the interaction, and this in turn materialises in linguistic features of the text. These connections are about interpretation, that is, they are inter-discursively mediated. Thus stage 2, which focuses on the interaction, is extremely key.

Interpretation or *interdiscursive analysis* (Fairclough 2001) involves the concept of *genres*. These are 'a way of using language associated with some particular form of social activity' (Fairclough and Hardy 1997:150), such as an interview, or in consulting, a training session, a consulting brief or report. Interpretation looks at which genres and discourses are drawn upon and analyses how these are worked together – hybridity is assumed. A text may have 'local distinctiveness, as well as recognising it as being constituted in a specific articulation of maybe two or three stable 'genres'.' (Fairclough 2001:241) This highlights distinctive material, particular to the actual consulting setting, yet locates it within a recognised genre such as 'proposal', 'brief', 'email' or combinations such as 'proposal-in-email' that 'are materialised in the texture of the text' (Fairclough and Hardy 1997:147). Fairclough also highlights the concept of *intertextuality* (after Bakhtin 1981 and Kristeva 1986): 'the idea that any text is explicitly or implicitly 'in dialogue with' other texts… Any text is a link in a chain of texts' (2001:233). Bakhtin's related notion of *heteroglossia* (Emerson 1997) suggests that every interaction is a relationship between two individuals in appearance only. Their words carry whole perspectives freighted with countless meanings that both reflect and reproduce power relations.[5] Intertextuality is vivid in public sector work, where policy and implementation are contested and discursive processes are represented in numerous competing material texts. The National Government work in Chapter 6 illustrates this with its long 'chain of texts' starting from a White Paper through consultations to the Act of

Parliament giving rise to work we were commissioned to do to support policy implementation.

Fairclough (2001) offers some questions to explore these issues:

- What interpretations are participants giving to the situational and intertextual contexts?
- What discourse types are being drawn on?
- Are answers to these questions different for different participants? And do they change during the course of the interaction?

These are questions I have taken up and involved participants in analysis with me where possible.

Explanation focuses on power and domination, on social struggle. It aims to:

> portray a discourse as part of a social process, as a social practice, showing how it is determined by social structures, and what reproductive effects discourses can cumulatively have on those structures, sustaining them or changing them. (Fairclough 1989:163)

Here the importance of past struggles that have shaped the discourse are highlighted: they create the power relations portrayed in the discourse. For example discourses of advice-giving have had impact over millennia on the processes we see today.

Fairclough and Hardy (1997) suggest analysing the broader contextual issues at three levels:

- immediate situational context – e.g. the work setting and the actors
- wider institutional context – e.g. the setting of the public body/ies concerned in the broader political scene, and the actors' connections to those power issues
- the widest socio-cultural framing – e.g. the nature of the work and its purposes, the subjectivities of the actors and the broadest drawing of issues of power between them e.g. patriarchy, managerialism.

They see this analysis as in fact a *synthesis*, suggesting texts may be holographic of power issues. How to identify these is rather glossed over (Alvesson and Karreman 2000). However, and crucially for my position as an insider researcher, Fairclough and Hardy comment:

> What is included within the domain, and what is not, is itself an interesting and significant question. Only someone who is a *cultural insider* ... is in a position to explore this fully. There is no attempt at objectivity here. We are interested in understanding social practice from within ... (1997:158 my emphasis)

The *text itself* underpins both previous elements: 'collections of inter-actions, mediums of communication (i.e. print or electronic message), or assemblages of oral and written forms.' (Putnam and Cooren 2004:323) Text comprises 'micro-level forms of discourse, which index macro-level expressions of power relations' (Lorbiecki and Jack 2000:S23). Text is thus a many-faceted term (and Fairclough (2005) regrets not having yet found a better term). Drawing on the schema in Fairclough (2001: 241–251), I have found the following elements of textual analysis most valuable:

– *representing* – how is consulting shown/talked about, for example through metaphors, vocabulary, direct or distancing talk
– *relating* – what relationship is there: 'we', 'you', 'they'
– *identifying* – what kind of identifying work is going on for actors as subjects, here as women, as consultants
– *valuing* – what is being valued and what is not, signified through strong or equivocal statements or terms (their 'modality')

This language analysis is 'highly selective and schematic' rather than exhaustively linguistic, but considers:

• Whole-text organisation and language
• Clause combination
• How clauses work: simple sentences, grammar, transitivity, mood, voice, modality
• Words – vocabulary, collocation, meanings, metaphor

Fairclough and Hardy (1997) suggest structuring textual analysis around three functions:

1. *Ideational*– about representing and constructing realities, attending to the type of process being expressed – for example '*nominalisation*'

where we make nouns out of verbs or processes. This is common in 'management speak', for example 'the deliverables', 'the must do's'. Nominalisation may have 'ideological significance' and hide issues of power, losing the sense of agency in a distancing (and technocratising) device. For example, the difference in impact between saying 'preliminary contact with..' and 'we spoke to ...' is dramatic in the National Government work (see Chapter 6).

2. *Interpersonal* – the micro-processes of enacting power, about projecting and negotiating social relationships, expressed through *grammatical mood*. Do we state, question or command? Are statements active or passive? Also power is expressed through *modality*, that is, how strongly statements are made that reflects commitment, values or affinity. Finally our choice of pronouns is key – who are the actors, are these clear or opaque? Both strong and weak modality statements and the pronouns 'we', 'you' and 'they' oscillate strikingly throughout my material.

3. *Textual* – about the links across parts of the text, how it is made whole through use of connecting words, repetition, cross-referring, overall structuring, shape or pattern. This helped me consider the genre of email and how it is constructed, for example how it begins and the personal touches that are included about the situation at that moment for the writer.

How has CDA been used?

Most CDA work focuses on overtly political published texts such as speeches or interviews by leading politicians, material produced by 'New Labour' in the UK (Fairclough 1992, 2001, 2003), parliamentary debates (van Dijk 1993), and more recently on issues of globalisation and transitional economies in Eastern Europe (Fairclough 2005, Fairclough and Thomas 2004). Others have analysed texts on diversity management (Lorbiecki and Jack 2000), company material on competence-based management development (Finch-Lees *et al.* 2005), video material promoting the 'voluntary transfer' of homes from public to private sector (Taylor 1999) and planners' ascendance in the redevelopment of Leith Docks in Scotland (Matthews and Satsangi 2007). Hackley's work (2000) in an advertising agency on silences has already been mentioned.

Wood and Kroger (2000) note there has been relatively less CDA work on naturally occurring talk. Some studies have used CDA on interactive material: the interaction of doctor and patient in diagnosing

ADHD in children (McHoul and Rapley 2005) and taped telephone conversations between local citizens and staff of a Spanish water company in the process of privatising (Morales-Lopéz *et al.* 2005). Studies have also used CDA on interview material following ethnographic work (for example, Hirst (2003) who examined new public management in English local authorities). I have located only two examples of a researcher analysing their own work or interaction using CDA: Fairclough (2003) uses his notes of an internal appraisal training seminar as an example text; Cella (2005) uses CDA with her own texts in auto-ethnographic work to change her approach to English teaching in a New Jersey high school. Using CDA on consulting interaction and texts from my own work therefore adds to the corpus of material applying the technique.

My use of Critical Discourse Analysis

Here I demonstrate how I used CDA in order to help the reader appreciate the method, before I present the material and its analysis in Chapters 6 and 7. Table 5.1 shows an excerpt from email interaction from the final stages of work for a University. Stella, the key manager leading the work, and I correspond. So far Mel, my consultant colleague, and I have led a series of workshops with Stella's team leaders to re-design the administrative system. We now have one final session before the teams and the Human Resources Department implement the changes.

I use highlighting and [tags] to indicate the CDA tools used for analysis in relation to the text itself. In relation to broader issues of the context and intertextual links between text and context I use underlining to show these, again with [tags] to explain them. Italicised material in brackets is information to help the reader.

While not all CDA terms appear in this brief excerpt, most important issues do arise here: the question of distancing language or passive voice which may obscure agency; particular vocabulary or metaphors show feelings or strength of view/values; strong or low modality statements indicate commitment or value given to what is said. Direct or indirect expressions of relationships, assumed connections to other texts and the broader context for example of economic relations are all present here. Following such an excerpt, I offer my own analytic commentary (Table 5.2).

This approach to excerpts will be followed throughout the presentation of material in Chapters 6 and 7.

Table 5.1   Example of CDA: 'this difficult project'

Subject: RE: notes of 9 Sept session
Sheila
Thanks for these [*refers to notes of meeting*] – it was a good meeting this week and certainly looks positive for the future. I am sorry not to be around on the 1st October when I think important progress will be [passive, distancing] made. I'm [first person, direct] beginning to think my absences [link to other meetings] have been a bonus !! [metaphor]
Thanks for your help with this difficult project [vocabulary]
Stella

From: Sheila Marsh
Sent: 17 September 2004 09:38
To: Stella   Cc: Mel
Subject: RE: notes of 9 Sept session
There is a tricky [metaphor] balance between support and letting them [relations] get on with it isn't there? [question] Mel and I think you have been really good [strong modality, evaluative statement, relations] at letting this go and trusting the process – quite a rare managerial trait we [relations] find [other consulting work]. Hopefully [low modality] as you say, 1st Oct will wrap up [metaphor] this phase productively. By the way my cheque came [commercial context,] this morning so the system [assumed processes] is working fine ! [evaluative statement] Thanks.
Best wishes
Sheila

Sheila
Pleased to hear the cheque has turned up [passive, distancing] at last – as you say at least something [low modality] is working! Good luck on the 1st
Stella

The unfolding research process

I turn now to charting how my inquiry unfolded in examining the multiple layers of my work:

> ...all social life is, first and finally, episodic. The essence of our humanness is contained and communicated through verbal inter-action, face-to-face or, at stages and places removed, telephonic and

Table 5.2   Commentary on 'this difficult project' excerpt

Here at the end stage, Stella talks in more abstract terms, perhaps as the difficult detailed implementation looms. She is self-deprecating about her own input to a 'difficult' project and keen to acknowledge our 'help'. I give her strong positive feedback on her hands-off approach, to which she does not respond. My reference to 'trusting the process' in meetings where Stella thinks her 'absences helped' draws in other discussions and implied voices, emphasizing the densely intertextual nature of the work. My comment about traits 'we find' equally echoes the interdiscursive nature of our consulting drawing on others we work with. The 'wrap-up' metaphor alludes to a film set and consulting as performance; it assumes an end point for the work, emphasized by me mentioning the cheque. This perhaps underlines for Stella the un-supported future she faces with the 'difficult' project, reflected in her referring to the cheque process as 'something' at least working – as though she fears the re-organization will not work or will at least disrupt things.

---

even electronic. ... the many moments of daily routine...everyday episodes, layered one upon another, occur contemporaneously across similarly interlaced institutional activities, constituting the immediate practices of daily life. (Boden 1994:6)

How did I work in practice with my chosen approach and maintain my critical reflexivity? The autoethnographer is potentially more overwhelmed by material and the problems of boundaries to her research as 'the cultural study of one's own people' (Van Maanen 1988:106) than others may be. Denzin (2003) explores autoethnography and the autoethnographer, who:

...functions as a universal singular, a single instance of more universal social experiences. ... Every person is like every other person, but like no other... The autoethnographer inscribes the experiences of a historical moment, universalizing these experiences in their singular effects on a particular life. (Denzin 2003:268)

Bruni and Gherardi (2002) comment that every ethnography is 'essentially contestable' and 'intrinsically incomplete' – a suitably modest note on which to begin this section. In order to meet my aims of exploring processes from the inside I needed naturally occurring interaction from my work, that is, it 'would have occurred even if it was not being observed or recorded' (Taylor 2001a:27), but not covertly captured. Wood and Kroger (2000) discuss 'naturalness' as problematic, commenting that the difference between planned and unplanned discourse may not be easy to see; all discourse is 'constructed whether it is planned or not' (2000:57); they conclude the issue is to examine 'naturally occurring' discourse; that is, not produced at the instigation of the researcher. 'Discourse is situated and must be viewed in its own context' (2000:64). It can therefore only represent itself '...representativeness is not an issue as long as we study the discourse in which we are interested.' (*ibid*)

A principal source was email exchange. Email stands up to the 'natural' test. If you use email you know there is a record and you inherently recognise the recipient may store, forward or otherwise use the material within the constraints of Data Protection legislation:[6] thus for email 'participants [are] sufficiently accustomed to the presence of the recording equipment to act as if it was not operating' (Taylor 2001a:27).[7] Fairclough also points to the importance of technology in mediating interaction: '[it has] transformed the order of discourse' (2001:231).

Gathering my 'live' material thus involved tracking email discussions and correspondence, taping key meetings/discussions and using my notes of events, such as telephone calls, when I could not tape them. This process was more problematic than I expected. Asking colleagues, and especially people commissioning work from us, to agree to taping meetings proved particularly difficult. I consistently felt such requests in relation to my (research) interests had the potential to compromise the consulting process we were in. This informed me early on just how near the surface of the consulting process is the commercial dimension: the person pays us to focus on *their* issues and not (explicitly at least) to pursue our own interests. It also reinforced my growing realisation that the accepted concept of the 'client-consultant relationship' was contestable: multiple, complex (and often long-standing) relations existed between numerous colleagues and people in the commissioning process and continued to develop throughout the work. All this bore down on the possibility or not to tape a discussion, and how that recording could affect the interaction and the relationships.

Hence it became relatively random what I recorded on tape, what I noted in my journal and what was captured in email exchanges, as I sought people's agreement and took the courage to ask to tape our work. Nonetheless I had taped material, recorded as the interactions happened, within four of six 'live' pieces of work[8] that I present in this book. These pieces of work were not principally concerned with training and development for individuals, but focused on organisations, their activities and their management.[9] I chose them as more compatible with definitions of management consulting and a more useful corpus of material to explore my research questions. Five of these six settings involved me, jointly working with a total of seven other consultants; all but one were women operating independently in the not-for-profit sector (one is male). The sixth involved two of my women colleagues.[10] As I began to pull together material on the earliest piece of work, and to pilot the CDA approach, I could at first only see the mundanity of this 'little, boring project' as I called it at the time. The work was still in progress and I tracked relevant interactions over five months. However, once I began to analyse transcripts and discuss them with others I realised that the material raised interesting themes. The CDA process helped me 'make strange' (Chia 1996) this material in which I was so closely involved. This encouraged me to replicate this process with other pieces of work.

Working with my autoethnographic material

This section traces how I worked with my large body of diverse material, especially how I brought together autoethnography with CDA. Van Maanen defines ethnography:

> the peculiar practice of representing the social reality of others through the analysis of one's own experience in the world of these others ... we are all fieldworkers whenever we must make sense of strange surroundings and pass on our understandings to others. (1988:ix).

He proposes that in fieldwork we must be 'concrete, sharp, complex, empathetic, and politically sensitive ...' in order to account for a diverse world in the face of increasing homogeneity (1988:xiii). His tales of the field include 'critical tales' that: 'make it clear just who they think owns and operates the tools of reality production' (1988:128). His view of fieldwork thus emphasises not only my concern with a 'critical consulting', but the challenges of ethnographic work.

> **Reflection**
> *Van Maanen reminds me of consulting itself, echoing the strangeness and closeness of the process and the sense-making entailed. For this reason too ethnography seemed especially right for my study.*

Early ethnographers considered 'how to set off their own work as different in kind from the writings of other travellers who also wrote about what they saw and heard.' (Van Maanen 1988:14) This echoes the divide between 'purist' academics who study consulting (Klat-Smith 2005) and consultants whose publications are not seen as serious study. My challenge was to ensure I was 'neither imprisoned within [my] mental horizons, …nor systematically deaf to the distinct tonalities of [others'] existence…' (Geertz 1974:30, cited Van Maanen 1988:17).

However, autoethnography blurs the question of the other: I am part of the studied group, not a temporary joiner-in. I therefore face the issue of the 'eye/I' as Kondo terms it (1990). In her seminal ethnographic work on identity, Kondo comments: 'that any account, mine included, is partial and located, screened through the narrator's eye/I' (1990:8). She recognises the difficulty of rendering something as multifactored as ethnography in linear written form. She is also concerned not to use depersonalised forms such as 'the Japanese woman'; similarly I avoid 'the consultant', 'the client', and use (assumed) names for actors in the interactions and stories, as Kondo does.

As I gathered my material, talked with others and reviewed my journal, I repeatedly looked for patterns or themes which I should follow up, to focus the inquiry on key emerging issues and to help select material

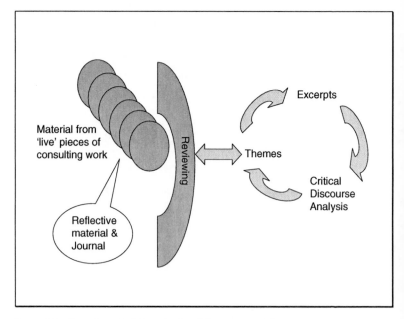

Figure 5.1   How I worked iteratively with my material

for detailed CDA. I undertook CDA analysis of excerpts from both 'live' and reflective texts that seemed to reflect critical moments, turning-points or dilemmas. I reviewed and annotated my research journal and my notes of others' reactions in 'public reflection' (Coghlan 2001) processes.[11] I kept notes of what seemed to be key ideas/themes, mapping how they seemed to cluster. I was especially alert to themes where links to the material were strong and persistent. I hoped emerging themes would deepen and make more sense within the framework of detailed CDA. Successive CDA exercises on excerpts from all the six pieces of work, separated in time, have also helped me see more and more in this material, so closely connected to my work, since 'interpretation is … checked via using it in further analysis' (Wood and Kroger 2000:97). How I worked with the material is represented in Figure 5.1. In this iterative work I recognised that variability is key – rather than looking for a structure or scheme to account for all the elements of material, I aimed 'to account for the discourse' (Wood and Kroger 2000:28). The process is one of *analysis* rather than synthesis: 'one essentially expands the data by breaking it down and examining relationships among the components' in contrast with other qualitative analysis which in effect produces 'progressively more abstract categorisation' (Wood and Kroger 2000:29). I also did this by seeking the perspectives of my colleagues on our interactions, taping some discussions with them and in one case with a person commissioning work. I sent excerpts to those involved in the work and shared my CDA commentaries with them. I incorporated our (email) conversations about their views into successive analyses; some quotations from these are included in Chapters 6 and 7.

Sense-making and presenting the material

> To be able to describe the world as it is, you have to be ready to be always dealing with things that are complicated, confused, impure, uncertain, all of which runs counter to the usual idea of intellectual rigour. (Bourdieu *et al.* 1991:259)

In the context of qualitative research, rigour requires accepting Bourdieu *et al.*'s observation while focusing on making one's research process transparent. This book is part of that process of transparency: offering my own insights for others to consider, develop or reject.

Discourse analysis requires excerpts from interactions be reproduced along with commentaries. CDA requires presenting a *transparent* analysis rather than researcher analysis supported by illustrative quotations from the material. Therefore in Chapters 6 and 7 you will find excerpts from each of the six pieces of work and from the varied reflective material respectively; you as reader thus have the possibility to make your own analysis, alongside my analysis and commentary. My goal is to present 'enough of the analysis for readers to see what was done' (Wood and Kroger 2000:180). Importantly though, this work represents 'interpretations of other interpretations ... mediated many times over' (Van Maanen 1988:95). This is the nature of intertextuality and producing this text is equally subject to this richness and inherent limitation. In addition 'seeing what we believe ... means that beliefs crystallised in earlier texts tend to 'edit' what is seen in current conversations' (Weick 2004:411), and requires a rigorous tracking of analysis. The broader discussions I held helped me refresh my analysis. Two groups were especially fruitful in both confirming and challenging my analysis:

- my *ongoing development network*, where all the members are women consultants working in the public and not-for-profit sectors, who have met monthly for ten years, know each other well and regularly work together. Meetings are free-flowing, sometimes around a theme or simply 'catching up' on work we are all doing, leading to extended discussions about tackling pieces of work. These are close to 'live' in discussing our work-in-progress of which the outcome is still unknown. Our thinking aloud about how to tackle the work is thus important material. In this way access to the sixth piece of work drawn on in Chapter 6 was gained.
- a *group of six women from a different locality*, who had heard about my work and wanted to discuss it. They all work in small-scale consulting and all but one works primarily in the public sector.

These different discussions confirmed and strengthened the issue of the struggle for power in the work process, the importance of the values of the consultants and how they felt about them. They challenged me to work on gender through the nature of the stories told about women and men in the process of consulting, and to clarify how I saw gender issues in consulting. Some of their stories feature in Chapter 7.

The choice of excerpts for CDA analysis is problematic as whenever material is abstracted from the interaction and ongoing processes something is lost. But the corpus of material for each piece of work is too large to present. Little advice about choosing excerpts is offered in the literature, other than to link choices to the aims of the study. Fairclough suggests choosing pieces that illustrate a particular problem of interest or which raise important questions (1992:230). Samra-Fredericks (2005b) suggests a focus on what is analytically interesting, that is, the researcher's interests. I have taken a similar strategy, choosing excerpts based either on some difficulty or contradiction within them, or based on their quality in demonstrating connected, emerging themes of the study such as power, emotion, and commercial process, or a 'feminine' discourse of consulting. Typically, following detailed analysis of texts, discourse analytic work is presented according to topics or issues raised, as in Chapters 8 and 9 (Perren and Jennings 2005; Teo 2000; Wood and Kroger 2000).

Power and ethics

The key ethical issues in this study concerned the power dynamics of consulting and how participants' differing interests affected how, when and with whom I generated material. I sought people's agreement to my using their words or emails as I went along. Where emails are originated by me or addressed to me and are not otherwise restricted or likely to harm the author or recipient, I have decided to use them as contextualised and legitimate material for ethnography.

It was easier to work with my consultant colleagues than to draw in those who commission us. Nonetheless presenting my analyses of excerpts to colleagues felt risky given my hope to continue our work together. The process has on the whole been constructive, but I suspect lack of response in some cases indicates disagreement they could not voice. People commissioning work were in contrast mostly positive once approached and offered comments on analysis when asked, with one exception. To this extent I inevitably lack all the perspectives at play in some pieces of work studied. Ellis *et al.* (1997) describe working with others in research as an *inter-subjective* process which contrasts with the hierarchical interview:

> a collaborative communication process ... sharing of personal and social experiences of *both* respondents and researchers, who tell (and sometimes write) their stories in the context of a developing relationship. (1997:121 their emphasis)

This sums up my sense of the discussions I had with people involved in the pieces of work, all in developing relationships with me.[12]

Critical to the ethics of the study has been my reflexive discipline. The links of ethics to notions of self and identity are well known (Foucault 1984c, d; Rose 1999; Sen 1999). Issues of self are key to the purposes of all research. In autoethnography I acknowledge the potential for narcissism; however, early on in collecting material I found I edited my own contributions out, or referred to myself in the third person. I needed to be *more* disciplined in bringing my subjectivity into the work.

My aim to show parts of consulting not represented in contemporary literature may be seen as self-promoting, but it arose from my reading of current work/research on consulting, rather than being a starting point. It reflects a genuine lack of material about women consultants, about small-scale work and about the public and not-for-profit sectors. Chapters 6 and 7 offer material to start to rectify this lack and explore what these different perspectives may offer to understanding management consulting in general.

6

Women Consultants in Action: Critical Discourse Analysis of 'Live' Consulting Interaction

Introduction

I examined consulting practice in action from the inside.

> ...practice is directional (one way, linear) relative to time and thus irreversible, a compromise between past experience and an imagined future. While one can try to "take back" an action or comment, this cannot actually be done. ... These qualities of practice – directionality, temporality, rapidity – place it in a different category of human endeavour than depictions of past conversations and physical actions... [and] complicate the study of practicing. (Martin 2003:351)

I did not rely therefore solely on 'depictions of past conversations'; reflections and stories nonetheless add important depth (see Chapter 7), but the core of my study was the 'live' material: so 'live' that my involvement in several cases continued after study was complete and one continues now. Chapter 1 described the six pieces of work. This chapter presents excerpts from these consulting interactions and their analysis using CDA. It charts themes I identified through the CDA work, and in summarising links these to the discourses of consulting identified in Chapter 4. In presenting her study of women engineers, Fletcher (2001) first asks the reader to:

> ...engage in a bit of 'poststructuralist paradox' – the practice of reading text as if it stands on its own, in order to understand how it does not stand on its own but is, instead, acted on by the dominant discourse. (2001:48)

Here I ask you similarly to see my focus on the interactions of women in small-scale consulting in the public and not-for-profit sectors as if they stand alone, and then later in Part III examine with me the overall

Table 6.1 The six pieces of consulting work viewed in terms of the three CDA dimensions

Title of work	Type of work	Social/political context/ issues framing the work	Intertextual/interdiscursive issues in doing the work	Issues in the text itself
The **National Policy** work	Producing a 'resource' to be used by local authority officers and elected members to assist in effecting the change	Government policy change to 'reform' how health services are held accountable to local communities. Involved shifting from direct democratic representation to arms length scrutiny. Change contested by local authorities and others involved in the previous system	Connecting to at least three other pieces of work going on in other organisations, to achieve similar goals. Framing the work within both government requirements and the sensitivities of local democratic bodies. Bridging notions of 'guidance', 'toolkits', 'competency frameworks' and similar genres in our work. The extended chain of texts involved	Struggle for power over the work linked to the broader context and to consultant values/identities. Emotions in the process especially anxiety for person commissioning and high stress of consultants. Importance of networks and reciprocal relationships to achieve the work required. Discourses of the 'client' the 'professional', the 'project transaction', but consulting as emergent work
The **One-to-one** work	Individual help with shifting roles and organisation development	A small voluntary organisation struggles to exert influence as the voice of an especially disempowered group in the population, who also struggle to be heard and achieve what they need in the health & social care system. Context of relying on voluntary funding and bidding for government funds	Links to OD approaches and strategic management concepts and the extent to which these apply in this context. The link of the one-to-one work with other discursive work by the manager in the management team and wider organisation, and to my work in other organisations. How I draw on other texts and discourses in the interaction	How the emotion and strength of feeling oscillates between the person and myself. Metaphors of the struggle of the organisation and its staff to cope with a managerial framing for their work – agency and structural tensions. Discourse of the 'trusted adviser' and its power implicit

Table 6.1 The six pieces of consulting work viewed in terms of the three CDA dimensions – *continued*

Title of work	Type of work	Social/political context/ issues framing the work	Intertextual/interdiscursive issues in doing the work	Issues in the text itself
The **Strategic Health Authority** work	Assisting with development of mental health strategy with local trusts and service users involving series of multi-stakeholder workshops	Constant structural shifts in health and social care which mean new local organisations commission mental health services for the first time, alongside national policies to improve standards in mental health and safeguard the public. The challenge of doing this coherently across an area, working with groups of service users, avoiding a fragmented over-localised approach producing even patchier services	The tensions of achieving structural change and new commissioning arrangements while working closely with mental health service users to set priorities. Bridging notions of 'consultation', 'involvement', 'partnership' and 'whole systems working' with managerial notions of 'implementation teams', 'delivery plans' etc. Genres of the 'project brief', 'final report' also important	The strength of feelings in the work for consultants, reflected especially in metaphors The struggle to make the best use of the work, to make a difference for service users The tensions between the team in the commercial process Discourses of the 'client' and the 'project transaction' Discourse of 'worthwhile-ness' for the consultants

Table 6.1   The six pieces of consulting work viewed in terms of the three CDA dimensions – *continued*

Title of work	Type of work	Social/political context/ issues framing the work	Intertextual/interdiscursive issues in doing the work	Issues in the text itself
The **Local Authority** work	Development of a new policy document in consultation with key stakeholders	National picture of fragmenting communities and government concern over racism and anti-social behaviour requires local strategies to combat these. Local authorities must do this to 'pass' performance assessment. Working to progressive aims despite the negative position of local politics	Developing a policy document which would meet the needs of the government approach while retaining local flavour and local political support given the authority was run by the opposite political party. Developing local involvement in this process not just a paper exercise	The complexity of negotiating across multiple texts and genres to weave one new document. The power dynamic and certainty of the consultant as 'adviser' asserting her view. The shifting relations of 'we', 'you' and 'they' between consultant and those commissioning her
The **University** work	Facilitating process for administrative staff to realign teams around academic structures and student support needs	Shift in education to a consumerist culture requiring 'student-centred' processes. Equally the demand to treat students as adults. Pressure on universities to reduce costs and increase student numbers at the same time. Culture of division between work of academics and of administrators	Connecting the conversations and perceptions of a number of diverse parties. Working both with fixed requirements and holding as much open to an emerging, staff driven process as possible. Bridging competing perceptions of 're-structuring', 'improvement', 'change'	Key role of emotions and emotion work in the process for all involved. Informal trust-based talk compared to formal talk in a new relationship. Shift over time for the person commissioning from the commodified 'project transaction' discourse to seeing consulting as an emergent process

Table 6.1 The six pieces of consulting work viewed in terms of the three CDA dimensions – *continued*

Title of work	Type of work	Social/political context/ issues framing the work	Intertextual/interdiscursive issues in doing the work	Issues in the text itself
The **Voluntary Sector** work	A brief to undertake policy development including a literature review of the core issue and a programme of participatory events	Policy context of increasing professionalisation of the realm of the family and how it works. Government priorities focused on children, especially disadvantaged children. Severe and growing poverty and health inequalities among large numbers of children especially in cities. Discourse of 'evidence-based work' feeds literature review emphasis	Bridging notions of 'consultation' and 'strategy development' with 'involvement', 'partnership' and 'whole systems working'. Working across managerial notions of 'implementation plans' within emergent processes. Contrasting genres of 'literature review' and 'participative event'. The 'chain of texts' as different actors get involved and the problems resulting	Strong emotions evoked for consultants How assumptions in the commercial process both in terms of power and of relationships, are brought to bear The nature of the task as surfacing and clarifying assumptions

themes and how they reflect or challenge dominant discourses of consulting or constitute other discourses.

Table 6.1 contextualises the six pieces of work, importantly locating them in the broader social and political context, in order to set the scene for CDA and its concern with the power dynamics discernible through discourse analysis. The table also summarises the issues and threads in the analysis for each piece of work, using the three dimensions of CDA that I also highlight in the excerpts presented.

The National Policy work

This work throws up a welter of interrelated issues of power, emotion, ownership of work and the 'contract'. It expresses the public and the private and hints at the critical role of our networks in getting work done. At the point of this excerpt Michelle and I have begun research into the kind of 'resource' that we need to produce and have spoken to key people in the department's 'expert reference group'. Michelle decides to up-date Carole, the key commissioning civil servant, on progress. Their email exchange is presented together with my contemporaneous reflections. CDA commentary on the whole follows.

Excerpt 1   'The Department has commissioned you ...'

---

2 October 2002 email from Michelle to Carole 14.27pm
C
Preliminary contact [nominalisation] with a number of the people on the expert reference group has clarified that the important, immediate need from the resource which we are developing is NOT a detailed [strong modality] description of competencies [social/political context, intertextuality]. ....
[*The mail continued in lengthy detail about what she felt the work was now about*]
M

Carole replies 2 October 2002 14.53pm:
M
thanks for this
I am currently bogged down [metaphor] with the regs [genre, intertextuality] and will have to come back to you on some of

---

Excerpt 1 **'The Department has commissioned you ...'** *– continued*

this. However, I am a bit [low modality] concerned that you appear [low modality] to be suggesting a change in what we commissioned [vocabulary] you [relations] to do. Can you confirm [vocabulary] that this is the case? The Department has commissioned you and Sheila [relations] to undertake a piece of work [vocabulary] and if we need to change that specification [assumed economic process], we [relations] need to discuss this. Perhaps [low modality] that's not what you are saying and I'm misreading your e mail.
I'm not accessible [vocabulary, passive voice] by phone at present, but perhaps you and Sheila could email me just to reassure [relations] me that you are developing the resource that we have agreed [relations].
Sorry [vocabulary] if I'm misunderstanding the situation
C

[Reflection : I had not been told [passive,] Michelle was sending her update – what is that about? What would I have said? The response from Carole was exasperating [strong modality] – could she not see that work is emergent and inevitably develops from the initial brief? But I have to consider how far our discussion with the expert group members [intertextuality, relations] was pitched to confirm with them our initial views of the needs, rather than Carole's views. We probably got the work through knowing the field, which meant that between us we knew most [relations] of the reference group, some of them really well [strong modality]. One of them recommended [intertextuality] us – Michelle had worked with her politically, she is a friend of one of my close colleagues and I had worked in her workplace years ago. We had a lot of links [relations, intertextuality]. She was also involved in producing some of the similar work that we had to take account of [intertextuality] in the project. At this point Michelle leaves me a phone message [intertextuality] saying she was fed up with Carole 'she's really beginning to get up my nose' [vocabulary, strong modality]

Excerpt 1   'The Department has commissioned you ...' – *continued*

Response from Michelle 2 October 2002 18.05pm
No, not suggesting any changes at all, just [low modality,]
updating you on what people from your reference group have
said to us [relations,intertextuality]! It's not at variance with
the comments from your consultation [intertextuality, political
context, relations, nominalisation], so no surprises [vocabulary].
The challenge will be [nominalisation] to develop the resource as
commissioned [vocabulary] by you bearing these comments in
mind. ... It was always envisaged [passive] that this resource
would highlight competencies [intertextuality] (although in some
creative [vocabulary] way), provide a diagnostic mechanism
[metaphor] and then route [metaphor] people to training
resources [intertextuality]. Or am I losing the plot? [metaphor,
strong modality]

Immediate response from Carole 2 October, 18.07pm
'sounds good to me ...! won't be able to give it any thought til
Friday at the earliest (and am on leave next week) but will
attempt to – possibly on the train in to London many thanks
though for the work you and Sheila are already doing
best wishes [vocabulary]
C

Michelle's reply 2 October 21.43pm:
You are under HUGE [strong modality] pressure!! I'm glad
[direct] you are having a break.
Can you discard the version of the flier [genre] which I sent you?
Our last correspondence and a session at the gym [social
context](very boring but good for reflection I find) has clarified a
few things for me and want to change the text a bit before
sending it out. ... Sorry, to be confusing. I'm [direct] spending a
lot of time thinking about this project at the moment and ideas
mature [metaphor] incrementally – or at least mine do! [direct]

Excerpt 1 'The Department has commissioned you ...' – *continued*

[Reflection: I would not have *sent this third mail, happy to accept her reply with* relief *[strong modality]! What is the* last word *[vocabulary] issue here – Michelle's control?? Are we all no matter our roles in consulting simply seeking control of our work??]*

Commentary

The opening of most of this mail is not softened by any greeting, rather launching in, the women addressing each other by their initial. The first from Michelle was blunt and arguably highly inflammatory in using capital letters effectively to shout at Carole, coupled with strong terms like 'important', 'immediate' and 'detailed'. This strong modality reflects our commitment to challenging the department's desire for a competency framework which we felt was a misguided approach to elected councillors. Michelle is asserting our power to act. The nominalisation of 'preliminary contact' however obscures what we had done and may have added to Carole's anxiety, in our appearing to take control.

Carole's reply telescopes multiple issues. She expresses both her sense of power and control in the situation, as well as how she feels. Her term 'commissioned' emphasises the commercial process. Carole uses 'confirm' in several emails to us – a term to do with control. 'I am not accessible' is also a phrase of control and distances her, reflecting her need to get away from the 'bog' of her work, but also perhaps 'I am not prepared to discuss this'. She sees our work as an object to be specified. She is assuming that a change is therefore outside the brief – her approach is the conventional 'good practice' of managing consultants through a 'tight brief'. In contrast Michelle is updating her about the work as an emergent phenomenon. Carole also evokes 'the Department': this is an organisation-to-individual situation, not two individuals corresponding and so asserts structural power. Given previous careful exchanges on the brief and letter of appointment, we knew the question of competences was important to her. It reflects a political difference. Michelle's mail then perhaps seems a clumsy attempt to take over the thrust of the work and re-cast it, using the expert group as a justification. Carole is clearly concerned and (appears at least) keen not to misread us – she uses questions or 'perhaps' rather than confronting statements – or is this to soften her reaction and give us a 'way out'? It may also be a gendered response to understate what she is asking (Yates 2001). Reassurance is her key stated emotional need – and recurs throughout the period of this work. But this relates too to control of the situation – she needs to feel she is in control of what we are doing, for her organisation will hold her to account for results and impact on their policy direction more than for the money spent.

My reflection shows passivity with Michelle taking the power to link to Carole. My feelings are to the fore regarding Carole's response; I am impatient with her discourse of the 'specification' which is at odds with my framing the process as 'emergent' – and which I pose as self-evidently right. Michelle's emotions are also vivid in her phone message – she is 'fed up' with managing Carole's anxieties.

In response to Carole, Michelle uses direct language, spelling out the agency involved; that Carole's own advisers are saying this, in line with her own consultation; that we linked to this group. Michelle acknowledges the power of the existing agreement with Carole. She uses the clichéd phrase 'no surprises'. This is rather a mantra with some consultants as a 'golden rule' in relating to those who commission; a 'common-sense' that contrasts with the frequent expectation of new thinking and challenge from consulting work. It represents the hegemonic process of the discourse of 'client is king'. Michelle moves to more distancing language and passive mood to deal with the consequences: 'the challenge will be ...', signalling a problem and the continuing tussle over the focus of the 'resource'. She also uses the word 'creative' to signal again our disagreement with the task as briefed. She echoes Carole's managerial tone in talking of a 'diagnostic mechanism', perhaps as part of the reassurance Carole wants. The consultant, Michelle, attempts to relate empathetically with the pressure on Carole and openly shares her thought process in carrying out the work. This seems to put more pressure on Carole to react and increases her concern about the work but she continues to thank us, despite her apparently anxious reactions. The impetus of the desire on Michelle's part to have a mutually positive relationship and to repair any damage done by her first email is certainly one reading of this text.

This reading was confirmed in discussing the text with Michelle, although she was also able to identify her sarcasm within the material: her mail ends with rather a sting in the tail – 'am I losing the plot?' How far is she confronting Carole's interpretation, or self-deprecatingly suggesting she herself is unsure? Or is she implying she is sure herself and Carole has lost the plot? 'Plot' is rather an ambiguous metaphor – either dramaturgic suggesting a prescribed script, or plot as conspiracy, either ours or Carole's. Michelle is pulling back from asserting power and expresses clear emotion in doing this. Carole raises the commercial contract and 'the Department' contrasts with two individuals, although at this stage her 'inaccessibility' effectively left us to focus things our way. It seems here that Michelle felt she had to be forceful in exerting her power and sense of knowing best for the project. This produced a strong reaction from Carole, which in turn produced hasty clarifications and softening of the original statements. This exchange points up the paradox of the 'client is king' discourse, yet the task of consulting so often demanding we challenge others' views, either directly or by disrupting their relationships to bring in others such as service users, long excluded from decision-making.

Carole's rapid reply is markedly different in tone. The direct message perhaps was sufficient, along with its echoes of others' words, others she knows and presumably trusts, in a way she cannot yet trust us. She pointedly thanks us for our work – showing perhaps awareness of the frustration her queries produced, expressed in Michelle's final question. The personal links between members of the advisory group and ourselves are not explicit here, although mentioned in general terms when we met Carole. She has perhaps no sense of the complex network of other trust-based exchanges that are going on during this work, and without which it could not be achieved in the timeframe set.

An attempt at empathy can be seen in Michelle's last mail, although again the capitalised word is striking. This may be a mixed message for Carole of 'you are overwhelmed and need a break' or 'you are not doing a good job right now'. Michelle expresses openly how she is working – redolent of Block's notion of authenticity (2000). But how was it received? We do not know since no further response occurred: 'the meaning of an utterance is in the very next utterance' (Wood and Kroger 2000:109).

There is a question of how far this exchange is gendered – do the tone and style speak more about two professional women corresponding than about person commissioning and consultant? Michelle expects Carole to appreciate the notion of a life where one only has time to think in the gym, that gym visits are a legitimate use of precious time. These assumptions may be reflected in her positive comment about Carole having time off. Are Michelle's assumptions correct and, if not, what is their impact on the relationship? Michelle's tone is perhaps one taken with a known colleague, possibly in a closer relationship than the one Carole may expect. My comment about 'relief' at Carole's final email reflects the emotional labour Michelle carried out in this exchange. I am struck by the multi-faceted persona Michelle presented to Carole here.

Summary

These exchanges are rooted in struggle for control of this work, in the emotional and personal responses this raises and in resolving these issues in the context of commissioned work, for which Carole's employer is paying us. The broader context of the shift of functions to local authorities through this work, and the political impact of this, frames the exchanges. We are keen to make this policy work but on terms that respect local authorities' democratic place in society. This partly underlies our resistance to setting out 'competences' for councillors. Michelle and I discussed this explicitly together in deciding to take on the work as something worth doing. Carole as a former local authority officer is aware of these issues, but now in the civil service is in a highly pressured, national political environment. Her ministers are looking for delivery of promises made rather than meeting what others want. The CDA highlights the multiple relationships and the way the consulting task is construed by the actors. Discourses of the 'project', of the 'client' and of the 'professional' are all visible here in contrast to discourses from the consultants of reciprocal relations, emergent work and values.

> **Reflection**
> *At the same time my reflection on this work in 2003 is striking: 'a boring and tedious small piece of work … going on in the background and terribly annoying and really frustrating at the time'. I am not focused on the work and its success. I focused on it only in short bursts when it came back into view. The issue of doing many projects at once and juggling them – what is its impact on what goes on?*

The One-to-One work

This excerpt comes from a session with Pat as part of ongoing work to help her develop her role as Director of Research and Development in a small national charity. It illustrates the tensions of the emotional labour of the consulting – and Pat's work – alongside the certainties of the adviser, drawing on a multiplicity of other texts. We have been working together for about a year at this point and have spent most time on the work Pat herself does and on strategic planning. She and her management colleagues have introduced systems and techniques such as project management, as the organisation has grown; this has caused some tensions. Here she turns to discussing how she works with her staff.

Excerpt 2   'I feel exasperated ...'

Me: You've travelled [metaphor] a long way

Pat: Got a long way, yes, and now we [relations] are asking people to go even further [*in changing how they work*] [metaphor, strong modality]

Me: and you [relations] won't do it in one huge bound [metaphor]

Pat: No but I want to do it by tomorrow!! [direct, strong modality]

Me: yes I know!

Pat: but it's just so, I haven't got time [direct, strong modality]

Me: so if you could have *a* meeting and just sort it, it would like be so much easier? [question]

Pat: yeah

Me: well I mean it's the drip, drip, drip method... [metaphor]

Pat: it is yeah

Me: ...isn't it? The endless re-restating, re-articulating, re-minding [repetition, alliterative] and endless [strong modality] questioning I think: 'how are you doing this?'

Pat: yes and some of those are more action learning-y type questions [intertextuality]

Me: yes, definitely, definitely, [strong modality] bring that stuff in

Pat: like 'what would you suggest?', 'this is an issue, what would you suggest?'

Me: yeah, yeah. You've got to force them to engage with it and you can do that through questions, because, they've got to [relations, vocabulary, modality] ...come up with answers! [*I laugh a bit here*]

Pat: mm, and that's where sometimes I sort of question my skills, cos sometimes [low modality] I just feel exasperated by it. I feel exasperated because I haven't got the time. I feel exasperated [repetition, strong modality] because it's usually built on a pattern of behaviour, been there before.

Excerpt 2   'I feel exasperated ...' – *continued*

Me: mm.

Pat: and I feel exasperated because actually you know personally I am having to struggle with quite a lot [low modality] myself. Um..

Me: yep, and you could do without [direct] all this..

Pat: and in [*name*]'s case it's further complicated, you know, he's a personal friend [relations] and I line manage him. That makes it complicated.

Me: is that something that will continue? Because it is [indirect, nominalisation] very hard when you manage a personal friend. I mean I just throw it in [metaphor, low modality] as a question, you don't have to deal with it .. you know is that a structurally unavoidable ..

Pat: it's interesting cos in, when we regurgitated [metaphor] the business plan [genre, political context] last time, [*name*] was sort of under [*another manager*] but structurally it was sort of [low modality] neater that he was in R and D kind of work. So, ... Another change would be ... [*she tails off*]

Me: yeah, not a good thing ... [*both speaking quieter here*] so it exasperates you to, like the endless asking of those kinds of questions would be, it feels like [low modality] that takes up a lot of time?

Pat: well I think because I get exasperated, sometimes I, what can I say, I am sitting here and God!! [direct] (*high emphatic whisper here*) Then I kind of go into ... giving a solution rather than asking a question, but sometimes I do go along that path [metaphor], but there's a pragmatism about, um, time. Because we don't have much time and we've got a deadline [funding context, intertextuality]. Unless we get this piece of work done and I know we [relations] are not going to have another meeting this side of Christmas, that sort of thing. And there is a real pragmatism about having to move pieces of work on. [distancing]

Excerpt 2 'I feel exasperated ...' – *continued*

Me: so the meeting is about setting the deadline for what he's going to do? Or is it about actually doing the work together there and then? [questions]

Pat: Um .. well ...(*pause*) there's always a long list of stuff that needs to be done [indirect] pretty quickly, like a training course [genre] that we're running and unless we've got it sorted (*laughs*) – it's those sort of pressures, but if you take something like objectives [genre] , I kept saying well ...[*not audible*] I kept [direct, strong modality] trying to get him to do the thinking and he just, 3 times he either didn't send back anything or it was pathetic what he sent back and I kind of then got exasperated [strong modality] and wrote them for him. Which I didn't feel happy about but I thought well otherwise we are never going to sign this off [intertextuality].

Me: yeah, well there's that and that's fine cos any human being [relations] would have done that. And then you are still left with practice which is that because he's not signed up [metaphor] to those objectives, he's still doing the same old stuff

Pat: absolutely

Me: and in a way I wasn't really thinking so much of the objectives around the idea of questions, but more the everyday work choices [intertextuality] he makes. I was trying to understand what your meetings [intertextuality] are about in a way. ... I don't know how safe [vocabulary] it is to [indirect] pose questions to him ...

Pat: it's interesting cos the, I mean I do wonder if I avoid stuff as well. Because in terms of a meeting around a piece of work, there's not really a problem [low modality].

Me: because you are doing it together

Pat: we do it together and really it's fine. He takes away, does his stuff, and I do my stuff. Absolutely fine, it's just not an issue at all. [strong modality] But it's the bits around the projects, the bits around this work. [metaphor, low modality]

Excerpt 2   'I feel exasperated ...' *– continued*

Me: it's how he constructs his work portfolio [genre] really

Pat: yeah and how he constructs [linking] his relationships with other people in order to do those things, get the work done in a way that isn't 'right I'll do this, I'll go away and do it in [*city*] and...'

Me: be in isolation

Pat: yeah. And that's the way he works – it's not problematic except when it's a project which depends on him communicating with others [relations].

Me: yeah. So I mean in a way, I mean maybe, and I don't know [low modality] for example how much he understands the impact of that behaviour on the other people... there is something I think about giving people responsibility through sharp [metaphor] questions that they, like you were saying to me, you can't sort it out, you have to go away and think about it. It should be left with thoughtful issues or questions that you do have to ponder over. [*Pat is mm-ing as I speak*] ...some of my best bosses [intertextuality] were like that, you left meetings with them and you were kind of, you had to really work out what to do, and then you could say back what you had done [intertextuality]. That was quite a good process [low modality].

Commentary

This interaction is notable for how frequently Pat and I shift the modality of our statements. We are tentative and direct in turn, our voices rise and fall. This may reflect me echoing and supporting her feelings, summarising and questioning, as she struggles to sort out what to do. It may reflect gendered speech (Tannen 1992) But some of my comments are very strong: 'definitely, definitely', 'force them', 'they've got to', 'sharp' questions; I am sending a clear message of what she can do. I am certain and taking power in the interaction. At the same time I 'just throw in' a question which she doesn't have to answer about the staff member who is a friend; this disclosure produces some distanced and nominalised language about 'it'. This expresses both our discomfort with her agency as this person's manager – my response relates to structure not feelings: is it 'structurally unavoidable'?

I notice now how much Pat is talking about 'time' and how I did not hear that so clearly then – judging by my summary note sent that day. Later reflecting on this interaction Pat comments that it seemed:

> a rather selfish need to manage my own time and expenditure of energy – I wonder whether some of my exasperation ... isn't related to my exasperation with myself. ...[or] my exasperation with [colleague] who working at distance is spared the everyday intensity and stress ...??

I am also struck by the intertextuality of the exchange, how many bits of knowledge and experience we are drawing on: strategic planning, own experience of being managed, own experience of managing time, meetings and people. In the rest of the session this is even more marked, since I draw on theories about culture, partnership and change in offering ideas to Pat. This suggests I am in the 'expert' role here as well as 'trusted adviser'.

This session focused on the tension Pat experiences between strategic and operational dimensions – both for her role and for those she manages. She must help them manage this tension. This assumes a managerial approach by Pat and her organisation, although in the interaction I try to question her 'exasperation' with individuals' approach. Overall the context of the need to achieve the work in time, in order primarily to keep the funders of the organisation content, is significant, along with the importance of achieving work for the organisation's service users – who as individuals are in a much less powerful position compared to its staff. The 'regurgitation' of the business plan is a striking metaphor which may sum up much of the problem here – that the small organisation (or Pat herself) may feel it is being 'force-fed' managerial systems that it doesn't want, need or value.

Summary

The interaction demonstrates the power of the adviser in working with the emotions of the person being advised and how certainty is produced. It is notable in *not* explicitly raising the issues of the commercial process that this session represents i.e. Pat commissions me. Her reflection on the process she has commissioned is that it:

> relates more to ringfenced time for me – a sort of luxury – in accessing expertise and accessing quiet and different thinking time – amidst a generally rather overpacked schedule

Pat's reflections have a ('feminine'?) subtext of reluctance to take what she needs to function well: 'selfish', 'a sort of luxury'. Pat is aware of her emotional labour and wants the consulting to provide time, space and expertise to work on it. The interaction is shaped by the wider discursive context of management and resulting pressures on her organisation.

The Strategic Health Authority work

The consultant team, Michelle, Karen and myself, held a meeting to discuss completing the project, a 'backroom' discussion where issues of control and purpose between the consulting team are to the fore. The strength of emotions here and their link to underlying values is notable. This excerpt comes after over an hour of discussion when we focus on the final report.

Excerpt 3   '... a bit of a polemic with some practical proposals ... would make it all worth while ...'

> Me – it's something about our commitment [strong modality] was to [send people back their own material] and waiting for the report and then only getting the exec summary [genre] which is nothing to do with their separate localities ...[intertextuality, broader social context].
> Karen – They'll hate that, service users will go mad [metaphor, strong modality]] if they don't see their stuff.

**Excerpt 3 '... a bit of a polemic with some practical proposals ...
would make it all worth while ...'** – *continued*

Michelle – Ok, all right, OK. So that's the purpose of the report
and there's something then about the aims of the project
[vocabulary] itself, which you've just identified, you know, which
was strengthening future planning, that's the aims of the project I
think.

Me – We've also got all sorts of text in the first report [other texts]
about the aims and scope of the project.

Michelle – So there's something about that. You know, and it
seems to me that clearly we've got to find some way in the
analysis, the discussion, further on, plucking out [metaphor]
some of the key issues under those headings. What I'm
wondering is did we add another, did the process of running
[metaphor] this project add another aim or objective which is
about getting a clear view of the moose [metaphor] issues.

Me – I was just thinking that.

Michelle – you know, these are gonna be the things ...

Me – the things that will get in the way ...

Michelle – ... that will get in the way [echoing talk] I don't know
whether they are just woven [metaphor] through or whether they
stand [metaphor] separately.

Me – I think it would be good to weave [metaphor] them into
those 3 headings but the introduction needs to say
[nominalisation] something about, the process enabled people to
raise the un-sayable. [intertextuality]

Michelle – I think there's a really important process discussion
to be had [passive] here, because of the critical, something about
whole systems working and complexity [intertextuality] here and
something [low modality] particularly about the needs of service
users [social/political context], and consultations [intertextuality]
with them and creativity in method and I really, really [strong
modality] think that is a central message [metaphor].

Excerpt 3   '... a bit of a polemic with some practical proposals ... would make it all worth while ...' – *continued*

Me – Well that needs to go into that third bit [distanced, indirect] on future development of stakeholders.
Michelle – It does as well but it also ...
Karen – There needs to be something about how we went about this, I suppose [low modality].
[*All speak – indistinct*]
Me: – ...that's all in the <u>interim report</u> [genre] and I don't think we should rehash [metaphor] all that, what we should do is refer to <u>that report as a kind of background</u> [intertextuality].... We shouldn't [strong modality] rewrite it all.
Michelle: you don't think so? [direct, relations, question]
Me: No [direct, strong]. Because we've said it all, went into whole loads [strong modality, metaphor of burden] of stuff on complexity [intertextuality], we talked about the <u>methodology</u> [genre].
Michelle: Couldn't we [relations] just [low modality] bring it forward [vocabulary]?
Me: We could [echoes low modality]...
Michelle: I think I'd prefer [qualified, low modality] to have it all in one place. I would. [direct]
Karen: As a <u>context</u> ... [broader context]
Me: Let's just...
Karen: <u>Cut and paste</u> ...' [intertextuality]
...

[*Reflection: At the time this part of the meeting was very emotive, the desire to do a good job [vocabulary] was for me creating tensions in terms of the time available to do it and feelings of exasperation and frustration were to the fore.*]
...

Michelle – In the watches of the night [metaphor] before I gave up and got up. I've been reading this <u>book,</u> [intertextuality]...

**Excerpt 3   '... a bit of a polemic with some practical proposals ...
would make it all worth while ...'** *– continued*

Marge Piercy, Woman on the Edge Of Time, all about mental
health. It is necessary [distance] to experience crisis and be
supported lovingly and to be able to emerge, shed a cocoon
[metaphor] and move on and that people have limitations and
strengths and that is so totally different – I mean what the service
users are wanting is opportunities [social/political context]. You
know I am going mad [strong modality] at the moment I can tell
I am having some weird psycho-somatic crisis it's obvious, it
happens, everybody [social context], you've just been talking
about yours. Service users are just abused [vocabulary, strong
modality] by the system [social/political context] and that's the
problem. ... the point about this is that every time you get that
cold hard edge [metaphor] coming into something where cold
hard edges don't need to be [strong modality], you know you're
up against [metaphor] a problem So I think that what I've
learnt is something about how we write the report as well and I
think it's all part of the experience of this project that you've
[relations] kind of got to follow your instinct [vocabulary].
Do you know what I mean? [relating, question]
Me – certainly to be true [vocabulary] to the service users
Michelle – how do you encourage, support, enable commissioners
[social/political context] to begin to free up even marginal bits
low modality] of time and money. To invest around the edges
[metaphor], that seems to me [low modality], if we can use
[direct] this report, as a bit of a polemic [intertextuality] with
some practical proposals [social/political context] that to me
would make it all worth while [strong modality].

Commentary

The 'we', 'you' 'they' and 'I' in this excerpt are clearly distinguished. We
each have a concept of the report different from the others. This reflects

how we take the power to make changes as we see things developing. I make strong modality statements, 'we've got to', 'we shouldn't'; these express commitment to the project but also my personal views of how to do this report. This echoes similar strong statements from all of us earlier on in the discussion. We keep rapport by chiming in on each other and echoing each others' words and by more tentative, low modality statements: 'I think I'd prefer', 'we could'. Hate and madness are stated emotions here for others – mirroring the issue which is about mental health services. Our emotions are not stated other than through the modality of our words. The report is discussed in nominalised, rather distanced or technocratic terms: 'aims' and 'purpose' are 'identified', a 'discussion' is 'to be had'; it is also referred to in terms of being a burden – 'loads of stuff': and I link it directly to other texts, assuming knowledge of a range of discursive genres, such as interim report, methodology. The discussion is not equally shared. Michelle and I have most to say. Karen is less present verbally at least in this part of the meeting. Michelle's questioning mode changes my resistance on how to structure the report. A power struggle is thus resolved. We are struggling with how to express a complex 'whole systems' piece of work in a short report to meet the needs of too many different parties, and with too little time to complete it. The pragmatics of consulting comes through with the conclusion of 'cut and paste'.

This excerpt, especially at the end, expresses Michelle's commitment to the work and how to make a difference; but it also demonstrates the personal state, identities and impact of the work on her as consultant. This ranges from waking up in the night, to considering her own mental state. She makes a series of strong statements about how she sees mental health issues and service users. Her passion for the issue is communicated through her connecting her concerns to herself and to us. Her identification with the issues and her self in the work are vivid, especially in the strong metaphors she uses: 'cold hard edge'. The ethics and commitment of working with service users comes strongly from us all in this meeting. Michelle's understanding of the position of commissioners in the NHS is also clear: she describes empowering them to act 'even marginal[ly]'. She oscillates between rather general, distancing statements, 'you get', 'you are', and clear personal statements 'I think what I've learnt'. She directly proposes an approach to deal with the hostile context for service users in the system and to make the effort in doing this work 'worthwhile' for her, that is by achieving investment to change services for the better. Even then she uses questions and qualifying phrases such as 'it seems to me' as we all have in this interaction. This may represent gendered talk, much as our echoing each other in 'rapport talk' (Tannen 1992) may do.

Summary

This excerpt is striking for the strength of feelings expressed, and the focus on how to make the best use of the report. The interaction focuses on how to achieve change in these mental health services, specifically getting service users a better deal. Implicit here is the discourse of 'modernisation' in the NHS and its requirements to change mental health. However we are concerned mostly with the user needs dimension rather than the public safety dimension that is probably louder in the broader policy context. The discourse of 'the client' is strong in terms of the report needing to work for them. Our values and what will be worthwhile for us are also highlighted, yet there are limits to the work we are prepared to do – we resist what we see as additional work in different ways.

The Local Authority work

This excerpt is taken from my meeting with Graeme, the senior policy officer. We are finalising the wording of the draft policy document on community cohesion the consulting team have produced through desk research, interviews with key staff in the local authority and discussions with leading councillors. We have also held a workshop with about forty stakeholders, including residents and community organisations. The draft has been circulated to all council departments for comment; some have said that it is not a strategic document; that it has insufficient clarity about what should be done. I selected this segment of the meeting for analysis as it illustrates a strong approach to advice-giving in an attempt to reduce the negative impact, as we consultants saw it, of an overly managerialist emphasis on 'targets'. The excerpt seems to encapsulate the issue of policy and the purpose of reports. It illustrates the tension of structure and agency and the multiplicity of ongoing relationships, processes and perspectives at play. We have been working through the document for about an hour at this point, poring over my laptop.

Excerpt 4   'Definitely that is not what you want ...'

Me – ... so 'the development of [distance] a detailed targeted' [vocabulary, social/political context] [*reading from report draft*], you see, ... 'the development of a thorough...' ...

Graeme – Yeah

Me – In a way you see I think we were trying to respond to the desire, we kept getting clear messages from you [relations] all about targets and da da da [paralanguage], so we keep talking [direct] about it, but I think our advice [nominalised] is definitely that is not what you want. What you want is [strong modality] something which has robust long term goals ... [intertextuality, vocabulary]

Graeme – hmm

Me – ...which each department then has to develop within its own work programme [genre] along with the other goals that they've got, from your budget strategy, your CPA plan, and your this and that and the other thing, this is, and your Equal Opps ... [[intertextuality, social/political context]

Graeme – yeah

Me – and all those other things.

Graeme – That is why it is supposed to be strategic isn't it! [low modality] [*laughs*] not operational [intertextuality]

Me – Yeah that is the definition of strategic [intertextuality] really isn't it? So – 'illuminating de de de de' [paralanguage] so 'it sets out' [*reading from the report*] – what's the 'it' here?

Graeme – the strategy

Me – Yeah... our strategy .... 'the draft strategy ... indicates [nominalised, distance] how the council can best do practical work' [*reading from the report*]

Graeme – does it do more than 'indicate'? 'indicate' seems a bit outline-ish? [genre, low modality]

Me – yeah it gives that clear framework of success factors actually [strong modality, intertextuality]. 'Sets out' I suppose. I think it does set it out but your correspondents [relations, intertextuality] don't think it does.

Excerpt 4   'Definitely that is not what you want ...' – *continued*

> Graeme – well I think we should go with what we think [direct, relations].
> *Reflection: I was in a mode here of getting it finished without too many changes as we were out of time. I was clear though that our position on the type of document i.e. <u>not a blueprint but a guide to action</u> [genre] was the* correct *[vocabulary] one. Shortly after* the report had been *[distance] completed, Michelle [who had worked on it too] rang me to say that it had* 'gone through' *[metaphor] the relevant committees and her contact in the authority (a key director) <u>said the councillors' reaction</u> [intertextuality] to it <u>'was racist, and why hadn't we mentioned dog shit'</u>. [social/political context] Typical! But she did say her contact had* chased our money *[metaphor, commercial context] and we are to get it next week. (excerpt from journal Dec 2003)*

Commentary

The importance of intertextuality is notable here: we draw on a complex range of discursive material to produce a newly woven piece – the draft strategy document. We take into account discussions that have gone on, feedback from others, other key linked strategies and the requirements of the broader managerial discourse stemming principally from government pressure on the local authority (without this specific strategy in place the council will be rated lower in its performance assessment). We also assume knowledge of several genres and subgenres around 'report' and 'policy document' such as 'work programme', 'outline' and of concepts such as 'strategic' and 'operational', and of a string of other policies and plans. The contrast of the formal written document in terms of its nominalised and distanced phrasing and our colloquial discussion of it is vivid: 'what's the 'it' here?', 'a bit outline-ish', 'supposed to be strategic'. My strong modality statements are marked: we as consultants have our view that we stick to regarding 'what you want'. I use a nominalised term 'our advice is' in order to raise the level of our view to 'advice', drawing on the 'trusted adviser' discourse. It is softened by starting with 'I think' but the 'definitely' conveys a strong position. In contrast Graeme expresses his view in low modality terms using questions and qualifiers ('isn't it?', 'does it', 'a bit') until the last line where he states in strong terms that what 'we think' is what counts.

My reflection is interesting for my assertion of our position as 'correct' and the reaction of councillors as 'typical'. I was adamant at what should be done and anxious to get it to happen. I felt cynical at the reported comments, possibly made for effect in a public forum and in contrast with relatively positive reactions at our meetings with councillors. We suspected their heart wasn't in this (government imposed) strategy so had been impressed by their willingness to take it on. I now doubted that we had made any difference – but was clearly reassured that we would at least be paid!

Summary

Relations in this excerpt begin clearly as 'we' the consultants and 'you' the local authority; they then shift into 'we' the consultants, 'you' the policy unit and 'they' the other council departments; finally relations are 'we', that is Graeme and I and 'they' are everyone else. This demonstrates the power dynamic of who is influencing the outcome and reflects the detailed work the two of us are doing as agents in our own right, separate from the local authority (and other) structures. We are creating a relationship in this interaction that is different from what went before.

The University work

This work engaged Stella's team leaders and their deputies – about 15 people – in an inquiry-based approach to the administration review, where they as 'project management team' reported to a steering group, including Laurie (head of the faculty), Stella and key others such as academics and (theoretically at least) students. The project management team met monthly facilitated by Mel and me and produced a thoroughly researched plan, which they presented to senior management. At this point our involvement ceased. The excerpt shows how relationships shifted over time and how the 'project' discourse changed. The dynamics of emotional work are also vivid here. This excerpt falls into three parts; initial email interaction including exchanging views on early events; comments from Laurie in the middle of the work; and email exchange with Stella as the 'project' finished.

Excerpt 5   'I wouldn't have the patience ... it would get on my bloody nerves ...'

Email from Mel 12 February
To: Stella; Laurie; Sheila
Subject: proposal for working with the administration teams
Dear Stella and Laurie
Thank you Stella for a very helpful [strong modality] meeting yesterday ...
Sheila and I have put together a proposal on the lines we discussed, which we attach.
Please do get back to us when you have had a chance to discuss it and with the team leaders [relations] if it looks as if it is feasible.
NB I am away from 13th to 20th Feb – Sheila will be around.
Best wishes
Mel

Email from Stella in reply February 25
To: Mel; Laurie; Sheila
Dear Mel and Sheila
We have now had an opportunity [distance] to discuss your [relations] proposal and would like to use this as a means of progressing [nominalised] both the issues of realigning the service provision [nominalised] within our admin teams and also as a vehicle [metaphor] to provide development opportunities for the team leaders.
I imagine [low modality] the next step is for us to meet again fairly soon with Laurie to establish the most effective way forward and also to work on the structure of the sessions etc. If you are agreeable, could you let me have some dates and I will ensure all parties [relations] are available for a meeting to enable us all [relations] to begin to plan a way forward with this venture. [vocabulary]

Excerpt 5   'I wouldn't have the patience ... it would get on my bloody nerves ...' *– continued*

Many thanks
Stella

Email from Stella 4 March
Dear Mel
Further to your last email I am pleased to confirm that we would like to meet up with you to further the proposal [distance] on 7th April at 12.30 in [place]. It is proposed that this meeting be used [twice nominalised] as a planning session [genre] to set the framework for the on going work, eg steering group, project management group [genre], membership, timescales, session planning, setting objectives and starting to explore a communication strategy [intertextuality] to support this activity. I will organise a sandwich lunch to be available [distance] for us and would expect the meeting to be at least a couple of hours. I hope this matches your thoughts. Looking forward to meeting you again
Stella

Email from consultants after the launch event for the project 10 May
Dear Laurie and Stella
Thank you for your helpful involvement [relations] in Friday's session.
The feedback on the day was positive – people were reassured [passive] about timescales and 'agendas', but there is still some concern about how genuinely open the project process [nominalised] is going to be... There was some anxiety [nominalised] about what the 'end product' is intended to be. We tried to reassure people that this is deliberately uncertain, and they will have to [direct, strong modality] help their staff live with this, as well as deal with their own response to lack of certainty – quotes from feedback sheets [intertextuality] – 'slightly reassured'; 'a bit happier'; 'some uncertainty still'; 'reassurance

Excerpt 5   'I wouldn't have the patience ... it would get on my bloody nerves ...' – *continued*

about timescale important'; 'disappointed not to have more definite detail'. The positives were about the day being 'interesting', 'useful and productive'; 'encouraging [vocabulary] to be consulted'; three people said it was good to have input from all depts – finding out what people thought; also 'good teambuilding'. ...

Response from Stella same day
Mel
Thanks [vocabulary] for the feedback on the day – I went away feeling that we [relations] had started on a positive footing with the group which we can then build on as the project unfolds [nominalised].
...
Thanks for getting the project [nominalised] off to a good start.
Speak soon
Stella

Email from Stella 1 June
Dear Sheila and Mel
Just to confirm that the programme looks great [strong modality] for tomorrow – I'm sorry I can't be with you but my daughter's wedding [personal context] looms ever closer on the horizon and we are off for the first dress fitting – breathing in all the way! Laurie has kindly [vocabulary] agreed to come along around 3.30 to take the feedback from the group in my stead. ...
Stella

Excerpt 5　'I wouldn't have the patience … it would get on my bloody nerves …' – *continued*

Excerpt from a discussion I held with Laurie on progress later in June
Laurie: take today's project, you are the right distance away, you know the organisation; you know that, the stem and the heart [metaphor] of what we want to do around students' well being. You've got the experience but you're [actor/relationship, direct/active] not bogged [metaphor] down enough with it to listen to all the carping [intertextuality]. If I was doing it I'd get so pissed off, I wouldn't do it the way you're doing it, I wouldn't have the patience. I'm too near it. But I wouldn't, but I know, I know that they've got to work differently and it would get on my bloody nerves [vocabulary] listening to how wonderful the service is they've got now .. it's not that, don't get me wrong, it's just they've got no insight. [relations] So I think you've got it right, because what you've done you've really, really [strong modality] got them thinking. … they are being moved from their intransigent positions. Someone's [vocabulary] actually saying sorry chaps [vocabulary] you can't stay there, you've got to move somewhere, so that's OK. You're doing what you're being paid to do. My observation [distance position] is you are raising issues [context] they wouldn't necessarily have raised. You are forcing [strong modality] them to at least think about it even if they don't agree with you. You are giving them a common entry and that's important… and it'll be interesting over the next few sessions how it changes them. It's norming and storming isn't it?! [distance, other text]

Email correspondence on 17 September about the penultimate project team session
Sheila
Thanks for these [notes] – it was a [distance] good meeting this week and certainly looks positive for the future. I am sorry not to be around on the 1st when I think important progress will be

Excerpt 5   'I wouldn't have the patience ... it would get on my bloody nerves ...' *– continued*

[nominalised, distancing] made. I'm [direct] beginning to think my absences have been a bonus !! [metaphor]

Thanks for your help with this difficult project [vocabulary]

Stella

From: Sheila   To: Stella   Cc: Mel

Subject: RE: notes of 9 Sept session

There is a tricky [metaphor] balance between support and letting them [relations] get on with it isn't there? [qualifying, low modality] Mel and I think you have been really good [strong modality, direct statement] at letting this go [metaphor] and trusting the process – quite a rare managerial trait we find [intertextuality]. Hopefully as you say, 1st Oct will wrap up [metaphor] this phase productively. By the way my cheque came this morning so the system [intertextuality] is working fine!

Thanks.

Best wishes

Sheila

Sheila

Pleased to hear the cheque has turned up [metaphor] at last – as you say at least something [low modality] is working!

Good luck on the 1st [October]

Stella

Commentary

The striking element of the early emails is the informality of the consultants compared to the formality of Stella. Our pre-existing relationship with Laurie probably influences our tone, whereas for Stella the relationship is a new 'venture'. Equally she frames the work in traditional linear terms: 'realigning' services and expecting straightforward conveyance of 'development' in a 'vehicle'. Her formality and distancing language are striking: 'it is proposed the meeting be used'. She also sets out a traditional project management agenda assuming a hierarchy of groups and rational planning processes, and knowledge of these discursive genres: 'steering group', 'project management group'. Relations are implicitly to be negotiated between 'the parties'. In the event we proposed, and she agreed, that the key recipients of the changes would form the project team themselves and with them we would pursue an emergent, inquiry-type approach in order to engage them and build ownership of change.

As the project begins the tables are turned, with we consultants in more formal mode, reporting back to our 'client' and setting out the substantive issues we see in moving the work forward (not included in excerpt). Mutual thanking is included in a possibly ritual fashion. But emotions are also visible in the way the work is going and how people experience it: feelings like anxiety and reassurance loom large, but there is also encouragement. Stella too now talks about how she feels and communicates less formally. She includes personal issues: 'my daughter's wedding looms'. Equally the nature of the project as 'starting points which will firm up' is echoed in Stella's 'as the project unfolds': there seems more connection here between how she and we see the work compared to the earlier mails. The experience of an intensive day with the affected staff had changed perspectives for us all.

What is striking in Laurie's comments is the primacy for her of shared values and emotional connection, and yet the clear separation of 'you', 'I' and 'they' throughout; each is viewed as positioned differently in the change process. She distinguishes the consultants as both strongly connected to 'the stem and the heart', but also 'the right distance away'. She also sees the consultants as both listening and 'forcing' the issue. She acknowledges that doing this work involves emotions as well as being paid for it: 'carping', 'angry', 'patience', 'pissed off'. Her description of this process emphasises her own distance, for what she sees as good reasons of emotional limitations. Laurie is concerned to take her own emotional reaction out of the process; she uses the archetypal female term 'get on my nerves' to describe how she thinks she'd react. She uses the consultants to achieve what she sees as a desirable approach – to divorce feelings from issues to be resolved at work. However it is hard to escape her sense of the situation as a woman who is commissioning the work and her need for the consultants in fact to do the emotional labour.

In the final stage, Stella once again talks in more abstract terms, perhaps as the detailed implementation 'looms' in its turn. She is self-deprecating about her own input to a 'difficult' project and keen to acknowledge our 'help'. I give her strong positive feedback on her hands-off approach which she does not comment on in her final response. I draw here on our experience with other managers working on change; Mel and I had discussed how helpful Stella's style had been compared to our fears at the outset with her 'project management' approach. The 'wrap-up' assumes an end point for our work, emphasised by me mentioning the cheque. The allusion to the film set 'wrap' and consulting as performance is notable. This may have underlined for Stella the unsupported future she faces with the 'difficult' project whose complex implementation continues.

Summary

This excerpt illustrates shifts in approach and feelings over the life of the work, especially for the person commissioning and how trust develops with her consultants. It also throws into relief the shifting of the emotional labour for change from managers to consultants and back again. Equally it illustrates how the starting point of a traditional 'project' approach for the person commissioning shifts to accepting a more fluid and emergent process. The frame of the commercial process is clear along with us as consultants assuming power to shape the work, taken as 'help' by the person commissioning. Our talk and concerns in relation to these issues can also be seen as 'citational' of gender (Butler 1999), reflecting and creating identities and working processes gendered female, both with Stella and with Laurie – though her attempt to reverse the impact of emotional labour is striking.

The Voluntary Sector work

The material here tracks a series of misunderstandings fuelled by time and changes in personnel which left the consultants paid less than their contract, as the people commissioning felt they had not got full delivery. Positive outcomes from the consulting work, such as the increased involvement of their users and stakeholders in planning new policy, did not outweigh their desire for the paper 'products' they felt they had commissioned. The excerpt shows the approach taken by Ros who led the consulting work and Nora, the person who inherited the commissioning role several months into the work, in a crisis at the end when they dispute payment. Various delays and slippage with decisions internally, as well as changes of personnel on both sides had complicated the process and skewed the time spent towards the literature review, leaving no time or budget for the final stage of getting the policy agreed. The email correspondence between Ros and Nora shows how they try to resolve matters.

Excerpt 6   'It would be useful to have your ideas about what is acceptable ...'

Email from Ros to Nora 9 November
Subject: write-up of participatory sessions

Following our conversation yesterday, Nora, for the write-up of these sessions I intended to include: [*Ros lists sections she will send*] I know we have kept talking about the 'final product' [vocabulary] it would be useful [passive, low modality] if you could say what your expectations are about this.
In retrospect I think the [organisation] [nominalisation] may have been [low modality] happier with nothing more than a very extensive [strong modality] literature review [genre]. However the process we all agreed [relations] to was one that was briefer in terms of literature review in order to have quite a [low modality] heavily 'participatory' aspect to involve other people, [organisation], non-[organisation] and other organisations along the way [metaphor] as this would support the implementation [nominalised] of the policy. In view of this it would be useful [passive, low modality] to have your ideas about what is acceptable [vocabulary] to you at this stage.
Best wishes
Ros

Email from Nora to Ros 11 November
Subject: write-up of participatory sessions

Dear Ros
Many thanks for your email and note re the write-up of the participatory sessions. There are three things here, feedback as requested on the participatory sessions report and on the remainder of our joint work relations] and a request for some dates.
...
Overall process and final product

Excerpt 6   'It would be useful to have your ideas about what is acceptable ...' – *continued*

You asked if I would clarify my expectations. I am working principally on the agreement we made [relations] on 16 June. Stage one – literature review – needs to be [passive] completed. Stage two – views of [users] – the agreed report is required [passive, distance] to complete this stage. Stage three – whole systems event – the report of the event is required to complete the stage. Stage four of the process is 'to draft ... <u>policy and implementation plan</u>' [genre]. This stage has not yet been [distanced, nominalised] started and we need to be clear about what you and Sally [relations] are able to propose from now until 26 November. There seem to me to be several options:

Option 1 – [*consultancy name*] [distanced, formal] complete stage four as per the agreement. This would mean some concentrated work [strong modality, nominalised] before 26 Nov. There are 6 days budgeted [for this] in the agreement. ...

Option 2 – [*consultancy name*] do not carry out stage four and the amount payable is reduced [passive, distance] by £3000 for the six days of estimated time.

Option 3 – [*consultancy name*] contribute to drafting the policy and implementation plan during November and possibly after 26 November. If you prefer this option, please could you propose what your role would be and when you would anticipate doing the work. I [relations] do not have a detailed plan worked out but see that there are several tasks [low modality] and action to be carried out.

[*she then lists numbered points 1–13 [structure] of the process she envisages to get a plan to the Board meeting in Feb*]

... Please would you give us dates to receive each of the following:
[*she lists the reports and other papers she wants*]
I'm in the office in the morning if you'd like to talk this through before starting any further work.
Best wishes
Nora

Commentary

Ros refers to a clear relationship in their prior agreement, but notably understates what concerns her and focuses the issue on the 'final product', a word implying a tangible item that can simply be provided. Her key points are of low modality: 'might have been happier', 'would be useful' (which is repeated). She also talks in a distanced way about the organisation and passively about what needs to happen now. There is little evidence here of the emotion she displays in private reflection on this work:

> what people commission and what they expect is driving me potty. ... They keep bloody changing what it's called

The response from the person commissioning is notable for a similarly low key approach using distancing, nominalised forms such as 'is required' and also invoking their agreement. However her stating of options expresses power in posing the consultancy's formal name in relation to her organisation's requirements. This places the commercial contract to the fore, an organisation to organisation issue, to the point where payment may be withheld. She takes the individual to individual relationship out of view. The mail as a whole is highly structured and deliberate with a setting out of three issues at the start, which are each pursued under headings, and several lists feature in the text. The 13 point numbered list of future expected processes to complete stage four contrasts dramatically with the low modality statement: 'I do not have a detailed plan worked out'.

Following the last email Ros told her story of this work to our development group. An excerpt from her narrative explains how she saw the process:

Excerpt 7   'They are stuck in a mindset ...'

Ros: First of all they chop off [metaphor] stuff which means there's a big delay and we don't start till June. All the way they say November is the end point. Then there's no agreement on the next steps. We ask them 'what are you going to do to bring [relevant] organisations together? We stick with it [metaphor, modality]. What they are talking about is campaigning. The open space happened in September and I know they were still inviting

Excerpt 7   'They are stuck in a mindset ...' – *continued*

people up to 2 days before it. So their chief exec is not happy that there aren't chief execs from other organisations there… So Sally is fortunately going away so we say we've only got this far and they expected that far. … So there's something about the timescale, something [low modality] about not being clear and then not making decisions – and then you're expected to be flexible! BUT every single stage was bigger than what we scoped. So 8 days for the literature review in June and July. At the end of October they send Sally an enormous [strong modality] re-write on that. … This has been so interesting. I know PA [participatory appraisal] techniques will produce the answer. … I know it's robust, I've done it a number of times and know we don't have [strong modality, direct] to keep repeating that [*process*].

… So we've run out of time. Last week, we agree to give them the literature review and the summary of the PA work and we will meet, last Wednesday and pull out the issues. Last week they ring and say we'd rather have more done on the literature review than meet you! OK, fine. So we used the day to pull out the themes, so obvious … I meanwhile write and say it would help if you were crystal clear [metaphor] about what you expect as the final product. … and then they set out 13 steps to complete the work: a meeting, revising the documents, consultation, redrafting – shall I go on?! – topics for the implementation plan, meeting to draft the plan, plan to Board in February and this is late as we've always said it must be November …! And this was in total a 32 day project … This process – 200 people have been heavily involved so surely [strong modality, rhetorical question] you don't need consultation? They are stuck in a mindset and on the literature review. … but this week's conversation we got [passive] 'we told you [relations] right at the beginning we just didn't have the staff, so you were acting as staff' ! (*Ros laughs*) We didn't work under that assumption.

Excerpt 7   'They are stuck in a mindset ...' – *continued*

> Me: they treated you like staff, as if you were on a salary..?
> Ros: when we said the maximum [*time*] we can give you is ... she said 'oh?!'
> She's a new person, not in at the start at the scoping ... I was gobsmacked [vocabulary] at her saying that. ... I felt that if we did more they wouldn't be satisfied. Sally is keen to draw a line [metaphor] even if we lose thousands.

This is an emotional story mostly of frustration at the problems in communicating, but also Ros's outrage at how the organisation's staff worked and their assumptions about the work. These problems were despite Nora being well known to Ros. Her feelings produce empathy within the listening consultant group. Her story describes the limitations of 'outsourcing' where the organisation tried simply to bring in pairs of hands. The agency of the consultants and their operating premises feature large in the story and they are not going to compromise: 'we stuck with it'. However there is passivity in the story of being given options and the conversation 'we got'. The contrast between the consultant going away as 'fortunate' and the negative response to a new person on the commissioning team changing the requirements is noticeably contradictory. The story is full of 'we said' 'they said' and 'they tell us', 'we told them', natural in a reported narrative, but perhaps reflecting a lack of listening and understanding. Strong physical metaphors are used: 'chop off', 'stick', 'heated', 'crystal clear', 'draw a line'. Ros is emphatic in her own sense of the situation: 'I know..' is a repeated phrase where she clearly draws on her ongoing other work and prior experience for this situation, but is frustrated that the people commissioning her do not accept her view.

Summary

The story illustrates the squeeze that consultants can be in, where time constraints affect them but not others, and others are perceived as expanding the work required without seeming to take responsibility for the consequences or to make the process work overall. It challenges how helpful it is to see consulting work as a discrete project with separate deliverables; it emphasises the power struggle for control of the work and the emotions this raises. Alongside all this are the commercial interests of both the consultants in being fairly paid as they see it, and the commissioners in getting what they think they are paying for. Sally reflected later that this work was:

> a lesson in how vulnerable we are as consultants. Not only is there very little we can do when a client refuses to pay, but I feel particularly in this case that my reputation is at risk. I do a lot of work in this field and it is a small area where everyone knows each other.

> It would be very unprofessional for me to discuss my side of this story with other potential clients, but I am not sure if the organization concerned has also been discreet. I still mix very much in their circles. I have a feeling that I have already lost a writing commission that was proposed some time ago.

The related emotional connections are implicit; much of the emotion is hidden from each other by the actors. The impact of such work on fragile feelings and reputations, which are permanent for consultants, but relatively short-lived for the organisation, is vivid here.

Reviewing the discourse analysis

This section sums up how CDA has illuminated the consulting interactions and signposts the discussion to come in Part III. It draws on the three dimensions of CDA: that is, what have we seen in analysing the *text*; what issues of *intertextuality* arose; and how are *broader social/ political issues* implicated? Interestingly we have seen all three intertwined as the CDA logic implies: what we say is not only part of our immediate interaction but shapes and is shaped by wider struggles over discursive resources and in society more broadly. The chapter ends with a review of how far the discursive resources drawn on by participants in these interactions reflect the discourses of consulting identified in Part I.

In each excerpt interlinked themes of **power dynamics, emotions and feelings, values and 'worthwhile-ness' within the commercial process** of consulting are vivid for all the actors. These are visible between consultants as we work together, as well as between consultants and those commissioning us. These themes produce the actors and their subjectivities and the structures which they help construct and within which they interact. The interlinkages of these themes are multiple and complex and will be explored in depth in Chapter 8, connecting also to the material analysed in Chapter 7.

CDA concepts for exploring *text* have helped to draw together this analysis of themes. Power and control have been seen in expressions of agency or distance. 'Agency is very much tied up with issues of power' (Wood and Kroger 2000:102). Noting the differing modality of statements and their directness has helped to illuminate emotions, values and commitments of the participants (Fairclough 2003). The material is full of strong statements of certainty oscillating with low modality statements qualifying our words or softening our edge, redolent of the 'certain but humble' approach highlighted in the genealogy in Chapter 2. Emotions are also shown in the vivid metaphors used, often violent or strongly physical, when we talk about our work. Vocabulary, metaphor and relations have highlighted the framing of consulting interaction as a commercial process. Analysing the text has also raised issues of gendered talk and practice.

The notion of *intertextuality* has illuminated the fundamental importance to consulting of the 'bricolage' of texts, as drawing on proliferating chains of texts and genres. It has enabled a view of 'knowledge' creation in consulting as to do with these chains of texts and the dense networks of actors who produce, disseminate and consume them. It has demonstrated the nature of the work as contributing to a complex web of processes, of working between and around these, in opposition to a strictly transactional or commodified discourse of boundaried 'projects'. This transforms how we view the commercial process of consulting and the relations that enact it.

Keeping the *broader social/political context* in view has enabled the theme of values and worthwhile-ness to surface clearly in the context of a public sector charged with a managerial and 'modernising' agenda. The discourses of consulting described in Part I are visible, both in the minutiae of the interactions, in the broader assumptions of the people involved and how they view the work. Questions of women and consulting, of autonomy and power in public sector work and of how challenges to institutional power can be made are all raised. Issues of the 'feminine' are implicit in themes of power and of emotion so that the broader discursive framing of gender, work and power is brought strongly to the fore.

In carrying out discourse analysis I have been sensitised to the discursive resources we draw on. Dent and Whitehead (2002) in their exploration of professional identities see power as 'a circulatory enabling energy through which subjectivity is engendered' and conclude that 'to exercise power the individual must present an almost seamless association with the dominant discourses … of their particular professional field.' (2002: 11) To become that professional we must keep up that association. How far did my colleagues and I work within the dominant discourses of consulting identified in Chapter 4?

The material predominantly reflects the discourse of 'trusted adviser'. There are many examples of the strong and confident voice of advice, although contrasting often with doubts, more tentative talk and negative emotions. There are some examples of the 'objective professional', of consultant as expert presenting her view as rational fact to the person commissioning the work, who needs 'help' in the 'deficit model' of consulting. The emotional cast of much of the material is striking however and contrasts strongly with notions of the 'objective professional'. The discourse of the 'client is king' is prevalent: the assumptions of the focus on the needs and desires of the person(s) commissioning, of hiding emotion work from them, of doing emotional labour for them are all strongly seen. To some extent this reflects the discourse of rhetoric and performance discussed in Chapter 4.

There is resistance to the discourse of consulting as commodity and the 'project'. While the prevailing social and political context is strongly present there is an absence of the 'permanent change' discourse or indeed that of 'knowledge work'. A discourse of values and 'worthwhileness' is visible in this material, which draws on the personal identities and commitments of those involved; this suggests a discursive resource which may help us work with the tensions of power, emotion and the commercial process.

7

Consultants Reflecting on their Work: Critical Discourse Analysis of Reflective Material

Introduction

This chapter presents reflective *stories* gathered in pursuing my inquiry, primarily reflection by my immediate colleagues and myself, both on the pieces of work presented in Chapter 6 and on other work. This material complements the 'live' texts and extends my approach of exploring consulting processes from the inside, offering another route to (partial) meaning and understanding of what goes on in consulting processes.

> the more complex and potentially unintelligible people's lived experiences become, the greater the significance of stories as ways of making experience meaningful ...but these meanings are always partial and in a process of becoming intelligible. (Dunford and Palmer 1998:217)

Stories are an important form in qualitative inquiry (Gabriel 2004; Lieblich *et al.* 1998) and may be seen as citational of gender (Butler 1999); they therefore connect to the issues of identity woven into the study. Women's stories not only describe the past but also form a mould for future action (Martin 2003). They also have to be viewed as partly about the performance of those involved: as social actors, as consultants and as women. The stories are one representation of our perspectives on the work in question or on consulting in general. They are not complete or coherent but emblematic of the 'ebb and flow' and fragmented space of 'antenarrative' (Boje 2001:137) As Gabriel comments, stories can be '...vehicles to enlightenment and understanding but also to dissimulation and lying..' (2004:62)

His concept of 'story-work' acknowledges the poetic licence needed to mould a story that 'is *verisimilar* … [and] accords with the psychological needs of the teller and the audience.' (2004:64–65, his emphasis). Gabriel suggests we pose three questions to the storyteller: so what? who are you kidding? and who are you to speak? I intend this chapter to enable the reader ask and answer these questions. The reflective material proved extremely rich, so stories became more important as I worked and provided apt texts for CDA, thus adding to analysis rather than distracting from it.

These are stories of consulting work, told in different contexts. I begin with reflective material from my immediate colleagues, mostly stemming from discussions of the work featured in Chapter 6 or from our monthly development group. Then stories are included from other woman consultants talking about their experience in the wider group discussions described in Chapter 5. I then add some of my own reflections about my work as I talked to others. The material concludes with two men's voices, in apparent contrast to my stated approach in the Introduction to researching women in their own right and not only in relation to an assumed male norm. I decided to include an excerpt from Sam principally in order to stay true to my corpus of material: he featured in the early part of the process of the National Policy work and his views on it contrasted with those of the women, so I felt it important to record this. I decided to include material from an interview with Martin as it was so different from the other (women) consultants' stories. The further very different reflections from him and Jan on each others' words were also striking. I felt that to include Martin's words helped challenge a perhaps reasonable assumption that all consultants working in small scale public or not-for-profit sector consulting may enact a 'feminine' discourse. Including male voices therefore both helps acknowledge that the world explored in the study is not exclusively female but also not exclusively 'feminine' either.

Reflective stories from my colleagues

The first three of these four excerpts are all short pieces full of emotions, dilemmas and unexpected connections within consulting work. They sharply reflect each woman's sense of self and values. The fourth is longer and taken from a discussion at the development group that raised issues of gender explicitly.

Excerpt 1 'Desperate' cry for help

Madge is a colleague consultant who left this telephone message on my answering machine. I had met her that day and she called in the evening to recount her subsequent experience.

Madge: I'm delighted that you are not taking my call, which is at about 5 past 9 on ..oh I dunno what day it is, … anyway just to say, an example really [low modality]. I got back this evening after our meeting, which I thought was good and I hope you did too [intertextuality, relationships], and there was an emergency [vocabulary] call from Jane and the [*government dept.*]. Their report was not acceptable to the Minister [distance, reported speech] and what could they do – it had to be published on [*date two weeks later*]. She knew I was busy but, you know, she was desperate, [strong modality] what could I do? It's just that kind of pressure, and thinking about that …, life work balance and all these things [other discourses], it's a nightmare [metaphor]… isn't, it? (*sighs*) I don't know how to balance these things. As she has to do, she's just started this new job, she has to produce something decent, [vocabulary, assumed norms] (*sighs*) how does she do that? She asks me (*laughs*) and that impacts on what I'm doing and so on. I don't know the answer to these things! (*voice tone rises to high note*)
Just, just, just somewhere that space between … that is what working is like, she wants me, I have these skills, she needs them .. what do we do, da, da [disjointed text]. And you know, working with people who are in these jobs [intertextual – arenas of action], dunno. I just offer it to you as a kind of living example of the dilemmas which I know are dilemmas, I do take Mel's points. But when (*sigh*]) work is **so hugely pressured** (*she stresses these words*) what does one do? What does one do [repetition, questions, distancing] when one is thinking about educational things as well? I leave it with you dear [relating, vocabulary]! Speak to you soon. Bye!

Madge is caught in the tyrannous pressures of other people's agendas, working in a senior government office. Her words express the vivid intertextuality of, on the one hand ministerial *diktat*, and on the other the debates and rhetoric of 'work-life balance'. She presents herself as wholly responsive, in a state of not knowing, privileging the needs of the person who wants to commission her. Her assumptions, that 'this is how it is', are clear, reflected in her emphatic words: 'nightmare', 'desperate', 'emergency'. Her sighs and changes of voice are also notable for their emotion, along with her stream of questions and unfinished sentences. All of these relate to her sense of what consulting is and the emotionality of her work pressure and that of Jane, the woman who rang her. Political pressures are bearing down on Jane and thence to Madge. She still takes a moment even here to hope I gained from that day's meeting as she did, valuing mutual gain in the work process. Her talk expresses a discourse of trust and values in consulting. She expresses professional work as about closeness rather than distance.

Madge is clearly undertaking emotional labour and sees herself, as do many women, as having to be open to others' demands. Reacting to Madge's story, other women consultants commented they had consciously learnt *not* to do this. They managed the expectations of those commissioning them as Madge's approach 'exhausted' them. They also saw this story as about the 'pressure of organisation being passed to the consultant' but in power terms 'a real omnipotence going on' for the consultant who felt only *she* could help.

> **Reflection**
> *This story reminds me how one of my concerns about deciding to move out of London was that I would no longer be able to get to a client in 20 minutes. How far is this something we put on ourselves? How far a fantasy about how we think people who commission us depend on us?*

Excerpt 2   'Not just what you get paid for'

Ros talked to me about her experiences of seeking and getting work and told this short story, which demonstrates how links to other texts have power to create action over considerable time periods. Ros is convinced the person concerned *felt* the type of event was right for him and that feeling meant he followed through even a year later.

> Ros: [*name*] had carried round [action] an open space flier
> [intertextuality, assumed genre] for a year. For an event I ran, that
> they never came to but that they liked the description of,
> instinctively [vocabulary] he knew it would be right for
> something. The old client (*whose contact was on the flier*) phoned
> to say do you mind if I give him your phone number and I said
> [reported speech] 'what do you think I do for a living?!' [indirect,
> questioning] (*Laughs*) 'yes give him my phone number !!' They
> don't understand how we [relations] get our living – and that was
> an event [intertextuality] I'd done for [*X charity*] for free.
> Sheila: the connections are amazing aren't they?
> Ros: yes and it didn't say much in the flier but obviously it said
> enough [intertextuality]. The interesting thing is the things I've
> done [other events, intertextuality] for free [social/political
> context], which I've just done for free and not because I thought
> it would bring future work, have always [strong modality]
> brought me future work. The batch [metaphor] of work
> coming in [distanced, passive] at the moment all comes from
> that sort of stuff. Not just what you get paid for [passive].

Ros is clear about relationships here, dividing 'we' consultants from 'them', people who commission work and this is expressed for her through the 'old client' asking permission to give out her number. Nonetheless she reports herself using a questioning, indirect style in response, rather than a direct imperative: 'give it out!' She is also emphatic that what she has 'done for free' produced paid work later. She emphasises that genuine 'free' goods have done this, that is not where she was fishing for future work: here a charity had no funds to pay her but she identified with them strongly in terms of values. She combines this value-based approach with a clearly commercial tone in getting her 'living' and seeing her work instrumentally though passively in 'batches' that 'you get paid for'.

Excerpt 3   'I can hardly function in the real world'

Michelle talked to me about the National Policy work, after seeing the transcript of the interactions, and we began to talk more generally about consulting work. She described how she sees her inner world in doing her consulting work, her feelings and dilemmas.

Michelle: 'I have a tendency [low modality] to beat myself up [metaphor] ... I'm over-fastidious, over-driven [strong modality, repetition] by values and scruples [shared reference points, socio-political context] – I can hardly function [strong modality] in the real world. [it's like a] mental illness, stress, vulnerability–I can't compromise [strong modality], a lot of fear [nouns] in it as well... My only armour [metaphor] is the power of my intellect. ... I [direct statements] am perceived as a fierce critic [strong modality]– people are pretty [qualifier] scared of me.'

Michelle uses metaphors of violent struggle: 'beat myself up' and warfare: 'armour'. The strength of her feeling emerges in her string of strong statements: 'over-driven', 'hardly function', her repeated use of 'I', only moderated by a more distancing use of nouns (stress, vulnerability, fear) and speech qualifiers: 'tendency to', 'pretty' scared. This story of personal struggle resonated with women consultants with whom I shared it. They recognised the extremes of vulnerability and yet simultaneously an extreme certainty about her position on which she 'can't compromise'. The issues of power/autonomy, emotion and values that surfaced in Chapter 6 are packed into her words. She is at the same time both overwhelmed by what she is doing but also seen by others as a 'fierce critic' – the closeness of seeming contradiction is striking.

Excerpt 4 Stories of 'betrayal'

This longer excerpt raises issues of gender and power explicitly, alongside questions of ethics and the emotional impact of the work. Here our regular self development group discussed our role as private sector businesses working predominantly for the public sector. This story was triggered by talk about relationships, ownership, mutual obligations and how we handle these. It is emblematic of several similar stories triggered at the time by its telling. Jan spontaneously tells a story of a male colleague she worked with.

Jan: it does, my very first experience when I first became a consultant, which, like, rocked [metaphor] me for ages, was when I worked with this load [metaphor] of blokes [vocabulary] – ha, ha (*she says this*) – particularly the one bloke that ran it. I got him a client [direct, active voice,], I got a client for the work we [actors, relations, repeated] were doing, which was about IiP, from a friend [relations] of mine and I took him along. I was not up to doing it on my own as I didn't know what the hell you did, fresh from education [assumption of a genre/discourse] and he basically took it over entirely and cut me out [metaphor, direct action] of the process whereas I had thought we would do it together [relations]. And, I was incredibly shocked [strong modality] and upset particularly as [*the person commissioning*] was a friend of mine and so it was like embarrassing. Um.. and so I tackled [metaphor, direct action] him about it and he said 'well you can't do it can you ? I got that work not you. You may have had the contact but I got the work. I sold it in.' [actors, relations, other's text replayed] You know they have all this language... [actors, assumed discourse] um 'I went in there, I did it' [reported speech] – erk, erk erk...' (*she makes noises and gestures to show a series of events happening*) ... so it's a.. so I'm going aargh ..! (*All make sympathetic noises*) [vocabulary – paralanguage] I was terribly shocked and very upset [modality] so I discussed it with some of the other people in the circuit [metaphor, relations] and in the end I was given [passive voice] a small part [metaphor] in it. Which was kind of like saving my face in a way in relation to this person that I knew ... head of the organisation, although I never could discuss it. And one of the others persuaded him to give me a finders fee (*someone gasps in astonishment and laughs*) and that was [passive voice] a small part [metaphor] in it. Which was kind of it. [low modality] And it was a really scarring [metaphor] experience (*all 'hm' in agreement*) as I felt entirely ripped off [metaphor, strong modality] in a way that I hadn't .., you know, well there was no discussion, no nothing .. [strong modality, repetition]

(*someone comments*: assumptions going on?)

... yes and I thought oh! <u>is this what it's like?</u> [assumed process of consulting] I can't cope with this at all and that is the sort of private sector type, macho type consultant behaviour I think isn't it? [identifying] ....

So when I met all of you I couldn't believe it. It's a totally [strong modality] different way of working. This type of conversation couldn't be had [passive voice] in that group, never [strong modality]. ... I mean he's not a stupid man by any manner or means and ... very skilled in the social interaction kind of stuff, just very [strong modality] nasty and <u>amoral</u> [assumed cultural values] I think. But not at all ... I'm just wondering actually, because ... (*pauses to think 3 secs*) ...his whole way of learning to be a consultant is 'you've got to <u>dominate the client'</u> [identifying, active voice, reported words, social-political context] (*expressions of shock from listeners*) that's the <u>first</u> thing (*more gasps and expressions of shock*) that's why ...

Madge: ... I've come across that, I recognise that man, yeah

Jan: so that's why I couldn't do it, and he could take that job, was I couldn't dominate the client, I didn't have the balls [active repetition, vocabulary] for it !!

Ros: oh!

The impact on Jan of this event is striking, expressed in her strong statements about emotions and the vivid metaphors she uses. He 'cut' her out, leaving her 'scarred', 'rocked', 'entirely ripped off': these are violent, violating terms, especially in referring to a male/female encounter. She is so overcome in describing him that words fail her and she resorts to noises to express what happened. She reports his speech directly, giving me the impression of words seared in her brain, which assume a totally different working approach. She reflects here too her self doubt about taking the work, but her assumption (implicit till the male colleague shakes it) that this will be mutual in terms of gain and learning for him and her. Her starting point of strength – 'I got a client' – is dismantled in this encounter.

Jan's story also shows she feels there is a way of doing things in consulting, an expected way that she may not know. She is left deeply concerned about whether she herself can work in the way he did. Her strong statements contrast with the weak modality and passivity of her account of what happened in the end, where things 'kind of' fell out and she 'was given a small part'. She is also acutely aware throughout of her continuing obligations to her friend, senior in the commissioning organisation. She is talking relationships and he is talking transaction – two differing discourses of consulting. She recognises this in her 'they have all this language'. She later characterises this as 'private sector' and 'macho' approach to consulting. She contrasts the story with this group of women – that the conversation would not be possible with this man and his group.

This story triggered two others to tell of women colleagues by whom they had felt similarly betrayed; they had operated in this transactional way. Another similar story from Madge about a male colleague also surfaced. In all these stories, the women's language was of strong modality, recounting stories vividly, using short sentences and repetition. They presented themselves as the watchers of (male) performances and astonished to see their impact. The metaphors used are strong and are either harsh or sexual in nature, as is some of the vocabulary ('balls'). They are also allusive, for example the male consultant 'going in there', 'be in there' with its penetrative overtone is consistently used by Jan and Madge. The external contexts also enter the scene, where power is used and quick responses are demanded from a changing political agenda, emphasising the intertextuality of the consulting process. The reaction from the group at the reported requirement to 'dominate the client' is strong and resists this viewpoint. In telling these stories the women also demonstrate 'rapport talk' (Tannen 1992) to connect to the speaker and show their empathy. This contrasts with the type of interaction being recounted.

Summary

These women perceive differences between themselves and what they see as male ways of working. Themes seen in Chapter 6 such as power, emotions, the commercial process and its values are strongly present. The dynamic between the women and their colleagues is founded on these interconnected issues. While power and emotions are vivid in terms of experiences, personal struggle and in relation to ownership of the work, the commercial issues are also live: the 'finder's fee', feeling 'ripped off' as well as the 'free goods' were all important. These also relate to how the women saw their values as different. They also emphasise the importance of personal relationships and support in doing their consulting work.

Stories from other women consultants

A different group of women (see Chapter 5) told a wealth of stories in response to my presenting the study and excerpts from the material. The three excerpts below especially demonstrate themes of contradiction in relation to the values they hold: one tries to balance ethics and earning money; one 'holds the line' in an interaction with a manager where power, conflict and how she experienced these are explored. The third concerns the emotions described by two of the women in pursuing their work.

Excerpt 5   Balancing ethics and 'the taxi-meter'

Pam specialises in equal opportunity work for the public sector. Here she struggles with the contradictions of this work and the resulting emotions, predominantly guilt, which she experiences.

> Pam: '...ethical standards which are about empowering the disempowered and cutting through bureaucracy, and the public sector should serve the public and not be self-serving. [social context and values]... At the same time on the other hand there is [passive, distanced] a job to be done. And there is a taxi meter [metaphor] to be put on that has to be clocked up. And there are some times when ... I'm just going out to put the taxi meter on. I feel guilty [evaluative, direct]. But you just do, you have chat with people and you shove a bit of paper about and you're not actually doing anything, but you've got a contract and you [distanced] are earning money. Sometimes the contract is over-egged [metaphor] because they think it's going to take you [relations] days to do something that you can do in half an hour. But at the same time underlying it there's always got to be the attempt [distanced, nominalised] to make

> this ethical change. And that, holding those in balance, that's what I find the greatest dilemma of the whole thing [strong modality]... but people do do unethical things ... one man told the client [reported speech] he'd had a heart attack and couldn't complete the work and they asked us to do it and we realised the man was a friend and we were horrified and rang expecting his distraught wife. And he answered and I said how are you? he said what do you mean? [reported speech] He was fine, he **made it up** (*she raises voice here and all listeners intake breath*), he made it up to get out of the job! Shocking, you can't believe this can you?! [strong modality, evaluative] So if you haven't lied or made up the data then you haven't done anything unethical and shouldn't [evaluative] feel guilty.'

Pam shifts from direct to more distanced speech when describing this dilemma: 'you just have to', 'there's got to be the attempt'. The 'taxi meter' is a vivid metaphor which is at odds with her declared stance. Her story of the man with a non-existent heart attack however gives her boundaries for her own values and ethics: 'if you haven't lied or made up the data' then fine. These issues were taken up differently by another group participant who commented:

> 'I have had 2 or 3 clients who have been absolutely amazed [strong modality] when I've bid for work on a £10,000 budget or whatever and I have actually said well I don't think it is going to be as much as this. They can't quite believe it, they think you'll pad it out [metaphor], and I have men say to me, you know you've just shot yourself in the foot [metaphor] there because you could have had an extra £2000 consultancy or whatever. And I said well the work isn't there and I won't do it and I say that to the client and you know more often than not they'll come back and say thank you for that. I for one will say can we use that time at a future job which is absolutely fine.'

This consultant doesn't believe in the 'taxi meter' approach and prefers to say so, trusting that future work will come her way as a result. Interestingly she identifies the 'padding out' as a male approach and describes men reacting with the violent metaphor of 'shooting'. Both women express strong feelings about how they approach ethics and money in their work and the tensions and guilt this produces. Both reflect assumptions of mutual gain as how to reconcile these issues.

Excerpt 6   'I held the line'

Pam shared the dilemmas of being 'deployed' by government agencies to work in organisations that are thought to need help. 'I get sent in – aaghh! People are hostile and resistant on equal opportunities – you have to find a human being who you can connect to.' Pam recounted a recent conversation, significant for her, with a manager in a public sector finance organisation. She was helping them improve their performance on national equalities standards, 'being pushed' by relevant politicians. She described this as a 'top down controlling' organisation and with a culture 'deeply sexist and often racist – yet people claim no law has been broken ever, very resistant.' She re-tells her encounter with the manager, Harry, where she reaches a point of no compromise with her values.

Pam: 'This is me talking to Harry – ...the key date is a meeting on 21 June with the equalities chair – unless all teams have set targets by then no way will I sign it off [strong modality]. So I have to confront this and I've been working with them for 9 months and obviously you have, you are human beings and you chat, how was your weekend [direct, relations], so it's getting into the conflict [nominalised, distanced] with this man [relations].

(she then reports what was said, reading her notes made earlier in the session)

Pam: we really need to talk about where we [relations] are going with these team equality targets [other discourses/texts, social/political context]

Harry: what do you mean? (*she then says to the group*: he's being evasive, been avoiding this meeting which was pre-booked, he's going out for a cigarette and now he's shuffling and stuff, already telling me he's [relations] not engaged with it) Well some of them [relations] have already done something , there are some [low modality] <u>business plans</u> [other texts, discourses] already in.

Pam: teams need to have [statement] the plans in place before the meeting in June with the chair of the equalities group

Harry : oh well I'll send them another note. Or perhaps we [relations] could set these targets ..

Pam: but the point is [nominalised] that they should **own** them

Harry: Or maybe we could get them [relations] to have the targets come back in by say the 17^(th)?

Pam (*'firm but anxious' she says*) but I need [direct] to be able to see them to see if they are robust and stretching enough (*aside from Pam*: as what they'll [relations] do is set things like, ... 'have access to a calendar which gives major religious festivals') or otherwise you **won't** (*said emphatically*) reach <u>level 3</u> [other text]

Harry: well the board and [*the politician*] will be very upset. But if we don't, we don't [relations, strong modality], (*she pauses to call this his* 'moment of realisation') you can take horses to water [metaphor] but you [distancing] can't make them drink. If we [identifying] can only get through the levels at a slower process so be it . [strong modality]'

Pam then sums this up: 'About how I held the line [metaphor] about something that was really important, cos the easy thing to do would have been to say, oh yeah it'll be alright. ... or I could shop them to the heavy mob [metaphor] (*i.e. the organisation who sent her in*) but that doesn't feel ethical as I am working with these people' [relations]

Here Pam is concerned with relationships primarily: 'we', 'they', 'you' – all the people involved and how she identifies with them. Pam shifts from 'I' to more distancing forms as she moves towards the need to confront 'this man'. In the encounter Harry gradually moves from disengagement – 'them' – to 'we'. Pam also focuses on the longer term purpose of change, rather than simply the interim target of the meeting in June. She feels that her clarity about how to handle the problem helps Harry move forward in how he sees this (difficult for him) process. She makes clear her potential power here 'shop them to the heavy mob' implying a violent outcome through that metaphor, but chooses to privilege her relationships with people instead.

Excerpt 7   'Heart-sink' work

Several participants told stories about their feelings in approaching their consulting work. Two such stories follow.

Jean: 'They can't hire me till we've got in a room together and I've [relations] seen if this is workable. My thing is, do I think this is a real piece of work, do they really want to do a piece of work [repetition] here. I don't think my psyche is [distancing] robust enough to bear the kind of work that is a hide into nothing. I would so quickly sink [metaphor], you know, if it didn't have some signals of going well, of having some substance. ... And it's me saying you lot [relations] have to prove to me you are serious [strong modality] about doing a piece of work. ...so I'll put in my precious [evaluative] hours?'

Chris: 'Like being in spin cycle in a washing machine [metaphor], every time I go in there even though I prepare very well for meetings and think it through, but when I leave I feel I need to lie down. It has become a heart-sink [vocabulary] piece of work. It's ...commissioned by a third party so nobody much [low modality] cares. So I am holding more of the direction or the ownership of it than I would normally expect. Every time I tried to negotiate back to the original client, he had gone, he's on priority number whatever... well off his radar [metaphor]. I could walk away but I don't really want to as that would look like a failed project as it wouldn't happen and I [direct, identifying] don't want that reputation. Also if I can help this guy get half a dozen people to behave differently in this huge horrible [strong modality] trust, that feels like it makes an impact.'

Both women are concerned with the impact of their work and making it 'real'. They connect this directly to how it makes them feel: 'quickly sink', 'heart-sink piece of work'. Jean cares about how she uses her 'precious' time and expects the same from those commissioning her, so she expects to move to 'we' in the contracting stage; Chris is not happy that 'nobody much cares' and while protecting her commercial reputation still wants to help 'half a dozen people' work differently. She talks directly in 'I' statements throughout, seemingly haven given up on the 'third party' and content to take on the lead role, provided she can make an 'impact' on a tricky organisation.

Summary

The stories from this group also express powerfully the themes of power, emotion, values and the commercial process and their interconnectedness, that were expressed in Chapter 6. They point up dilemmas in the consulting process: of earning a living, keeping one's values and the emotional results of this in personal struggle and identity work. They valorise relationships over power and focus on purposes, 'making a difference' through 'real' pieces of work. They seem unaware of the paradox that their confidence and certainty contrast with their apparently fragile emotional response: 'no way will I sign it off' but 'you have to find a human being who you can connect to'; 'do I think this is real..' but 'my psyche isn't robust enough ...'

My own talk about consulting

Throughout the study I recorded reflections on events in my work. I also had opportunities to reflect and/or talk about how I perceive my work. I found a different kind of reflection is possible by taping myself talking to others and later using CDA on my words. Taped stories seem more immediate, closer to feelings and events, less mediated than what I wrote down.

Excerpt 8   Where is the client?

This story recounts events from a piece of work I did with several colleagues to review workforce development for a large NHS organisation. I tell an involved tale. The shifting processes of actually engaging with senior people and of conflicts over the final report and recommendations are vivid. The struggle for control alongside a preoccupation with having impact is also striking.

...as we went through the work those people [relations] kept changing the terms even though we had bits of paper and signed letters. Every time we met them there was a different slant – even to the end they wanted to change the report, and we [relations] changed things in ways we thought were legitimate [strong modality] to what we'd done and also met their need and put it back to them. Then it came back again 'no we still want' – they literally edited some of our stuff [relations, strong modality]. So we had a little tussle [vocabulary] even at that very end point 'no this is our report, our name is on it, you wanted an independent view we agree with this, this and this but this here we are not taking it out' [strong direct, reported speech, other text]. Here two organisations had commissioned us so we behaved as if they were joint clients, scheduling a review meeting [genre] and saying 'will you involve the others?' – 'no why would I?' – 'Well we thought it was a joint project' – 'no they're just funding it.' Then as we get into the work, we realise there is no (*workforce*) strategy [genre], a huge gaping gap [metaphor, strong modality] and this is the HR director, it's her jurisdiction so why hasn't she got this. So we decide [direct] the Chief Executive needs to be the client and the board, as it's such a strategic issue. So we suggest to her where is the CE on this? She agrees so we meet him to get him on board and get his Board involved. We think this is great. He [relations] has another view altogether. I say when [indirect – use of questions] will you want to take this to Board we are happy to present it and he looks astonished and says we keep the board for strategic issues [assumptions, discourse] not this training stuff .... So a very strange moment this is a very large organisation and workforce is their key issue that is what they spend most of their money on, there are huge changes in external context and huge [repetition, strong modality] recruitment and retention issues [social political context] and they really have not got a handle [metaphor] on it and so he didn't see himself as the client even though he'd come into the meeting and bought [metaphor] the director's line that he should be there. so you've got a very slippery [metaphor] weird process and strangely that meeting had a third person in it who we'd never met before – introduced as the person taking over from the HR director going on maternity leave. So all the people we thought were the client weren't. The one person [relations] we'd not met before, in a way she's really the client as she is the one who over the next months will be doing something about the report or not. That's another issue what will happen as a result of your work. For me the point of consulting is for something [low modality] to change. ... [the] Chief Executive [tried] to chop [metaphor] a bit out of [*our*] report about a recommendation they do more work on staff talking across the organisation ... I was proposing this, he said we [relations] don't want this. So we had a discussion and we managed to get them to agree, they were trying to impose stuff which wasn't about how people at the bottom [relations] saw it."

The see-sawing of 'he', 'we', 'they' and 'people at the bottom' is vivid here signalling complex, shifting and conflicted relations. This story conveys strongly through repetition and emphatic language my sense of the absurdity of what went on here: the image of the independent consultant attempting to impose her view on a large, complex and highly political organisation. The gender dynamic of the male chief executive coming late into the process of a female team is also notable.

Reflection

This piece of work remains in the memory of the consultant team. It took a lot of energy and cost £25,000 of public money to no effect that we could discern, despite pursuing this after the report was complete to no avail. We also discovered golfing partners and other hidden relationships that affected the processes. The report had not even been circulated internally although this had been promised. We felt finally that this was a 'tick-box' exercise with no commitment to change – we ended feeling guilty at profiting from it

The struggle to control the work and the report is vivid. In the final lines, I feel it is fine to impose my view on him but not for him to impose his on me! I 'get agreement' and they 'impose'. This conveys I feel I am right and he is wrong to resist this – I use a violent metaphor 'chop out' to express my view. What makes me so sure? My presence in the discussions held with staff gave me a view that they needed and would value more cross-communication. But does this explain my assumption of a right to confront those who run the organisation and who may have other information that suggests other action is better? It did not occur to me I may not have power. I am sure I can act, that I know what to do, what is required. That they want me to act is an assumption I make on being commissioned. Once commissioned, I am an independent agent in a set of power processes; hence the tortuous path recounted here.

Excerpt 9   Not just 'a pair of hands'?

Here I describe the beginning of the Local Authority work featured in Chapter 6 and my concerns about how those commissioning viewed the consultant team. Again the themes are of struggling for power, recognition of an independent identity and for the work to have impact. My certainty as the consultant is again strong.

Sometimes they just want a pair of hands [metaphor], they're too busy to do the thing themselves and they want to treat you like an employee. The [local authority] want to treat us like employees [repetition], [we've had] an email where the client has written this list of what he wants from us to do this piece of work and it's all about reporting in and control in an employer/employee kind of way [social context, discourses] and we've said [reported speech] 'no forget it we're not [strong modality] going to behave like that, you take us on as independent people [identifying] or you don't.' ... I suppose I want maximum autonomy to do what I [identifying, direct] think is needed. The power stuff in here really. They want it completed [distancing, passive], a policy document [genre] by September and it's really problematic and we are going into a time when there will be no one to talk to. We say this is mad [strong modality]– but no they must have it, they [relations] just want a document to say we've got one of these [political context] they are not interested in implementation. For me [identifying] in developing the policy you do it with a view to how it will be implemented but they are not interested in that, they want the object, the solution [nominalised]. That's incredibly common. We all find ourselves trying to slow down processes, get people to think about what is the point and the purpose and sometimes people just don't want to hear that. You [relations] then have a choice you either do it the way they want it and take the money or you don't do it and I've done both those things.

... We feel [our contact] is not senior [social context], we're not going to get the support we need ... We feel [repetition] the Chief Executive is the client really, ...That's what we're going to do, to insist [strong modality] on a meeting with him early on and insist [repetition] that we come back to him with the draft later on and then it comes down to our power. ... I think our power over the relatively junior [evaluative] contact, he's not going to stop us contacting the Chief Executive's office... But then even with the Chief Executive whether he will take it on, whether he will have us portray [metaphor, passive] him as the client, whether he'll be willing to be recruited [metaphor, passive] as client. ... we're going to try together [relations] to see him as powerful and make him see he should [direct] take up that power, ... it will always depend on what you are trying to achieve, what is the work in question. It isn't a matter of hierarchy of position or even, straightforwardly our influencing skills or anything [strong modality] like that. It's to do with the work really. What does it need [nominalised] to achieve what we think [strong modality] needs to be achieved and so who needs to be involved [relations].

As I comment in the text, this story is about power, how it is perceived and created within the consulting work. I start from a position of asserting 'independent' autonomy, sensitive to early signs of being constrained. This links to my frustration at the limited approach I see in the local authority about this work. I am angry that they left the work, so that they now want it in a hurry and at the least conducive time. I use a series of strong modality, active phrases, often repeated: 'insist', 'make him', 'we're going to'. The political context is very present and shapes how the people in the local authority are acting. Still I want to ignore this and focus on implementation in developing the policy. Our intention of working more with the chief executive is portrayed as crucial, something we must exert power to achieve – based too on our vivid certainty of what the work requires, that is, a 'senior' lead. In the event we met the chief executive and together engaged leading politicians in the work to increase the possibility of action as a result.

Excerpt 10   'How does she know we are going to be any good?'

This excerpt concerns perceptions of trust: mine and those of the person commissioning me. I tell the story of how several years ago Mel and I began to work with Laurie, who commissioned the University work featured in Chapter 6. I also include Laurie's reflections looking back to that time.

> It's a very interesting thing as I think she really does trust us. We have got a real [strong modality] roving brief in her organisation. Every year we discuss with her what she would, sorts of things she might like us to do for the coming year. But she always says what do you want to do? ... [strong modality, question, reported] ... She's very interesting, she is such a strategic thinker. That's great as it is so unusual [strong modality], she's always looking way ahead [context]. And it's stimulating to be in a meeting with her ... She trusts us, tells us stuff [intertextuality] I know she doesn't tell her staff. About how the university's future is shaping up. She's ... involved at the highest level. It's, that's great you feel trusted, you know, we're going to do interesting work, the work changes. It's also it's a constant thing, there's something reassuring about having this contract that continues. I feel she does listen [relations] she listens to us she appreciates the fact we come from a very different place from her academic staff they've

been there for years they are not outward looking, not adjusting to the [*changing*] environment of the public sector [political context]. So she likes our fresh thinking and she likes [repetition] that we deliver stuff. [vocabulary] She asks for stuff [repetition] from her staff and she just doesn't get it. And she's very good at putting people together. She [relations] sort of collects lively thinkers … And how did we get her? Well – the Vice Chancellor was … someone Mel had known years ago when he was some humble lecturer somewhere and she'd been involved in some programme or other [low modality]. So we were looking for a university to accredit [intertextuality] a programme we were doing … So she said well let's go to this university 'cos I know this guy … So we did that and we accredited our programme… And that got a bit boring [vocabulary] so 2 years later we go and see him again and he said [reported speech] well you should meet this woman, she's about the only other lively [vocabulary] person in the whole university, you should definitely meet her, she'd have things for you to do. So we literally rang her up and said hello your VC has suggested we meet … And she must have had, thinking about it, she must have had a conversation with him about us, she must have [repetition] done because I can't understand it otherwise. I remember coming out of that first meeting and she'd basically commissioned us for like a large amount of work, like on the basis of that one discussion like that, and she was giving us a lot [strong modality] of autonomy. So we came out and I said to Mel that was pretty amazing [vocabulary], and she said well yes, how does she know we are going to be any good? I said well I don't know really. Then we stopped worrying about it and got on with it really. It's interesting as she exhibited massive [strong modality] trust right from the start. I don't really know why, where that came from. She may have had a conversation with the VC, but what did he know? He didn't know very much and nothing recent and he knew almost nothing [repetition] about me anyway, so where did that come from? So something must have clicked (metaphor) in the meeting anyway.

My description emphasises the positive feelings I experienced with this person, 'feeling trusted', 'reassured', 'listened to', 'liked' and in a trusted circle of advisers/consultants, given 'autonomy'. The terms used for her: 'lively', 'strategic', 'amazing', 'stimulating' verge on the sycophantic! All this contrasts strongly with the apparently accidental process of the connection being created, signalled by a stream of low modality phrases. My use of the transactional discourse for consulting ('we deliver stuff') makes a notable, rare appearance here contrasting with the story about trust.

In talking with Laurie during the University work she said she had not talked to the Vice Chancellor about us:

Laurie: 'We never had [that] conversation, my assumptions are, in retrospect, [that he thought] we keep [*the faculty*] as it is or develop into new interesting areas and [*the faculty*] is very traditional. I knew we needed to go [direct] somewhere else but I was not very clear and not exactly surrounded by people who thought like that, there weren't a lot [low modality] of people thinking: what is the next thing? What struck [metaphor] me was you had a different view on life, different take [metaphors], you weren't the management of the university looking for growth or development, anything like that. I guess you were punting for work to put it crudely – but what struck a chord [metaphor] with me was your [relations] breadth of vision about the public sector, the values [intertextuality] that seemed to come over, and I knew I needed help' [direct]

Laurie's reflections emphasise her desire for the long view and to develop her faculty more actively and strategically, but within a set of public sector values. She also sees our dissociation from university management as a source of disinterested help – while recognising we are 'punting for work'. Her position echoes the 'objective professional' discourse of consulting and the notion of consulting as reassurance for the manager trapped in the discourse of 'permanent change'.

Laurie poses her position in a series of low modality terms: 'somewhere' 'not very clear', 'not exactly', 'not a lot'. This contrasts with her metaphors of 'striking a chord' and being 'struck' which sound as if she had a sudden insight in our meeting about shared 'vision' and 'values'. Later her close use of 'you' with 'I' and 'me' signals the relationship forming and enabling her to seek the direct help she wanted. Her view of her position, as not knowing and needing help, the 'deficit' discourse, contrasts with my description of her as strategic and enabling – I see our work as supporting a strong person. On the other hand we say almost the same things about why the relationship has worked: we consultants come 'from a very different place', and have 'a different take'. We are 'other'.

Excerpt 11 'What really it takes to do the work'

Below I talk about how I see the process as messier than those who commission do and how I doubt the notion of skills. I emphasise connections and space needed for 'worthwhile' work, a recurring term in all my material. My certainties and doubts oscillate palpably in this excerpt.

> 'What's tricky is it's always much messier [metaphor] than the processes in literature, it's very iterative and emergent and one of the problems is the clients have read the literature [intertextuality] and they think it's a straight line [metaphor] process, so convincing them, letting it be shaped [passive] and emerge and depending on what we are getting determines the next step, they think they [relations] are losing control of the process as all the books say [intertextuality] you manage your consultants very tightly [metaphor], you have a clear brief [genre] and you have milestones [metaphor] and a procedure and life's not like that, [evaluative, strong modality] they feel they are doing it wrong [vocabulary] and that the consultant [distancing] is taking advantage or something. So it's quite a tension, this mental image [nominalised] of the procedure and what really it takes [direct, distanced] to do the work.
>
> Interviewer: so what skills do you think you use in the initial phase?
>
> Me: In a way, in a way, it's all in the moment, it's being able and willing, willing [repetition] to enter [metaphor] that co-creation,

that relationship of, what are they trying to do, how can I be part of that in a way that I think [relations] is worthwhile [vocabulary]. So in a way [indirect] that is what they are getting, it is absolutely outside [strong modality] that idea of skill, it's that energy, a bit like complexity theory [discourse] you bring the energies together and maybe that kickstarts [metaphor] something or moves something on in the organisation. So it may [low modality] be, I don't think that's a skill, an ability or a characteristic, I don't know what it is, but it's between human beings. [relations] Sometimes it's hard to know any more than that really. Sometimes [low modality, repetition] I think what it is, is the capacity to think [nominalised] which often people in the organisation haven't got the space [context] for that. They might get that space by having a consultant, we might force [vocabulary] them to think, we might [low modality, repetition] do some thinking and then offer it back and then that triggers [metaphor] their thinking. But there's not a lot of space for reflection out there at the moment, everyone's very pressurised, they're doing three jobs, being reorganised and all that stuff [socio-political context]. So maybe [low modality] what we offer is space, which is a kind of emptiness and paradoxical.

I am asserting the power of popular management discourse about consulting and the use of genres like the 'brief', and how it affects working processes. This seems to be a combative situation between 'we' and 'they'. I am talking ambiguity and emergence versus the commodified 'project' discourse I experience from people commissioning work. Notably I use 'mental image' rather than directly saying they are thinking wrongly. I baldly state 'life's not like that' and sound immovable in my assessment that the process happens as I perceive it.

My view of what is worthwhile is also striking. Colleagues and I ask ourselves 'should we get into this?' – this decision is key, since it will entail so much entanglement. There is a similar reference to 'enter' as in referring to male colleagues earlier, but in order to 'co-create' raising a rather different sexual image, that of reproduction. I talk about the process rather than expert input or transaction. Although I use a strong term: 'force', I also use a string of low modality terms: 'might', 'maybe' and 'something' in indirect expression of my opinion. My concerns with what is worthwhile, and making connections between people emphasise value and emotion rather than the commercial process – which is nonetheless still present in terms of 'getting' and 'offering'. The broader public sector context of others' work and their pressures are very present, resulting in the 'paradox' of space as the key consulting 'offer'.

Summary

My reflections are concerned with power, but not as a finite object passed between people in consulting. This rejects the 'commodified' discourse of consulting as transaction. My stories illustrate the limitations of notions of 'client' or 'project' in these settings; terms quite elastic and meaningless. There is a trail of relationships (processes) that have led to the point of work being commissioned. These relationships and the 'project' extend into the past and endlessly into the future. The themes of certainty with doubt and concern with 'worthwhile-ness' recur for me.

> **Reflection**
> *Similarly my colleague, Mel, and I reviewed a not-for profit consortium, working on health issues. The management committee commissioned us as they were concerned about viability. I interviewed a senior manager in the local council who were funding the group. She walked in and said 'I think this council should have commissioned this, what are these people doing, commissioning their own review? They are independent but we fund them.' Everyone has a point of view born from their take on the relationships involved, and especially about who is the client.*

Men's voices

While most of my material has involved women, some involved men. Here I analyse reflective excerpts from two male colleagues, both self-employed consultants, also working predominantly in the public sector. The first is well-known to me and the second is not a direct colleague.

Excerpt 12   Avoiding 'a pig's ear'

The National Policy work featured in Chapter 6 involved Sam, who specialises in editing and writing, in the early stages of tendering. Later reflecting on the email transcript he described his overall approach to his work and how he saw quality in his work.

Sam: 'In fact, unless I am explicitly excluded [passive] from production, as an editor or a writer I try my hardest *not* [strong modality] to let people get on with it by themselves. And if people [relationships, distance] want to exclude me [strong modality] I think hard about accepting the job. This is because in my experience most clients unused to publishing, and even some who are, need all the help they can get to avoid obvious disasters [strong modality, vocabulary]. Therefore, I want to be closely involved at all stages up to and including delivery/dissemination. I also don't want to end up with being [passive] associated with things that look like a pig's ear [vocabulary] Hence I have asked for my name [identifying] not to be included in a couple of publications. This is part professional [vocabulary] pride, and part wanting to make sure that end-users get something that bears as close a likeness [metaphor] as possible to the original conception [metaphor] (including the conception that the client had)'

Sam describes a transactional process where he tries to control 'people' in relation to his own input of work. He identifies his approach as 'professional' and involving his 'name'. He uses strong words to talk about the possibility of the other people getting things wrong and affecting his own standing: 'disaster', 'pig's ear'. He will use strong sanctions such as withdrawing his name or not taking the contract to ensure his control. Nonetheless he uses words like 'conception' which suggests developing a project 'child' to help the end users. His words show a clear desire for autonomy and control, with the associated emotion and identity work, but he takes a very different view of relationships within the commercial process, where he is the professional and expert, than do the women's reflections.

Sam's story highlights a discourse where the assumption of specialist knowledge work wins out despite his concern for the end user. In contrast women frequently refer to making sense of their work as a whole, connecting it to others' work and to broader issues such as the politics of the public sector. Time and again in the consulting interactions especially, my women colleagues and I emphasise our commitment to the people using public services, to the needs of those commissioning us in order to serve the public. We are undoubtedly more comfortable with this notion than that of being private sector businesses – as we in fact are. This is explicitly stated by me: '... for us it's a political thing of public spending and it ought to be worthwhile, especially if we have unwittingly been the beneficiaries...' (Development group Dec 2003) Again *worthwhile-ness* recurs.

Excerpt 13   Throwing work 'over your shoulder'

Martin is not a direct colleague of mine but was willing to discuss his work with me. Here I asked him to talk about interactions between consultants in doing the work. Martin described various ways he works with colleagues in a rather dry, matter-of-fact and task-focused way. At the time I wanted this question to lead to talk about interactions between him and his colleagues, but he responded by focusing on the structures and contractual relationships, which seem rather instrumental, reflecting what might be termed a 'masculine' approach.

Sheila: ... a lot of in the nature of the thing has been about <u>between</u> us as consultants, so interesting to hear about when you've worked with colleagues, how that interaction, that process goes ...

Martin: yeah, done quite a lot of work where there's been a team of us, associates. A recent project was, uh, quite complicated in terms of how it was contracted. I was contracted [passive construction] to be a <u>third tier</u> [assumed hierarchy] associate, if you like, to the main company. It was loosely a partnership, but really they [relationship] were running it. The main consultancy had got the piece of work and offered work to the other consultancy that I was working for. They were taking quite a large cut, the consultancy that I was working for had another cut, [metaphor] and so I got what was left, <u>that's how it works</u>. [assumed power relations]

Sheila: so you weren't part of that deal [vocabulary]

Martin: no not in that instance. Yeah that is a classic [vocabulary] one where I just get invited in to work on a contract that someone else has set up. Another way of working is I work with an organisation or for myself to contract for work, it might be a

---

bid or just again someone I know through a network that wants something doing [low modality, relations]

Sheila: do you do much bidding or quoting?

Martin: Yeah, yeah. I do quite a bit of bidding, quoting, it's an essential part of the work. If you've got your own [business]…, unless you are doing all associate work … where you are just working for someone else [low modality, relations], then you don't do that. Fine, but basically what happens is you do the up front [metaphor] work – you may or not get paid for doing the up front bidding, negotiating with the client, doing the design work for the product or whatever it is programme, research whatever it is. And then if you don't get paid for that, you take a large cut, you take a cut [metaphor] off all the delivery [metaphor, transaction] work that's done whether it's done by yourself or by other people. So you might take 10 or 15%. Then if there's any delivery work you undertake, you take that [direct]. So that's generally, in general that's how it works [assumed process, discourse], there's lots of variations, that's good. It's good experience doing that. And …. it means that you don't have to do it all yourself, you throw it over your shoulder [metaphor], let other associates take it on. But because you've done the ground work setting up the deal, then you're compensated [vocabulary] for doing that. So sometimes you get paid retrospectively for doing that. So that's another arrangement. Let's just think. There you're really a programme manager in that role. And then the other way is where I directly contract, not using another organisation's brand [vocabulary, intertextuality]. Which is the reason I'd do it the other way, I need that brand. You know a larger organisation has got a track record [metaphor] in that sector and the other way is I'd contract for myself and my company. There's a kind of unspoken understanding [other texts] about sources of consultancy. It's always, if you do a good job for a client under another brand and the client comes to you with 'can we contract directly next time and not have to go through ..' [reported speech] that's a no-no.

This is not an emotional account of shared work like Jan's. Martin uses rather distancing phrases with the passive construction: 'get invited' 'get contracted'. The same metaphor of the 'cut' is used differently here: it is about division of money, and not a butchery metaphor, but that of the card game – how the 'deal' is done which I mirror. 'They' are running things and 'that's how it works'. Martin accepts this and sees its positive aspect as he too does this when he initiates work. He works through his networks, like the women in the study, but he is not talking about them in the emotionally connected ways the women do: 'just again someone I know', 'just working for someone else'. His metaphor of 'throwing over your shoulder' the work for others is striking. The image suggests throwing a bone to dogs at a medieval feast. In this text the underlying issues of power and of the commercial process are present, but emotions are not really visible. Issues of identification are coupled with the instrumental marketing discourse of the 'brand' although linked to a clear ethic in relation to accepted behaviour in such relationships.

The text sets out a structural, hierarchical process, not informed especially by notions of reciprocal relations that the women discuss, although his opening statement in the interview was that he preferred 'to work collaboratively with the client'. For Martin being 'compensated' or getting 'your cut' as just reward for effort in a commercial transaction stands apart from the women's talk and interaction.

Martin's and Jan's stories were so different that I asked them each to read both and to comment on them. Their responses were equally different. While different in length (I have cut Jan's but not Martin's) this may be due to my closer relationship to Jan than to Martin. The major difference concerns Jan's not accepting 'this is the way it works' and wanting a different approach to power in doing her work. As a woman she seems to be aware of gender differences and patterns in a way that Martin is not: for him 'there are sharks' and 'who knows what really happens' rather than socially constructed gendered relations of power. Her response is also notable for the emphasis she lays explicitly on the emotions in the work: 'holding the anxiety' and noting Martin's lack of emotion.

Martin's email after reading his and Jan's words:
Two things for now: one is that these are just two accounts so who knows what really happens. Secondly no surprise regarding your other account – there are sharks [metaphor] in this business like every other and I've heard very similar stories.

Jan's email after reading hers and Martin's words:
Rereading my story and Martin's I was struck by the difference between our views. I was talking from a personal point of view and generalising from an early experience. [I described it very badly too. There was a great deal more complexity in the whole thing than I have shown e.g. how I was introduced to that guy and the work and therefore my expectations and the role of the other associates who all also got burned [metaphor] in different ways and reacted differently too. There was a gender difference with the women in my view being treated worse and boundaries being very badly breached all round but hey!]

Martin seems to inhabit another world. [image] One of clear hierarchies and power relations where it seems to be mutually understood and agreed who gets paid for what, in relation to the selling in/bidding process. [No emotions!] I don't mind that hierarchy, if it's understood in advance, it seems fair to me for people to be paid for what they bring to the work and not to pretend that everyone is equal in skill, experience and connections. I don't think it works as seamlessly as he seems to suggest however. ...

Sometimes it's great not to have to take the responsibility for setting something up, being the front person and holding all the anxiety [metaphor, vocabulary] so I sometimes like the associate position but prefer it when it's joint and collaborative. But is it always fair? It makes me think that the way we work is dependent on a high level of trust and communication which isn't always there of course and when things go wrong they are hard to untangle. ... I'm not sure how much all this is down to gender difference or down to styles of dealing with the nitty gritty of competition and rivalry over sharing the resources i.e. power and ... how political principles operate in all this and shape the working relationships.

Summary

The men's voices show a glimpse within the same working context of different discourses in use than the women's emphasis on trust, emotion, reciprocity and 'worthwhile-ness'. Sam reflects the expert 'objective professional' who is concerned for his identity in achieving outcomes he is happy with; although he acknowledges the emotional labour, his aim is to avoid it. Martin draws heavily on a commodified transactional discourse devoid of emotion and full of instrumental assumptions about roles and rules in commerce. This contrast suggests it is vital to explore links between femininities and consulting in order to make better sense of the women's experiences and talk.

Learning from the CDA process

This section briefly sums up how CDA has illuminated the reflections and stories about consulting, signposting the discussions to come in Part III. As in Chapter 6 this section draws on the three dimensions of CDA: the *text* itself, *intertextuality* and the *broader social/political context*. These highlight similar themes of power, emotion, and the commercial process and its values, and how these are mutually shaping, as in Chapter 6. The section ends in summarising the dilemmas highlighted in these excerpts and their connection to the discourses of consulting identified in Part I.

CDA concepts for exploring *text* have helped draw attention to strong feelings, through the powerful metaphors and consistent strong modality of statements. Tensions and contradictions, for example in shifting power and relationships, are shown through our oscillation between direct and distanced talk, and between strong and low modality of expression, as in Chapter 6.

Overwhelmingly the emotions displayed here are strong and strongly expressed: 'scarred', 'fierce', 'shocking'. Mirrored feelings are rife, for example, the fear Michelle feels and fear felt by those she works with; desperation of both Madge and of Jane who called her. The contrast of certainty and vulnerability among the women is sharp and reflects themes from Chapter 2 of the certainty of the adviser, yet their position as marginal 'Other'. As stories, perhaps the excerpts inevitably dramatise the experiences in re-telling to others. But my journal and much of the corpus of material I gathered bears witness to strong emotions evinced within day-to-day mundanities: how we feel about the work, the angst of computing glitches, the traumas of actually making contact with people. A frequent emotion is frustration, reflected in my own partner's comment in carrying out my administrative work: 'consulting is about a lot of people taking ages to not do what they promised!'

The notion of *intertextuality* shows, as in Chapter 6, the chains of texts and the webs of interconnected actors involved in them. The complexity of processes before, during and after consulting work is clearly illustrated in a number of stories. The actors draw on varied discursive resources to achieve their work such as 'skills' or 'brief', alongside implicit assumptions of commerce such as what constitutes a fair 'cut' or 'free goods'.

The *broader contextual issues* of power are especially notable in these excerpts, connected to the actions of the consultant. This predominantly concerns our autonomy to act in relation to those commissioning us, in order to work with emerging events and issues in the broader context. The material contains striking examples of the consultant taking power to herself. Madge takes this in relation to her 'desperate' government caller; my stories are full of how I and colleagues take decisions to act and influence, in ways we see fit, to shape and control the work, its direction and relationships, as in the local government work and the health trust.

In contrast Jan's story shows a concern for 'power with' in work with colleagues coupled to attention to relationships and connections with people commissioning her. Pam's story of Harry also reflects these priorities, privileging keeping connection over exerting her power through 'the heavy mob'. The sense gained is of women struggling for enough control to see through what they think is 'worthwhile' – a word that has recurred among us all. Pam commented a piece of work had been 'worthwhile' when one police officer 'agreed that not all gypsies were thieves'.

The voices of the men seem to show a different approach to power: that of transaction, of professional expectations about standards and acceptance of 'how it works'. For the women the decision to engage is key, as once you 'get into' something then to walk away is very hard. As one discussion group participant commented 'the core power as a consultant must be to walk away'. This power is inextricably linked therefore to what can make us walk away – our own values, emotions or motivations about what is worthwhile. This set of notions about power link to the 'trusted adviser' discourse, much more than to the 'objective professional'.

it always boils down to – well I could lose my job. That's why consultancy is so fantastic because every time you have to be prepared to lose the job, it's grounded on [that] (discussion group participant)

The excerpts sharply delineate core dilemmas in the process of consulting for the women. Their talk both reflects and challenges contemporary discourses. They implicitly draw on the 'trusted adviser' discourse more than that of 'objective professional'. They reject the discourse of commodified project in favour of a discourse of connection, relationships and 'worthwhile-ness'. While rejecting a 'power-over' approach they remain, like the premodern advisers, certain of their views and advice, yet still marginal. At the same time as experiencing this certainty, they work from a set of emotions and sense of self that encompass doubt, fear and vulnerability.

The tension of the commodified 'project' discourse with the role of relationships in the commercial process stands out. Jan's highly gender-inflected story and Pam's experiences are working with this tension of connection versus transaction. Madge's story focuses on a close and mutually dependent relationship, while Ros recounts the power of 'free' goods in the commercial process for building relationships. My own paradoxical conclusion about consulting as an empty space stands also against the commodified 'project' discourse. The assumptions of mutuality in the commercial process and between colleagues are strong and co-exist with the certainties and choices asserted by the consultants in action. The stories demonstrate an alternative to (masculine) models of entrepreneurship. They show women operating commercially but in different value-based ways which presume a mutual relationship. They are demanding engagement and change of people commissioning work from them.

The material shows other dilemmas abound in the commercial process: ethics and the 'taxi meter'; 'free' work and making a living; completing the contract and keeping the relationships. The role of values and ethics within the commercial process is especially keenly felt by the women. These issues produce a range of emotions and pain as the women struggle to reconcile what they see they have to do with what they wish to do – and what others wish or demand they do.

Overall the reflections show a 'complex web of storied relationships' (Boje 2001:135) that holds the key issues of power, emotion, values and the commercial process in tension: each equally, consciously and intentionally interwoven rather than a hierarchy. This weaving is held by

Table 7.1 Connecting themes, dilemmas and discourses of consulting

Theme	Dilemma	Discourse
Power/control	Certainty vs. vulnerability & marginality Power over vs. power with Autonomy in work vs. 'client' control	'trusted adviser' 'Rhetoric' vs. 'partnership' 'objective professional'
Emotion	Confronting vs. keeping connections going Balance of strong emotion with earning a living	'partnership' 'performance'
Commercial process & its assumptions/ values	Ethics vs. earning a living Consultant values vs. values of people commissioning work Project or product vs. emergent process	'worthwhile-ness' 'commodification'

the increasingly strong place of gender in the material – here the experience and discourse of women consultants – and the added clarity the reflections have given to the themes of Chapter 6 through surfacing key *dilemmas* in consulting. These are summarised in Table 7.1. Part III explores these themes further, drawing together what has emerged from Parts I and II.

Part III

Making Sense

8
What is Going On in Consulting Interactions?: Exploring Meta-themes of Power, Emotion and Values

Introduction

Here I explore what is going on in consulting interactions, through a focus on meta-themes derived from the analysis of my material in Chapters 6 and 7. These meta-themes seem powerfully inter-connected: *power, emotion,* and *values in the commercial process*. They surface throughout and were immediately noticed by others reading the material. They are not only striking and consistent, but are themes not convincingly dealt with in the contemporary consulting literature. There power is mostly assigned to either consultant or client; emotion is barely discussed; classical norms of economic rationality are simply assumed in the commercial process; and the pejorative discourse imputes negative intent to consultants, far from any sense of 'worthwhile' values.

This chapter highlights the inter-woven nature of public and private in consulting work.

> the arrival in an outer form of something intensely inner and personal; and the act of working itself – a bridge between the public and the private, a bridge of experience which can be an agony and an ecstasy to cross. (Whyte 2002:68)

Gender inflected-ness reverberates through the meta-themes: women working in a commercial process, engaged in power struggles and emotion work, experience 'agony and ecstasy' in enacting their values and spanning the public and private as we saw in Chapters 6 and 7.

These meta-themes echo my early concerns, especially those of strong feelings, of worth and value of work, and of identity. They also mirror issues raised by the genealogy in Chapter 2: the importance of relationships, feelings, purposes and values in advice-giving. Thus they offer a helpful focus for sense-making in order to explain what may be going on in (these) consulting interactions, what this may mean for women consultants, for discourses of consulting and for 'critical consulting'.

The meta-themes encompass important sub-themes, summed up in Table 8.1 and linked back to the material analysed using CDA. My exploration here of each meta-theme draws on these and aims to enable a deeper understanding of the dynamics and implications of power, emotion and values in the commercial process.

Power in the interactions and stories

The struggle for control of the work and its direction is the clearest meta-theme in my material, the most consistently identified in the CDA and in comments of colleagues and others viewing/ reading the material. Power is expressed or displayed

> *'There's nothing much on management consulting and power [in database searches] – it's all about the energy industry!'* (journal 21 February 2004)

in the text through the modality of statements, in how relations are portrayed, in passive or active statements, in how other texts are invoked by actors and in how the broader context affects what people do and say. The struggles visible concern both a discursive tussle to link our micro actions to (our) broader social/political concerns and a linked tussle over discursive resources in terms of negotiating meaning (Wenger 1998). Power for consultants in the study is about our autonomy to act, our sense that as agents we not only can act, but are expected to act and wish to act, including on our own account in pursuit of what we think is 'worthwhile'. Such struggle is prefigured in the framing of the CDA approach and reflects the crucial link of power to discourse; it confirms the fruitfulness of viewing of consulting as a discursive practice.

Wenger sees the construction of identity (through engagement) brings power issues to the fore. Power is 'primarily ... the ability to act in line with the enterprises we pursue' (1998:189) rather than about conflict with others, competing interests and so on. Power then is *agency*, the capacity or choice to act on what you see as *your* projects (Weick 1995). For Wenger power is 'the negotiation of meaning and the formation of identities ... a property of social communities. ... a social concept of

Table 8.1   Meta themes and sub themes in my material

Meta-theme	Sub-themes	Examples
Power	Ownership of work & 'making a difference' Politics of settings Agency, confidence/ advising Knowledge & its use	Strategic Health Authority work: 'what will make it all worthwhile' and helping people to 'invest around the edges' Local Authority work: 'the politicians hate this policy area', 'our advice is ... that is not what you want' Development network: 'dominate the client' vs. expectations of mutual relations
Emotion	Feelings about people involved and colleagues Feelings in the interactions, emotional labour & hiding emotions Passion for the task Trust	National Policy work: importance of anxiety and producing reassurance; 'terribly annoying and really frustrating at the time'; University work: 'If I was doing it I'd get so pissed off, ... it would get on my bloody nerves'. Strong emotions: 'she is toxic', 'betrayal', 'exasperation'; 'what people commission and what they expect is driving me potty..' Jean: 'prove to me you are serious'; Ros: 'I just know PA will work' Emergence of trust in the University work; trust of Laurie in consultants; assuming reciprocity: Sam, Jan, & Pam's reflections
Values in the commercial process	Worth, value & values	Colleagues' reflections: 'I'm over-fastidious, over-driven by values and scruples.' 'I just did it for free', 'what will make it worthwhile is ...' Concern for service users in the Strategic Health Authority work and to avoid simplistic 'targets' in the Local Authority work
	Impression management	Strategic Health Authority work: 'I call it analysis', 'let's cut and paste'
	Planned, commodified 'products' vs emergent processes	University work: 'a vehicle for development', 'the project unfolds'; National Policy work: 'you appear to be suggesting a change in what we commissioned'

identity entails a social concept of power' (1998:189–190). His concept of 'economies of meaning', founded on our 'ability, facility and legitimacy to contribute to, take responsibility for and shape the meanings that matter' (1998:197), illuminates my colleagues' and my desire for autonomous action within our work. We thus display elements of a 'community of practice.'

A Foucauldian view of power also speaks directly to my study of interaction and how power shifts in the consulting interactions studied.

> For Foucault power does not reside in things, but in a network of relationships which are systematically interconnected. ...located in the micro-physics of social life, in the 'depths' of society ...minute and diffuse power relations exist, always in tension, always in action (Burrell 1998:20)

The 'micro-physics' and 'minute and diffuse power relations' of relationships in the National Policy work are typical. There were multiple social, political and work-based connections between my colleague, me and our contacts, overlapping with people connected to those

Reflection

'Carole couldn't pull the plug of course, she needed the work done, she had no other place to go. So an interesting set of power relations. The fact that processes can only go on, you can't undo processes – they have contracted you and there are limits about starting again as people always want it quickly.' (Journal July 2003)

commissioning us. Drawing on these undermined normative notions of power in the commercial process and, once commissioned, we exercised power in the emergent process, determining the direction of the work. Many, many processes prefigure consulting work and carry its unfolding: in this case the work of an advisory group, many of whose members were in our social/work networks, affected not only our getting the work but how we carried it out in concert with those people among many others. The intertextuality of the work, connecting to the work of many people outside the government department, and the other demands of that department on the person commissioning us, constrained her actions and gave us more space to act. Power and agency are of course mutually reinforcing. Consultants' power will be greater 'in times of instability in the inner power structure' (Gammelsoeter 2002:226). Conversely these overlapping networks potentially reduced consultant power in the Voluntary Sector work where Sally feared her reputation compromised. The denseness and closeness of connections to those commissioning us may also produce oppressive expectations or a sense of our 'omnipotence' as with the example of Madge and Jane.

In the Strategic Health Authority work, the power dynamics were complex: we, the consultants, took the power to re-define the work as it progressed. We chose whose interests to highlight (service users) and whom to influence (commissioners), in relation to what we thought would be 'worthwhile', regardless of the influence of broader, mainstream discourses of government regarding mental health. In deciding how best to achieve this we ourselves struggled for control of the report, its content and presentation. Similarly Clegg sees power as relational within 'a more or less stable or shifting network of alliances extended over a shifting terrain of practice and discursively constituted interests.' (1998:30). Mumby too defines a critical view of organisational work as about 'political sites where various organisational actors and groups struggle to 'fix' meaning in ways that will serve their particular interests' as we did here (2004:237).

The Local Authority work and the University work are notable for the evidence of shifting relations as the work progressed. Who linked to whom and who identified with whom created power. Questioning who should lead enabled us to connect to key local politicians; Graeme and I forged a link over the humming laptop that gave us the power to complete the report our way; our developing relations with Stella influenced her away from hands-on project management to a more hands-off style, empowering her team leaders. Similarly in Chapter 7, Pam 'held the line' and Harry shifted his position. At the same time these interactions were influenced interdiscursively by other interactions: the meeting of stakeholders, discussions with councillors and comments from other departments in the Local Authority work; the intensive days with Stella's staff in the University work; Pam's experience elsewhere of pursuing equality standards.

We are (per)forming our power relations in the exchanges as well as (per)forming the work, and from both we (per)form our sense of who we are in what we are doing. At the same time we reject the 'dominate the client' perspective of Jan's male colleague, but we still take pains to assert our views of what we think is right or 'worthwhile' with the certainty of the premodern advisers seen in Chapter 1: 'I plainly tell you.'.

The Voluntary Sector work alone seems to illustrate the normative view of power in consulting, that is the commissioning person holds the power to pay, or not, on her judgement of contract completion. This framed the relationship: the consultant had little power and took a near supplicant role. However, here there was no exit, as the strangers who are 'quits' in the classical economic market transaction (Callon 1998); there was a lasting effect as power was enacted on the identity of the consultant who feared for her ongoing reputation and chances of being commissioned.

Deetz's exploration of Foucauldian power draws directly on consulting (1998). For him the level of autonomy, lack of clarity about the work, together with professionalised 'expertise', all militate against 'sovereign power', as it is hard actually to see the work process. Consultants, then, are 'constantly anxious' about their identities though imaged as confidently certain (1998:168). My material however shows that confidence and anxieties are *both* present. Deetz feels consultants have to choose loyalty (to those commissioning) or exit but not voice, which would produce negative consequences for them. Loyalty produces identity but requires consenting to dependent power relations. What the pieces of work and

> **Reflection**
> *In working for a government department Ros and I struggled with the woman commissioning us at the consultation events we were running: she felt we weren't asking the 'right' questions as people were not responding as specifically as she wanted. We changed the questions several times, but got the same kinds of response; she remained unwilling to agree with our view that these responses and their broad nature were actually the data she and we needed to absorb. People said what they needed to say regardless of the question: that was the point. I felt she never changed her view that we hadn't done it 'right'.* (Journal January 2004)

stories presented raise are the possibilities of (critical) voice and the extent to which these produce negative consequences or positive change. We can see that Sally fears the negative, and that others, such as Michelle, Pam, Jean, Chris and Ros, experience major emotional labour in achieving 'voice' for change. Notions of voice, emotional labour, power, anxiety and identity are all highly gender-inflected with implications for women's experience of work. It is hard therefore to read this material and its theme of power, control and autonomy as other than about *women* at work in consulting processes.

The Foucauldian view of power has spawned a debate about how agency, power and knowledge intersect (Legge 2002). Consultants in my study take up agency through assuming power in the interaction, not expected under traditional notions of power in commerce. Why do we assume we have power to act? We assume 'the capacity to shape, facilitate and generate practices, processes and social relations' (Cooper 1994) in our work. We see power as productive. We seem to embody the agency/structure tension: people in organisations are using consultants to bridge this tension, reflecting consulting as 'liminal space' (Czarniawska and Mazza 2003). At the same time we oscillate between certainty and softer tones, echoing the rejection of 'unmitigated agency' that Bakan (1966 in King 2005) saw as male and needing the mitigation of female 'communion'.

In our work issues of power and control are not only linked, as we might expect, to the economic process of consulting and to issues of our autonomy and expertise but also to our emotions in undertaking it and our commitments in terms of values and ethics. We experience a tension in enacting our desire for control of our work with our desire also to do something 'worthwhile' *with* others, not controlling them.

Emotion in the interactions and stories

> ...practical reasoning unaccompanied by emotion is not sufficient for practical wisdom (Mangham 1998:51)

Mangham's view is implicit for the women in the study and largely absent from the contemporary consulting literature. This section explores emotion in the material, but recognises the link of power with emotion in the commercial process. The material in Chapters 6 and 7 showed how closely power and emotion are linked in consulting work. While control and constraints are key terms in relation to power, along with trust and distrust, the latter also connect strongly to emotion. For example in the National Policy work, Carole's anxieties oscillate with her desire to control the consultants; in the Strategic Health Authority work my feelings of frustration and anxiety connect to my attempt to impose my view of the report structure on the consulting team: in Jan's story the power play with her male colleague produced (ongoing) strong emotions. The power of the 'trusted adviser' is also highlighted in my advice to Pat and Graeme in strong terms, linking my views and intent to the intimate one-to-one setting. My corpus of material is full of examples of power and emotion linked in relations between consultants, and between consultants and those commissioning us; for example in the Strategic Health Authority work we discuss our work being 'hijacked' by other interests and how 'fed up' we feel. I have been struck throughout by the sheer strength and ubiquity of this emotional dimension that is strangely absent from contemporary literature on consulting.[1]

The emotions visible in the analysis (for all actors) centre on mutual feelings of trust and commitment or their lack, on anxieties and the resulting desire for reassurance, and on the strong desire to achieve the work in the best way. Again this is complex, and not only as these feelings relate to the way we evoke and experience power in attempts to control the work. Interestingly these emotions link fundamentally to the commercial process we are engaged in and our sense of self as autonomous actors. We are not keen to be viewed as quasi-employees, as in the Local Authority or Voluntary Sector work. Yet we are paid directly to substitute our emotional labour (Hochschild 1983) for that of managers, as in the University work. The framing of the National Policy work was threaded with emotional issues connected to the broader policy environment and how other actors experienced the changes before we were ever commissioned.

Emotion and organisation research has grown in last decades, arguably in parallel to the growth in service industries where much of this work is located (Fineman 2000; Harris 2002; Sturdy 1998). It remains a contested area and 'the conversation about emotions has been strange to the prevailing Western organisational discourse' (King 2004:424). For me emotion:

> ...has everything to do with the social and cultural contexts that provide the rules and vocabularies of emotion. [is] intersubjective, a product of the way systems of meaning are created and negotiated between people. (Fineman 2000:3)

This intersubjectivity is precisely what I examine in my material, where the interactions express or suppress emotion. Fineman's focus on 'systems of meaning' also echoes my discursive approach.

Frameworks for studying emotion include: why it is produced, what happens and what impact it has (Morris and Feldman 1996); research approaches and the consequent insights, privileging and silencing they produce (Sturdy 2003); a typology of workplace emotion (Bolton 2005). Kerfoot (2002) discusses the role of (non)emotion in professions: where the manager must be 'disengaged' and emotion regulated. Hatcher (2003) comments on the 'ordered passion' achieved in organisations through 'feminine skills'.

In my material emotion is either labelled specifically ('I am concerned', 'I am fed up') or is signalled by strong modality statements ('we can't do that', 'they'll go mad') or through use of freighted metaphors such as 'bogged down', mess, burden, defence, cutting, penetration, suffering, 'nightmare', violence. Emotions too are overwhelmingly negative in relation to the work: fear, vulnerability, betrayal, frustration, despair, despite recurring themes of trust and feeling something is 'worthwhile'.

Reflection
Interesting too that issues of the compression of time and space in the pressure of completing work comes out for us as <u>emotion</u>. We get cross at how people commissioning work want such speed yet don't respond quickly to us. We are frustrated at the emotional side of managing this process. (Journal 20 March 2004)

Positive emotion is visible at the edges in more personal exchanges: Stella and her daughter's wedding, Michelle being pleased Carole is taking leave. In our relations with each other as consultants, we also take care to weave positive feelings into emails: 'in solidarity in this hellish process' I wrote during the National Policy work. During our stories we support each other's telling and laugh or gasp accordingly. The material reflects Mangham's view that 'emotions are *embodied* and conveyed in discursive acts' (1998:56) his emphasis); they reflect our judgments, how we perceive, 'a fundamental first cut at a situation where mine or someone else's "weal and woe" may be at stake' (1998:62).

Like Mangham, Fineman (2000, 2003) challenges separating emotion from rationality: 'emotions lubricate rather than impair rationality... thinking and deciding is always brushed with emotion.' (2000:11) The two are mutually constitutive so 'pure, emotionally neutral, cognition cannot exist' (2000:12). This fits closely to the notion of the 'trusted adviser', working across the public/private divide and rational/emotional realms. King notes how in contrast the process consulting school takes an 'instrumental view of emotions, encouraging consultants to notice their feelings and the emotions of the client and to treat them as an important source of information' (2004:465). This, she argues, sets a 'premium on rationality that sets up a body-mind dualism where emotions are treated as a handicapped appendage' to reason (op. cit.). Such authors do not consider the effect on the consultant of dealing with feelings that result from the interaction with the client and King deduces they assume 'a heroic individual: aware of her feelings, able to manage them in and after the moment, in a rational fashion and seemingly all by herself' (2004:467). King and her consulting colleagues explored patterns in their work with 'clients' where they seemed to expect consultants to:

> smoothly adjust to the dominant feeling rules in the system (ranging from aggressive self confidence, to meek compliance) or they expected the consultant to model an alternative pattern, e.g. remaining calm, pleasant and nice in an aggressive and confrontational client organization. (King 2004:457)

She concludes that navigating these different 'feeling rules' comprises emotional labour.

My material in Chapter 6 communicates in contrast extreme anxiety on *both* sides, along with enormous emotional labour in doing the work, and in commissioning it. Is this how women experience consulting given the majority of the actors here are women? (King was working with a mixed group) Or, is it to do with the context of small-scale work in the not-for-profit sector? (King was working in a consulting firm setting with predominantly large private sector organisations) Of course the presence of both is also striking, that it is women who are doing this kind of consulting. Or is it that for consulting in general emotion is suppressed in favour of the 'objective professional' or 'performance' discourses? For example, King comments that generally she and colleagues suppressed negative feelings and tended only to express more positive feelings.

Distinction is possible between emotional display (or suppression, entailing similar labour) to those commissioning work and/or to colleagues in different spaces at work. My material often reflects the notion of 'front stage' and 'back room' raised in the service industry literature (Harris 2002; Lewis 2005) and dramaturgical approaches to organisations. Emotion work is done in public interactions through careful talk (in the National Policy work emails) and suppression of emotion (in the Voluntary Sector work emails), in contrast to the expression of emotion in the 'backroom' of consultants' own meetings (in the Strategic Health Authority work or in the development or discussion groups) or in intimate settings with the person commissioning, for example with Graeme or Pat. The development group's talk reflects a female 'back room' space, the site of 'collective coping' by women in their emotional labour (Lewis 2005). The reciprocal nature of this group process echoes Fletcher's 'relational practice' (2001) and Sass's 'storytelling' (1997). Our collective strategies for emotion work may also link to the notion of 'bounded emotionality' (Mumby and Putnam 1992).

Most research on emotion at work has focused on the service encounter in everyday settings, such as air travel, restaurants, call centres, rather than on professional services. The service encounter is seen in the power terms of the 'master/servant' drawing on embedded paternalistic relationships formed through centuries of domestic labour – especially by women (Williams 2003). However, recently studies of professional services have addressed emotion (Dent and Whitehead 2002; Fineman 2003; Lewis 2005). Consultants are affected by the emotional assumptions of the 'objective professional' discourse: where we suppress emotions in my material, we are enacting this discourse of (masculine) professionalism.

Kerfoot (2002) suggests that 'the constitution of professional identity entails a personal price, not least with respect to the expression and experience of emotion' (2002:93) but also constant self scrutiny and 'work on the self'. Professionals are also constructed as different from 'frontline staff' in terms of the nature of their work (Harris 2002; Morris and Feldman 1996). Their relatively autonomous working mode, especially if they are self-employed, and the wide range of settings and audiences they cover seem to make the difference, along with drawing on (often long-held) work traditions. Historically situated context is important to emotional exchanges (Fineman 2000; Fineman and Sturdy 1999; Sturdy 2003); it acknowledges the greater power position of professionals and how this affects their emotional labour.

The importance of emotion as a meta-theme in consulting interactions here reflects its growing acknowledgement as key to the work of professionals in service settings. Its gender inflectedness bears further exploration and affects sharply how we understand what is going on in consulting interactions – is it emotional labour to instrumental ends[2] or a form of Fletcher's 'feminine' 'relational practice'? (King 2005)

Values in the commercial process

As I worked with the material the commercial process itself seemed central to what was going on; but what concerned people went beyond the immediate transaction and getting paid for it. How we approached the commercial process of consulting seemed always connected to values in the interactions and stories, how we enacted our beliefs in that process and what for us made the (often frustrating) commercial process 'worthwhile'. The material presented shows how economic interests in consulting are organised socially rather than by the occupation of positions, such as 'client' or 'consultant'. Drawing on the work of Callon (1998) and Sayer (2005) among others I consider what kind of commercial process this is and the implications of its expression by the actors in terms of their underlying assumptions and, crucially, their values.

The commercial process concerns the contracting for, transactions about and payments for consulting work, references to which proliferate in all the material.[3] Importantly it also concerns assumptions people make as they engage in the commercial process, specifically the *values* they hold that affect their purposes, assumptions and actions.

The commercial process here is not about simple power relations, that 'who pays the piper calls the tune' but is a *political space* (Laclau and Mouffe 2001 cited in Wilmott 2005). In the National Policy work it appears that a powerful government department is contracting two individuals to carry out a relatively small piece of research and writing work. However, issues below the surface undermine this reading of power: the project is a small but key piece in a jigsaw about the implementation of a major policy shift; its critical role in placating particular noisy, political and disgruntled stakeholders; the few people with relevant knowledge whom the commissioner could access; and that it had to be done within six weeks. All these elements combined to reduce the economic power of those commissioning, especially once work was agreed and letters signed.

Processes can only go on, they can't be undone. There are limits to starting again with consultants who take less control, as people commissioning, like Carole, always want work finished quickly. The context

---

Reflection

In discussing my analysis of this case someone said 'the client is paying and so has power'. Every fibre of me was screaming 'no they haven't, we have a lot of power. That woman had no control over what we did in the end'. (Journal July 2003) [Further reflection April 2006: my thoughts then illustrate both the strength of emotion in the work and the importance of power and control to me, the consultant...]

Carole faced limited her day-to-day control and changed the commercial process to enable us to act. In this we pursued our aims and values, for example not to foist competences on elected councillors (as we saw it). My material shows a commercial process enacted by people embedded 'in a social or cultural frame' (Callon 1998:5) where they are 'entangled' in the marketplace. This is the opposite of the classical assumption of rational calculation, where after a transaction the agents are 'quits' and 'leave the exchange as strangers' (1998:3). Similarly Abolafia (1998) sees commercial actors 'socially embedded in a network of important social relations and culturally embedded in a meaning system of norms, rules and cognitive scripts.'(1998:69) The National Policy work, the One-to-One work, the University work and stories from Ros and Jan challenge us to see 'rationality as a community-based, context-dependent cultural form' (Abolafia 1998:74). The network of reciprocal relations through which we seek, gain and carry out our work (and our efforts in maintaining this) is vivid. Time and again we assume values of reciprocity.

For Callon, a pure market transaction 'must be decontextualised, dissociated and detached.' (1998:19). This is exactly the opposite of what we see in the excerpts – as consultants we are not 'dissociated' commodities as we always have our own agendas and aims driven by our values as well as by our commercial interests; we operate within tightly linked chains of texts reflecting multiple power dynamics. Callon maintains that if the commodity and the agents cannot be 'disentangled' then they can never be 'quits': 'the one who receives is never quit and cannot escape from the web of relations. The framing is never over. The debt is never settled.' (1998:19) Thus the classical economic view of consulting is *disentanglement*: the 'objective professional' sells a clearly defined service; the 'client' specifies what they will receive and takes steps to control the process to ensure this. The critical management literature equally holds this view: its critique is that we cannot see what is being bought and sold, so that it cannot be measured nor its value determined, thus leaving space for the power of the consultant in 'systems of persuasion'. The processes I have analysed demonstrate Callon's notion of *entanglement*; whether with the person commissioning or between ourselves as consultants, we are in a continuing 'web of relations'. Callon comments that 'disentangling a service relation, [that] frequently requires the effective co-presence of the supplier and the consumer, is obviously a brain-teaser' (1998:34). He demonstrates that the more agents try to 'disentangle' themselves from goods or services to produce rational transaction, paradoxically they find 'the more the ties proliferate and multiply' (1998:37), exemplified in the 13-step process suggested by the person commissioning to 'end' the Voluntary Sector work.

The commercial process is also about *perceptions of worth* and links strongly to values and identities in the consulting process, where we are a 'mind for hire' (Smith 2000). Deetz (1998) links this to emotions:

consultants 'discussed the good feeling that came from knowing that a client rather than employer was willing to pay for what they did.' (1998:161) He concludes this is about worth being measured by money:

> Consulting, as the discursive self-conception, produces consent to worth's being determined by money ... the transforming of self into commodity. ... Rather than the self being an end with labour and money as means, the self becomes a means to money. (1998:162)

He goes on to comment on the forms of *unpaid* labour and control that come with this: the under-reporting of work hours and related emotional labour. He describes issues seen here in the Voluntary Sector work: unrealistic demands, on the basis that 'I have paid for this' so it doesn't matter what it takes to achieve, and in addition the consultant having to placate and maintain relationships. On the other hand my material shows that resistance to this approach, for example from Jean, who requires people to convince her to put in her 'precious hours', also requires emotional labour. Those who seem to operate to the norm, such as Martin, seem less affected.

The notion of worth and 'worthwhileness' and the prevalence of talk of 'making a difference' relate to ideas about cultural political economy and 'moral economy' that highlight the social process of commerce alongside its material impact (Sayer 2005). These concepts de-stabilise the stereotype of the commercial transaction of consulting, emphasising values and ethics, as the women do in my material. Moral economy links ethics and emotions to the economic sphere, drawing on the historical evolution of economic ideas by Adam Smith and others (Sayer 2000). Sayer (2005) discusses relationships in the commercial process and how 'thick' relations, shared understandings and constructed expectations produce behaviour and power, predicated on trust. This resonates with my material, extending our thinking beyond the normative approach to the commercial contract found in the contemporary consulting literature (van Es 2002). It echoes Hoggett's conclusions (2006) on ethics and the public sector:

> organizations of the public sphere perform ... functions which link them directly to the ethical and emotional lives of citizens. This adds to their complexity as unique moral institutions where questions of technical efficacy ('what works') can be integrated with value questions. It follows that to work as a manager, consultant or

change agent in such organizations one needs tools and capacities which can meet the challenge of this complexity. (2006:188)

Sayer's discussion of moral economy also helps construct discursive space for moral or ethical consulting within a frame which allows for complexity of emotions and ethical values and commitments as well as the expression of power: 'the moral dimension is pervasive, indeed power often depends on actors having moral commitments' (Sayer 2005:80).

Trust and assumptions of mutually supporting social relations recur in my material.

> ...thicker transactions and relationships involving cooperation, enduring responsibilities or specialist expertise. ... [are] not only exchange relations but organized systems of cooperation ... inter-personal and enduring, ... especially likely to take on meanings and expectations and sometimes commitments which go far beyond those assumed by liberal economic theory. ... Trust is essential and it presupposes a level of trustworthiness, involving probity as well as competence. (2005:88)

For Sayer, as in this study, trust and the economic connect with feelings, implicit values and power relations and he highlights the key idea of 'fellow feeling' from Adam Smith's early work: that people are capable of tremendous sensitivity to the emotions, needs, thinking and experiences of others, which challenges prevailing assumptions of individual self reliance and self interest in the economic system. This is especially challenging given the discourse of entrepreneurialism applied to self-employed people such as independent consultants, that promotes the myth of the individual achiever. The process of earning a living as a consultant is intimately connected with how we feel about the work, our colleagues and those who commission us; economic processes are socially embedded and admit of more variations in enacting power than we may assume.

The public sector setting is also important in considering the values dimension of consulting interaction. The women in the study are at pains to distinguish their consulting work from what Jan terms 'a private sector, macho style' and even to elide their position as private businesses. Their concerns hold to a public service ethics and the values of the common good, within the commercial process of consulting. Similarly, Conroy found that embracing private sector ethics when enacting change in the public sector would create 'virtue clashes' (2007). Drawing on MacIntyre's work on values, he concludes 'the moral construction might be that organisational change embedded with private sector ethics and managerialism is not healthy for people who hold a public service ethos.' (2007:147) Perhaps it is also not healthy for those working with the public sector and holding to this ethos, as Hoggett implies in commenting on the challenge for 'change agents' (2006).

The recurring issues of power, emotion and values remain entwined with the commercial framing and reflect the context in which we work. The meta-theme of values shows how the commercial process we experience both reflects the discourse of consulting as commodity, but also challenges this in seeing power as equivocal and shifting within economic processes driven by a range of values and social aims. My material also makes clear how much more complex are the relational processes than the typical discourse of 'managing the project' or the reified 'client-consultant relationship'. Connecting values to the commercial process makes more sense of the economic issues in my material and opens up (gendered) questions of worth and especially the struggle for identification and self-worth within dominant discourses of consulting.

Interwoven themes with gendered dimensions

We have seen how the three meta-themes of power, emotion and values are interwoven and also entail key linking issues of relationships, identities and the commercial process. Figure 8.1 offers a view of this set of issues within the consulting interactions studied and within the broader social and political context. The three-layered figure mirrors the three dimensions of CDA: the *text* reflected the three meta-themes of power, emotion and values, shown at the centre; the linking issues constitute the *interdiscursive*, the multiple texts implicated in the interactions and that people draw on. Both these are shown within consulting interactions; the final layer of the *broader context* and orders of discourse frames the interactions. Viewed together in this way, the gendered dimensions of the meta-themes, the linking issues and the contextual elements become more visible. Arguably the interwoven-ness of the issues in the figure especially affects women consultants.

Power issues have a dynamic relationship to emotions in the interactions studied, with each shaping and constructing the other; emotions are frequently hidden in enacting the commercial process, yet this process also evokes strong emotions in the actors; particular power relations and values are assumed within the commercial process which

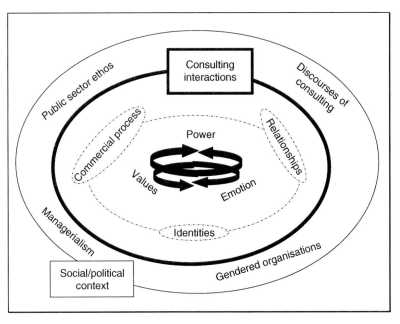

Figure 8.1 How we can view consulting interactions in the study

are both reflected in and challenged by my material. One utterance in an interaction may express all these issues. For example, Carole in the National Policy work says: *'I am a bit concerned that you appear to be suggesting a change in what we commissioned you to do. Can you confirm that this is the case? The Department has commissioned you and Sheila to undertake a piece of work...'* She is not only referring to a 'commissioned' commercial contract – expressing her assumptions of where power lies – but also to her feelings of 'concern' about how we are tackling it given her aims. She asserts the power of 'The Department' in relation to two (mere) individuals.

So the expressions of emotion in the interactions and the evidence of power struggles to control the work and the interactions seem traceable to and/or stem from the nature of *relationships* between actors. For example a colleague urges me:

> ...make early contact with their proposed designer(s), ... if only for your own peace of mind. If they don't have one earmarked, try to push them to get this sorted. In my and Madge's experience getting the designer on board – and establishing a direct line to them rather

than through the client – as soon as you can saves endless headaches (Sam)

He is encouraging me to forge certain relationships and to 'push' for
this control, in order to ensure the work not only happens but to save
'headaches' and ensure 'peace of mind'. The message is clear: if I don't
do this I can expect a process full of problems and negative emotions.
Equally his connection to me as a colleague, on my side as it were,
means he offers his (painful) prior experience. The reciprocity of relations among consultants is a strong thread in the material and links of
course to values also.

The material that expresses emotion often connects directly to talk
about the commercial process and raises key issues of identity and
values. For example Laurie says: *'if I disliked someone I wouldn't commission them again. I like the way you work with others …. You don't bullshit
in any way, shape or form.'* She links her emotional response to the commercial process and later her values, one part of her multiple identity:
*'I recognise in you a shared value system and I can get that more pushed out
into the [organisation] by what you do.'*

A striking example of these links is also given by Jan describing her
male colleague who 'took over' an assignment: *'I wasn't even saying it
would be 50/50 I was happy for him to have more money etc etc but he just
took it. And that's why it was so… appalling.'* The connection between
the commercial process and her values and feelings is clear and raises
vividly issues of power. She identifies the interaction as gendered, concluding: *'I can't cope with this at all and that is the sort of private sector
type, macho type consultant behaviour I think isn't it?'*

While the meta-themes are fundamental in making sense of my
inquiry, my CDA work and sense-making discussions show that the issues
of *relationships, identities,* and *the commercial process* suffuse all three.
They encompass the core trio of power, emotion and values, so inter-
connected are these. They are vital to the study – for example identity
has been a key focus since the start linking both to women consultants
and to me as researcher. The impact of relationships is striking in the
material; they affect values in the commercial process, perceptions of
power and how people feel. While each connecting issue provides a different lens, they too are significantly intertwined. For example, issues of
identity are enfolded in relationships, values and how business is done.

In Figure 8.1, discourses of 'permanent change' and 'knowledge work'
are almost invisible. This may reflect the different context of the public
and not-for-profit sectors where the exploitative links between these

two discourses seen in private sector consulting apply less. Arguably there is an element of knowledge work to be seen in how we work inter-discursively to assemble new texts but we do not view it in these terms. Our certainty seems much more to relate to our values and identities than to 'knowledge'.[4] We take up the 'trusted adviser' discourse and reject the discourse of commodification of consulting work. We are affected by the discourses of rhetoric and performance and 'client is king' but express a discourse of 'worthwhile-ness'. The discourses visible in the material that are different from those previously identified primarily concern the emotional dimension of apparently objective work, the prevalence of concern about what is 'worthwhile' within the commercial frame, consulting work as emergent rather than a specified commodity and the reciprocity of commercial relations.

The mapping in Figure 8.1 responds to my research questions about what goes on in consulting interactions. The interwoven issues it portrays point to key gendered dimensions of what goes on. All the meta-themes are issues which are not only fundamentally gendered as social constructions, but also intimately associated with women in terms of a large literature dealing with women and work, women and power, women and emotion. Similarly notions of identity, relationships and values hold gendered assumptions. So this mapping begins to respond to my questions about women consultants and their work.

The discursive resources implicated in these themes contrast with the identified dominant discourses of consulting in Chapter 4. Thus the mapping in Figure 8.1 also begins to respond to my questions about how the interactions affect discourses of consulting and the notion of 'critical consulting'. Importantly the review of contemporary literature reflected a masculine norm for consulting as an order of discourse in contrast to a more 'feminine' premodern perspective. Therefore it is clear that the next task is to use the lens of *femininities* to illuminate consulting work (for men and women) and explore the discursive implications of gender for consulting.

9
Femininities and Consulting: (Re-)animating a 'Feminine' Discourse of Consulting

Introduction

This chapter develops the findings of Parts I and II, using gender as a lens, but with *femininities* in the foreground. The importance of femininities grew as the study developed. My material raised the importance of women and consulting in contrast to the lack of any substantial focus on women in the contemporary literature; yet the genealogical material showed advice-giving by women and men that we can characterise as 'feminine'. The women in the study also expressed, in their interaction and stories, an approach to their work substantially missing from extant studies on consulting and which rejected several of the dominant discourses of consulting I had identified. I also gradually recognised how gendered were my starting questions about distance and closeness, about confidence in my knowledge base, about my identity. My process based approach to the research itself is mirrored in the emergence of the 'feminine' as I worked.

I explore the feminine in relation to the meta-themes of power, emotion and values discussed in Chapter 8. This chapter will (re-)animate a 'feminine' discourse in consulting without getting trapped in essentialist notions of gender, through holding a discursive and constructivist approach within a broad socio-political context. I draw on feminist thinking about gender, identity and the power of normative masculinities in order to frame my work as challenging a 'masculine' *discourse* of work, in this case of consulting, rather than challenging what male consultants or managers do, or engaging in an essentialist argument on gender.[1] This framing asks how consulting processes contribute to a masculine hegemony of work and what might be the contribution of a 'feminine' discourse of consulting?

Following Bruni *et al.* (2004b) in their study of gender and entrepreneurship, I focus on gender as consulting practice and consulting as a gender practice, drawing on ordinary experience rather than that of 'exceptional' women. I intend this to help conceptualise a 'critical consulting' practice in Chapter 10. I select from the substantial literature focused on women and work (particularly on management or professional work and women entrepreneurs) material which develops my discursive focus and relates to the meta-themes of the study. In particular I use Jean Baker Miller's seminal work on women, power and emotion (1976, 1982) and Joyce Fletcher's (2001) linked concept of *'relational practice'*, exploring gendered work in the organisation. Her notion of the 'feminine' being 'disappeared' by dominant, taken-for-granted discourses of work and organisation is especially helpful in exploring a 'feminine' discourse of consulting. Their work frames a discussion of values, alongside material on women entrepreneurs, relevant to this study of independent women consultants.

I begin with a brief theoretical discussion that locates the 'feminine' and discusses the key implicated issue of *identities* raised in Chapter 8; I then review the findings of Parts I and II using the meta-themes presented in Chapter 8: *power, emotion,* and *values.* The further key connecting issues of *relationships* and *the commercial process* identified in Chapter 8 are woven into these sections. I conclude by setting out the elements of a 'feminine' discourse of consulting and the discursive resources with which it is enacted.

Locating the 'feminine'

As soon as the word 'feminine' is uttered, there is a sense of the lack of the concomitant masculine. Weedon comments on the marginalising of the feminine in language – relegated to 'mysticism, madness and magic.' (1987:9) The feminine can hardly stand alone, especially in relation to the domain of work, and convey meaning. The pervasive 'ideology of separate spheres' (Padavic and Reskin 2002:22) prevails.[2] The world divides into public/private, rational/emotional, home/workplace, such that these are not only highly gendered as 'masculine'/'feminine', but also represent and reproduce male hegemony (Ross-Smith and Kornberger 2004). The apparent neutrality of work and the organisation masks the male standards applied that devalue women's or 'feminine' work, leading directly to job segregation, lower pay for women (Acker 1990; Davies 1995; Maddock 1999) and the gendering of occupations (Crompton 1997) and of work space.[3] These effects are illustrated in my material, as in Jan's story of her male colleague and in how the women experience the tensions of home/work, rational/emotional. We experience too an oscillation between the spheres – certainty and softness – which may be a 'feminine' experience linked to the permanent 'dual presence' of public and private for women throughout their lives (Gherardi 1994).

The hierarchic binary of Other

A feminist poststructuralist view (Ahl 2002; Cooper 1994) sees these reified, apparent binaries as hierarchies not amenable to fixed meanings. Placing or 'casting' woman as Other (Czarniawska and Hopfl 2002; Fournier 2002), and 'second-sexed', creates 'the systematic de-valorisation of the female' (Gherardi 1994:597). Knights and Kerfoot (2004) conclude that gender analysis deconstructs this hierarchy only by disrupting male hegemony. They suggest this be achieved through temporarily occupying 'a space between representations of gender and the conditions of subjectivity and language that make them possible' (2004:430). Linstead and Brewis (2004) comment that this means taking up neither a fully discursive nor a fully realist critique, that is, a position similar to my own.

The other-ing process highlights the invisible woman (Collinson and Hearn 2003; Crompton 1997) who must fit into the male context to survive (Maddock 1999) and work on her impression management (Gherardi 1994; Padavic and Reskin 2002): the subject is 'always already masculine' (Kondo 1990:310, drawing on Butler and Irigaray). However, attempting 'masculine' behaviour may not help (Maddock 1999; Powell and Graves 2003), attracting negative attention. Woman's experience in addition of the 'dual presence' (Gherardi 1994) where the private and public permanently co-exist for her, conversely makes her femininity only too visible and exposed in the male workplace: a classic double-bind. This experience echoes the premodern adviser whose private and public roles, both visible, produced a vulnerability that could lead to verbal or physical attack. It also offers clues about how consultants are perceived in a 'feminine' discourse of consulting. Deetz (1998) comments on consulting:

> the often hidden and mysterious work... leaves identity to be acquired from the projection of the subject ... Often the [consultant's] symbolically produced identity was more secure and lasting (and accounted more for a client's product assessment) than the work product. But a *lingering sense of falseness and insecurity* comes with the symbolic identity. (1998:157–158 my emphasis)

Deetz here expresses something approaching what I often feel in consulting and recognised by Perriton (2001): feminine identity as 'other' or impostor, permanently challenged in the public sphere of paid work:

> in a permanent impostor role because of the construction of their gender as 'the other'. Their labour is ... first and foremost the labour of mimicry and simulacra. This will mean they always feel this sense of imposture. (2001:295)

So femininities are subsumed in a broader discussion of gender and overwhelmed by normative masculinities. A substantial literature[4] has accrued concerning gender and work, and especially since 1990 on the notion of gendered organisations (Martin and Collinson 2002). The continuing 'nature/nurture' debate[5] creates a tension in gender studies: how far are gendered effects viewed as discursive or material in nature. However a social constructionist approach at least explains our experience and perception of gender differences and how we produce behaviour that assumes they exist, thus enacting difference (Powell and Graves 2003; West and Zimmerman 2003). The power of the discursive context to construct gender is clear: 'the very word 'gender' encapsulates all the symbols that a culture elaborates to account for biological difference.' (Gherardi 1994:592)

Martin sees gender as an institution and thus is concerned with its practices:

> If the gender institution failed to provide a repertoire of practices for societal members' use, they (we) would be at a loss about how to 'do gender' at work (and elsewhere). (2003:344)

Martin privileges here notions of structure over individuals' agency. Conceptualising gender in this way produces notions of gendered cultures (Collinson and Hearn 2003; Maddock 1999), gendered roles and language (Harriman 1996; Tannen 1992). Crompton (1997) explores how gender stereotypes remain constant in a socially constructed world and concludes that discursive processes are key to their robustness over time, despite examples of stereotypes overturned by individuals. This underlines the power of the taken-for-granted (male) discourses of consulting for women and men.

Normative masculinities

A stream of notable work (e.g. Acker 1990; Collinson and Hearn 1996; Barrett 2002), highlights the false neutrality of organisations, as portrayed in much organisational theory, and signals a consequent male hegemony: 'the assumption of power by men in a way that seems normal and commonplace' (Barrett 2002:159). This process draws on the 'separate spheres' assumptions, for example of reason as normatively masculine, which is then imbued in management discourse (Ross-Smith and Kornberger 2004; Samra-Fredericks 2005a and 2005b). Workplaces are thus infused with gender:

> Concepts ...key to organizational life such as competence, leadership, effectiveness, excellence, rationality, strength, and authority (among others) are moreover conflated with the practicing of gender in ways that differentially affect women and men. (Martin 2003:345)

She comments that hegemonic masculinity allows men in western societies to call on women 'for practical, as well as emotional, support' as of right (2003:348). Kerfoot (2002) quotes Connell's description of the 'masculine' in the professions:

> ... constructed historically as a form of masculinity: emotionally flat, centred on a specialised skill, insistent on professional esteem and technically-based dominance over other workers. (Connell 1987:181 cited 2002:87)

This definition resonates with both Sam's and Martin's words in my study and with the image we gain of Jan's male colleague. It describes the opposite of how the women see their consulting work. Kerfoot sees this idea of masculinity as about power and being in control. This entails denial/control of emotion, the valorising of rationality and instrumentality and represents the work process as primarily about individual, independent (male) endeavour:

> [The] myth of self-reliance and independence, even though most people have a (largely female) network of people supporting their "individual" achievement (Fletcher 2001:10)

The hegemonic effects of this process are seen in micro-level interactions at work; these draw on and also constitute discursive practices which achieve the normalisation and masking of gendered power: gendered working practices and discourse that 'disappear' the 'feminine' (Fletcher 2001).

Identity/ies and the 'feminine'

How does a 'feminine' identity matter or work in consulting? Casey (1995) summarises feminist work that 'male identity ... is characterised by a preoccupation with difference, separateness and distance in ways that female identity is not.' (1995:55) She comments (drawing on Benjamin 1987) that privileging male separation effectively denies a female self. We must choose between paradoxical gendered poles of nurturance and freedom.[6] Miller (1976) challenged this view of human development, since inevitably the hierarchical gender binary valued separation over connection. In the discursively male world of management, connection is valued for its instrumentality rather than in and of itself, as in the discourse of 'partnership' in consulting or Martin's associates he 'just' worked with.

For Gini (1998) 'work is one of the primary means by which adults find their identity and form their character' but fragmented in modern life:

> ...so few of us see, understand and participate in the whole purpose, process and the final product of our work. We are, to use Marx's term, alienated from our labor. (1998:708)

There are echoes here of consulting, being on the outside where you cannot see the whole, and have little control or even access to key information, as in my experience of the health trust where we never could establish who was key. Gini concludes:

> we find identity and are identified by the work we do. ...we must be very careful about what we choose to do for a living, for *what we do is what we'll become*. (1998:714 my emphasis)

This brings together notions of performing identity with emerging identity in a mutual process. Exploring self and identity involves enduring, ontological questions, such as the relation to Other, experiences of fear, anxiety and doubt, and the link to ethics. All of these are raised in my study and are important to the women involved. Two connected paradoxes stand out from current ideas about identity/self:[7] the fragility yet continuity of identity; its fragmentation and yet coherent narrative.

Feminist debate on identity asks: are we 'always already' female and/or do we create gender in interaction? (Mills 2003) – as in my discursive framing of consulting, studying interaction. Butler famously introduced the notion of gender as performative. She argues for an 'understanding of performativity... as that reiterative power of discourse to produce the phenomena that it regulates and constrains' (1993:2); thus a multiplicity of situated actions reflect back or 'cite' previous acts. These 'congeal over time to produce the appearance of a substance, of a natural sort of being' (Sullivan 2003:82) Hodgson concludes performativity produces 'the elision of discourse and action ... [and] identity ... seen as constructed in and through conduct rather than as pre-existing conduct ...' (Hodgson 2005:54–55) This approach helps find an anti-essentialist path of 'becoming' for conceptualising gender processes and offers 'a persuasive conception of subjectivity that is in no way predetermined but is nonetheless 'always already' compromised by its formation through power' (Hodgson 2005:55). It explains the complexities of how women in the study both enact and challenge gender stereotypes in doing their work. We assert our power to act as autonomous agents yet we doubt our worth. Butler's view adds depth to the notion of a dominant male discourse that 'disappears' the 'feminine', through iterative, citational, situated conduct. People who commission us consistently assume the 'project' can be 'managed' in a discourse of commodified consulting that denies the emergent and processual character of the work as we experience it. Our work to build different relations and outcomes is valued less than 'delivering outputs' as in the Voluntary Sector work.

Kondo's ethnographic study of identity (1990) notes the 'inextricability of power and identity' (1990:43). She intended to focus on the workplace, but in practice she found that multiple selves are crafted through multiple processes and the 'matrices of power' (1990:25) in the whole context of a person's life, not solely in one setting such as work. She discusses the connected sense of fragmentation she found in women's narratives of their (working) lives compared to the 'maturational' and coherent narratives of the men:

> the fragmentary, almost contingent nature of the women's stories... No commanding, masterful performance of a coherent familiar story ... culminat[ing] in a linear scenario of the ever finer polishing of skills and maturity; ... equally striking was a sense of urgency and economic necessity. (1990:260)

The theme of the fragmented self is notable here, along with the focus of the women on their economic needs. Similarly women consultants focused on the commercial issues throughout – and told complex tales of their work compared for example to the ordered tale told by Martin. Kondo also sees paradoxes for the women workers:

> they provide the young men with a humanized work atmosphere; a source of support and care. ... a feeling of togetherness ... a locus of emotional attachment. (1990:295)

This is double edged – the women are relationally powerful but structurally marginalised in the workplace, exactly like the premodern advisers. Kondo sees selves as 'never beyond power', as 'subject-positions – shifting nodal points within often conflict-ridden fields of meaning' (1990:46), echoing the processual, discursive view of work that this study illustrates for consulting.

So, work on self begins to explain the way in which (women) consultants focus on their own identity and its links to how they see their worth, their work and their life as a whole. For the independent sole trader this is even more the case, engaging as fragile individuals with the modern, corporate economy. For the woman trader, such as those in the study, the interconnections are denser still as the ensuing discussion will show.

The 'feminine' in my study

This section discusses the 'feminine' as it has emerged from my work and discusses how this may help explain what may be going on in consulting interactions. This discussion is aimed at what affects women and men. It leads us to the final part of the chapter that focuses on a 'feminine' discourse of consulting and the discursive resources it may provide to understand consulting interactions.

Chapter 3 offered contemporary images and critiques based on an overwhelmingly male view of the commercial process and nature of consulting, drawing on professional and managerial concepts which we can see as 'masculine'. Indeed Berglund and Werr (2000) describe the consulting dichotomy they explore as about 'men of reason' and 'men of action'. Bohm's 'montage' (2003) uses male images of the gambler, the *flaneur*. Harvey uses the military metaphor of 'no man's land' (2005). There is relative silence in the consulting literature about women, and relatively little by women.[8] Material from women that challenges established discourses of consulting is not much taken up, cited or discussed, such as Shaw (1997) on complexity in consulting, which pre-figures much of what Clegg and colleagues (2004) raise.

Frameworks from the limited contemporary literature on women and consulting are shown in Table 9.1 alongside key findings of this study and key elements of the premodern highlighted in the genealogy. The genealogy shows a process-based view of advice-giving, focused on the building, challenging and repairing of relationships, working on a constant flow of rather hidden interaction to sustain the fluctuating fortunes of those in power through multi-faceted work. These activities are built on an identity of 'other' yet a connection of trust. Certainty and humility co-exists; reciprocity and the 'good' of others in your network and of society at large are expected outcomes. The two frameworks from contemporary research on women consultants echo much of this as the table shows, and my own findings confirm and reflect similar issues. This section links these dimensions to Fletcher's 'relational practice' (2001) derived from the relational theory of Miller's work on women's psychology (1976): a 'feminine' view of power, connection and mutuality. It will also link my findings to theoretical work on identity, on professions and on the woman entrepreneur in order to examine the 'feminine' in my study from the point of view of the issues raised in Chapter 8.

Summarising the story so far ...

The exploration in Part II of consulting interactions by women, connects strongly to extant studies of women consultants as shown in Table 9.1. Each of the issues shown strongly raises the 'feminine', once explored. They link to the picture of consulting interaction developed in Chapter 8, echoing the connecting issues of relationships, identity and the commercial process which infuse the meta-themes of power, emotion and values (see Figure 8.1).

The material in Part II illustrates a female view of women in consulting work. It raises issues of how far women's socialisation is implicated in how we do this work, how we see power, how we feel, how we express ourselves. For example, do we avoid confrontation in favour of keeping relationships positive? Do we 'perform' to each other to keep intact our identities as women with public service values?

The power of sexual allusion turns up the volume in the more explicitly gendered excerpts. Equally the interplay between the individual woman's sense of identity and her socially constructed roles are visible in the consulting interactions and influence how she approaches her work. We see women's view of our consulting work as about creating and drawing on relationships and mutual connection to achieve social change. We emphasise the importance of power and action by the consultant, but not dominating the client; we demonstrate the emotional labour of the work and

Table 9.1   Relating findings in Part I to Part II

	Part One: Genealogy	Contemporary literature on women in consulting		Part Two: Women's consulting interactions in this study
		Rehman & Frisby 2000	Kaplan 1995	
What was studied?	Individuals & roles equivalent to the public and not-for-profit sectors	Sole trader women in Canadian leisure industry	Women organisation development consultants in the US	Sole trader women in UK public and not-for-profit sectors
Key issues arising	Relationships	Social context	Relationships	Relationships & emotions
	Personal and work issues intertwined	Personal situation	Individual journey	Identities/ values
	The Other	Gender relations	Oppression	Being a woman
	Multi-faceted, hidden work	Nature of the work	The work	Nature of the work, commercial process

its pressures; we talk of openly sharing our thoughts in the process, and of getting both the right distance and making connection at the same time. We act often with sureness and certainty despite voicing doubts and vulnerabilities.

For the women in my study (and me) the prime issue of connection between people is vivid. We work across our networks, assuming aims of mutual gain, and aim to keep the relationships positive. The relationships mean we are working with the emotions of others, both colleagues and people commissioning us. We make connections through liking, empathy, trust and a consistent sense of responsibility to others. Connections are vital:

> Ros: 'To do the work, to get the work, to share the work when you've got too much, to do it together 'cos you need complementary skills ...
> Me: To get support 'cos it's a nightmare sometimes ..
> Mel: And it's much more fun ...
> Ros: And you can learn different things, different perspectives.'
> (development group discussion Dec 2004)

There are extremely personal issues and concerns portrayed in the study. We have aspirations to change things. We feel deeply the emotions of betrayal, of wounding and of vulnerability. The texts express how we see ourselves, our role, our (shared) values in carrying out consulting work in the public sector. A discourse of 'worthwhile-ness' is visible which echoes the concern with ends rather than means in the genealogy. We experience being the 'other' as consultant as a struggle.

The voices in my material also express gendered dichotomies discussed earlier, such as subjective/objective, rational/emotive, mind/body, public/private. These tensions and their importance for women are illustrated time and again: by Laurie and her desire to distance herself from the emotive yet to commission consultants to do the emotional labour; by Madge in her turmoil for the 'desperate' woman calling her. They are shown also as false divisions for the women in the National Policy work where they struggle to integrate mind/body and public/private dimensions of how they work and interact. They express a discourse of consulting that reflects a focus on connection and 'power with' rather than a discourse of transaction and 'power over' (Follett in Tonn 2004).

So the emerging story is of experiences and constructed meanings that seem very different from most contemporary consulting literature. The nature of consulting as seen in the study (and in the genealogy) is one which is not linear project work but iterative and densely networked, not transactional but about fundamental reciprocal connectivity. This consulting stresses the emotionality of 'objective', 'professional', or 'knowledge' work and its links to the desire to make a difference for others. Alongside this runs a paradox of doubting self-worth yet a certainty in action. All these issues are identified with the 'feminine'.

Power: professional subordination of the 'feminine'

In considering the importance of power to the women in the study I am struck by how similar their experience as consultants was to their experience simply as women. Power is 'an essentially contested concept ... [how] power is conceived is a political issue, highlighting certain social relations and marginalising others.' (Cooper 1994: 452–453) It is noteworthy that to focus on small-scale consulting in the not-for-profit sector has meant a primary focus on women both in commissioning and in carrying out consulting. Who works where, and with whom, affects the many interactions that together create power effects.

The genealogy charted a gradual shift from a 'feminine' advice-giving to a more masculine, professionalised approach. The inseparability of power from identity is noted by Kondo (1990) and Macalpine and Marsh (2005) use the term 'power/identity' to:

> express the complex intersection of ... the way that individual identity produces differential power depending on context and [on] the specific identities involved. For example a white male doctor can exercise power that a black female nurse in the same context cannot. ... power/identity ...combine[s] the crucial micro-effects of a Foucauldian analysis of power dynamics ...with a more material reading of the nature of power. (2005:432)

How power/identity is enacted in the (professional) workplace in relation to gender affects consultants, men and women. In the interactions and stories our resistance to the managerial discourse of the organisation is clear, yet the pressures of the 'taxi-meter' that Pam describes force a conformity to prevailing norms of consulting with which we are not comfortable. In the increasingly managerial environment of the public and not-for-profit sectors, we must 'immerse [our]selves in the masculinist culture of endless competitiveness and instrumental measurement' (Dent and Whitehead 2002:6). This is not a gender neutral process and suppresses our aims and values. For example, the aims of connecting large numbers of people into the policy development process in the Voluntary Sector work were subordinate to the 'delivery' of required tangible 'products' in the eyes of those commissioning the work.

Professional power as male

The assumption of power by professions is long-established – however contested their claims to authority or knowledge. Davies (1995) in exploring nursing makes clear the highly complex, gender-inflected nature of the professional power process. She emphasises the impact of the gendered organisation as well as the actions of individuals in producing power effects that marginalise women's professions in the densely gendered terrain of health. Such marginalisation is described vividly by Jan and Madge in describing male colleagues and in the professional power expressed by Sam and Martin as they assert their view to those commissioning work or construct the professional dimension of the process.

Dent and Whitehead (2002) show how professional power is produced, locating the discourse of professions in the midst of changing economic processes, of gendered subjectivity and in issues of power and emotion in the workplace. Kerfoot (2002) notes 'intersubjective dynamics' in her examination of (male) professionals and their power and concludes that 'the notion of 'being a professional' can be regarded as mutually inter-constitutive of masculinity.' Both are 'idealised ways of behaving' such that 'their successful display and performance confers organisational legitimacy and the prospect of a secure identity.' (2002:92) The professional ideal involves 'valorisation of instrumentality' as a way of working. Kerfoot questions what therefore gets 'suppressed, marginalised, demeaned or trivialised' and what this costs people and organisations. She views professional and management discourses as proscribing: 'the articulation of specific masculinities and behavioural displays commonly associated with men' (2002:82). Jan's story expresses both the hostility this can produce and her shock at experiencing it. Feminist analysis of male power in a patriarchal world makes further sense of the dynamics of such gendered work practices. Not only does the power differential between men and women exclude women from desirable positions at work (Calas and Smircich 2003), but connected hostility to women is key to their experience (Maddock 1999; Puttnam and Kolb 2003). Collinson and Hearn (2003) also describe women's shock at the aggressive and competitive nature of male-dominated management settings and the resulting exclusion it produces for them.[9] Madge, Michelle, Pam and I talk of our struggle to respond to others in consulting work but keep our own aims in view. Similarly Maddock (1999) describes the struggle of women to lead, challenge and innovate in the face of their socialisation to listen and help others.

Women, power and work: subordination and connection

The women consultants in the study show doubts and vulnerabilities that echo the popular viewpoint that consultants are incapable in managerial roles. This feeds a sense of inferior power and produces a struggle in terms of identity, when power is conceived as domination rather than as productive of social relations. Reciprocal relations and the power these give us to act represent a key finding of the study.

Jean Baker Miller produced original thinking about power from her work on the psychology of women (1976) proposing that women operate from an assumption of 'growth-in-connection'. She challenged the prevailing view that separation/independence was the desired adult psychological state as privileging a male perspective. Miller set out her views of the 'dominant-subordinate' relationship and how she saw this affecting both parties – in this case focusing on gendered power difference, although referring also to ethnicity, class and other inequalities (Miller 1976:3–12).

She points out the subordinate (like the consultant) may be hired to do work or perform services that the dominant group is unwilling to do; how 'subordinates are usually said to be unable to perform the pre-ferred [here managerial] roles' (1976:7); and how then subordinates find it hard to believe in their own ability. Interestingly, Miller's ana-lysis of the dominant-subordinate relationship seems to echo aspects of the popular (and negative) view of relationships in consulting, which may be further sharpened when the consultant is a woman. The per-spective she paints is visible in the pages of the popular (management) press about consultants as useless, mere talkers and unable to be leaders or managers themselves. Miller concludes the subordinate group culti-vates characteristics pleasing to dominants and focuses on their desires in order to survive – as in the discourses of 'client is king' or of consult-ing as rhetoric and performance. Alternatively 'some may try to treat their fellow subordinates as destructively as the dominants treat them.' (1976:12) This reminds us of the stories of betrayal by colleagues that so affected the women in Chapter 7. Or they may become more like the dominants 'if they are willing to forsake their own identification with fellow subordinates.' (*ibid*) This fits closely to the critical manage-ment view of the consultant 'out-manager-ing' the client in autocratic and charismatic behaviour, in the opposite of the 'trusted adviser' discourse.

Power and emotion: re-defining power through 'relational practice'

My material is riddled with emotion, implicit or displayed. Talk between women in the study is notably about and expressing emotion – perhaps exemplified by my conversation with Laurie about the University work. My work identifies two discourses of consulting which represent emo-tional poles: the 'objective professional' and the 'trusted adviser'. The latter discourse is what we hear overwhelmingly from the women in the study.

Power as trusting connection vs. professional detachment

Miller explores how women enact power in their own terms, that is, privileging growth and development. I quote her at length as she speaks strongly of the (adviser) role behind the scenes, in the 'backroom', where resourcing others is the reality of much consulting work and reflected in interactions in the study:

> women's traditional role, where they have used their powers to foster the growth of others ... might be called using one's power to empower

another – increasing the other's resources, capabilities, effectiveness, and ability to act. For example, in "caretaking" or "nurturing," ... is acting and interacting to foster the growth of another...emotionally, psychologically, and intellectually. I believe this is a very powerful thing to do, and women have been doing it all the time, but no one is accustomed to including such effective action within the notions of power. It's certainly not the kind of power we tend to think of ...

The one who exerts such power recognizes that she or he cannot possibly have total influence or control but has to find ways to *interact with the other person's constantly changing forces or powers*. And all must be done with appropriate timing, phasing, and shifting of skills so that one helps to advance the movement of the less powerful person in a positive, stronger direction. (Miller 1982, my emphasis)

Miller advances ways to define power which challenge the received view and echo the nurturing of the strong, seen in my genealogical review, and in the oscillation of power between consultant and person working with them. We see it as emergent work not wholly in our control. We are certain yet diffident. This view of power and emotion in relation to women is not essentialist, but about processes and becoming. It resonates with a feminist and Foucauldian approach to power despite stemming from a very different psychological base. Miller sees power, like Foucault, as enacted, shifting and contested, but also surfaces a paradox: underneath equivocal feelings of being doubtful yet feeling 'I know best', for many women 'power makes you feel destructive.' The link of power to emotion is critical for women.

Any discussion of emotion is pivotally about gender even if implicitly (Lutz 1996; Williams 2003). It is seen as a 'naturalised' aspect of women – and hence not valued (Guy and Newman 2004). It derives from the 'separate spheres' concept posing rationality as the ('masculine') opposite to ('feminine') emotion. Parkin suggests: 'a gendered division of labour divides emotions and the way they are expressed, by whom and where.' (1993:168) For Parkin, men 'dominate the sexual and emotional agenda, most profoundly by not perceiving they have one' (1993:169), in assuming rationality as the norm. Mirchandani comments that 'it is not always easy to separate the paid and unpaid, or public and private parts of a job', that emotion work for women may straddle all these. (2003:726) She finds that a 'significant portion of self-employment work involve[s] the management of feelings' (2003: 730) in her Canadian study exploring the intersection of gender, class and ethnicity among self-employed women. She was not concerned with emotion at the outset but reports, as I have, that the question of feelings in doing the work permeates her material. The women not only express emotion in doing the work and in relation to others but in terms of how they define their work. For Mirchandani 'Emotion work in self-employment involves negotiating the exclusions which are encountered' (2003:737).

This gendered terrain is also reflected in work on professions and emotion. Fineman (2003) and Lewis (2005) note the professions are associated with male detachment (as in the 'objective professional') as opposed to female attachment (as in the 'trusted adviser') – a tension for professionals in their work. Lewis (2005) notes that Bolton's typology of approaches to emotion at work (2005) omits a gender dimension, but characterises her 'prescriptive' approach as gendered 'masculine' and her 'philanthropic' approach as 'feminine'. The philanthropic links to Fletcher's 'relational practice' (2001) in offering support as a 'gift' and assuming connection and reciprocity (Guy and Newman 2004; Waldron 2000). This contrasts with the rather instrumental 'banking' concept of the 'socioemotional economy' suggested by Clark (1990 cited in Fineman 2000). Paradoxically however, male professionals are 'allowed' to show strong emotion as part of the job, reflected here in Jan's story of her male colleague 'doing a number' (see also Guy and Newman 2004), whereas women showing emotion run the risk of being labelled weak and inadequate as they embody the emotional 'other' (see Harris's (2002) study of barristers).

'Relational practice': the 'feminine' in work processes and how it is 'disappeared'

Miller sums up much of what the women in the study enact: 'most women are keenly aware of an essential truth that we all need others, need to live in the framework of relationships, and also need to increase the powers of others through our activities.' (1982: 7) Fletcher's fascinating study (1998, 2001) of women engineers offers a framework for this through her 'relational

> **Reflection**
> *In a review of my doctoral work I was challenged by a male colleague: 'why are you so concerned with your own processes and relationships, why are you not taking a hard look at the effectiveness of consulting for example?' I felt very defensive at the time and unable to counter this – now I see it as an example of the masculine discourse 'disappearing' the 'feminine'.*

practice',[10] building on Miller's work. Her work helps link my findings to how dominant discourses of consulting 'disappear' the 'feminine' in consulting. She exposes the way in which gendered power in organisations 'disappears' the very attributes and behaviours modern managerial rhetoric promotes, for example the 'soft' or 'feminine' behaviours in the learning organisation discourse, due to the 'masculine logic of effectiveness ... that is accepted as so natural and right that it may seem odd to call it masculine' (Fletcher 2001:3). First I set out the elements of 'relational practice' and how I identify these within the study. I then explore how it is 'disappeared'.

'Relational practice' describes what Fletcher sees women do that connects to Miller's ideas about women, power and emotion. Miller's relational theory helped her see the effects of male hegemony described earlier and the hierarchical binary that devalues women's activities, as outside the public sphere and/or as emotional. In discussing my work I use her four categories of relational practice as a structure.

These are:

1. *preserving*
2. *mutual empowerment*
3. *self-achieving*
4. *creating team*

Preserving is about getting work done through relationships. We can see 'preserving' work in the consulting interactions where we 'hold the anxiety' as Jan put it; in Michelle's repairing efforts in the National Policy work; in how I work with Graeme to reconcile views in the Local Authority work; in how Mel and I absorb the emotion in the University work. It is about keeping work connected to the people and resources it needs, maintaining relationships, especially reciprocal connections between consultants and between everyone involved, 'translating' between parties, 'absorbing the stress or acting as a buffer between people' (Fletcher 2001:51), to 'operate in a context of implications and consequences' (*ibid*:54). This also echoes how the premodern advisers worked. 'Preserving' can feed the discourse of consulting as commodity, about delivering the work at any cost, putting in time and effort unseen (and often unpaid). But it is also about 'looking at the whole' and 'expectation of integration and interdependence' (*op cit.*).

Mutual empowerment: assumptions of mutuality and reciprocity are striking throughout the study, including in the genealogy, as consultants/advisers work to empower others, yet not lose sight of their own power and benefits. Sam and Madge make these assumptions in contributing to securing the National Policy work; Ros holds this view in her work with the Voluntary Sector; Michelle works to achieve change for mental health service users within the Strategic Health Authority work. My material is full of this element of relational practice. Power and expertise shift, along with emotions, within the interactions in order to achieve reciprocal benefit, for example in Pam's story of holding the line on equalities, in the Strategic Health Authority work to complete our report, in the framing of the University work, and in the One-to-One work with Pat. For Fletcher mutual empowerment 'enable[s] others' achievement and contribution', where mutuality is key – both parties have to feel they benefit/grow from this interaction.[11] (*ibid*:60) 'Protective connecting' is a form of mutual empowerment that eliminates barriers for people such as 'cutting others slack because of some emotional situation they were dealing with, even if ...outside the work context.' (*op cit*.). For example, our self development group constantly shares or offers information that may be helpful (such as important policy developments) and supports each person to survive tricky situations, such as the problems arising from the Voluntary Sector work.

Fletcher's respondents had 'a mindset that saw needing help as part of the human condition, not as evidence of individual deficiency' (2001:61). (This approach is how Laurie saw her need for help and how Ros worked with her charities 'for free') They assume reciprocity until they feel strongly it is absent, as Jan did until it was blatantly shown not to exist: but her male colleague saw her need for help as deficiency. Stella wanted help with her 'difficult project' and in the University work we 'helped' her empower her staff and saw 'power and expertise shift from one party to the other, not only over time but within the course of one interaction.' (*ibid*:64) Fletcher concludes this fluidity requires the skill to be empowered yourself, that is, to be open to learning, not always the expert, 'both emotional and practical considerations ... require[s] an ability to empathize with another person's reality and recognise it as different from one's own.' (*ibid*:65)

Self achieving is about 'using relational skills to enhance one's own professional growth and effectiveness' (King 2005), for example, maintaining relationships with colleagues that keep open 'future growth potential'. This means keeping connections positive and a real sense of urgency in putting right any possible damage, as well as 'relational asking', that is, ways to ask for help that increase the likelihood of getting it – and it being mutually positive. The self development group works like this; the consultant teams in the pieces of work studied often explicitly discuss our learning, how the work may develop us. Equally we are swift to repair relational breaches as Michelle and Carole did in their email exchange or with each other as in the Strategic Health Authority work. Arguably this 'feminine' response may result in occluding immediate conflict or disagreement for longer term gains or simply for an easier life. In the Voluntary Sector work which ended in

> **Reflection**
> *This echoes for me the hours colleagues and I spend in discussions about the work and its impact, about how to pose tricky issues to those commissioning and how to ask for what we need to do the work.*

irreconcilable differences with those commissioning, this approach by Ros does not help Sally, who felt future relationships were compromised. Fletcher sees self achieving as 'an exercise of power, the power to call forth tenderness in another... Making visible one's "not knowing" is a way of calling forth enabling behaviour in others.' (2001:71)

She felt her respondents' focus on self achieving behaviours stemmed from a belief that both personal and professional growth depend on connection and that the effort of maintaining relationships produces long-term benefits.

Creating team, finally, is about activities 'to foster group life', about a team's emotional experience rather than creating its identity. 'Creating team' occurred in the University work where Laurie feels we acknowledge people and we felt Stella enabled people to work differently as a team; it was part of the connection with service users in the Strategic Health Authority work; it featured strongly in the focus group held during the National Policy work; and it underlay the discussion with Pat in the One-to-One work about her staff. Facilitating good group processes is of course fundamental to much consulting work – hard to get right, easy to take-for-granted. Fletcher refers to other research about women's para-linguistic work, attention to speakers and making space to listen to feelings, and to her respondent who saw women as 'inherent facilitators' always asked to sort things out in groups. She sums up 'creating team':

> the belief that individuals have a right to be acknowledged or noticed as unique and that part of what it means to be a good co-worker is to do the noticing.... (Fletcher 2001:81)

Such work creates intangible outcomes embedded in people, such as trust, respect, values, rather than task-based outcomes. Fletcher concludes women work through interdependence rather than 'an atmosphere of separation and specialisation' (Fletcher 2001:54) which we saw in the men's voices and how they describe their work.

So in summary, Fletcher's work demonstrates how relational practice is not recognised in the dominant organisational discourse: because women do it, it is therefore devalued, and 'disappeared' as she puts it. People say it does not add value: 'things would have gone OK without it' or it shows women's own incapacities to act for themselves. It is written off as deviant behaviour. The paradox is that women are simultaneously both expected to do this work and then devalued for it.

> society in general and organisations in particular use female sociali-
> sation as a free resource, simultaneously requiring and devaluing
> support activities. The result is a gender-segregated workplace that
> appears to be the result of natural selection rather than an exercise
> of power. (Fletcher 2001:33)

What is valued and how what women do is viewed both link to notions of discourse and discursive practice, and to power and emotion in workplace practice. Paradoxically 'relational practice' is hard to see and apparently simple to do. But we all know people, both women and men, who think they do this 'relational practice', but whom others see as insensitive, crashing through delicate interpersonal webs, never realising the damage they wreak, or who remain narcissistically focused on self rather than mutual empowerment. We can see that relational practice links powerfully to the question of the values we hold in doing our work and how we enact them.

Power, emotion and values in the commercial process: how women do business

We have seen how pervasive are underlying assumptions regarding gender and the economic process. Conventional dichotomies of public/private, rational/emotional, production/reproduction, and essentialist views of gender difference emphasise the 'othering' of women in the workplace and the valorising of masculinities over the 'feminine', for example in 'disappearing' relational practice. Fragmented and shifting notions of the self and the impact of the consulting work setting on our identities add an important layer to this picture, along with the sheer emotionality of the work process. Turning now to the meta-theme of values, this section considers the woman entrepreneur, how the women studied see business and go about it; this links once again to the work of Miller and Fletcher on mutual gain, reciprocity and enacting 'relational practice'.

The women consultants in the study all operate as sole traders and see themselves running their own businesses, forming *ad hoc* links with others in informal partnerships. We engage in entrepreneurial activity as women, a topic that has not received much scholarly attention until relatively recently despite the emphasis on 'the entrepreneur' in the 1980s and early 1990s as a result of the policies of the Thatcher and Reagan Administrations in the UK and USA respectively.[12]

'Worthwhile-ness' for women in business

My study emphasises the practice of women in their businesses, and their struggle to enact their values while earning a living – their discourse of 'worthwhile-ness', whereby the women want to make a difference. That they do this through their networks is highlighted in the study. These are used to support their work, not just to get work but to be able to carry it out. They focus on reciprocal connections and relationships both with colleagues and with those commissioning work. They experience strong emotions and dilemmas in doing this. The story-telling in consultants' groups and the support it engenders is vital to the participants. Ros comments in one of our meetings: 'I hadn't realised till now that almost all the people who commission me are women!' Jan comments that these conversations could 'not be had' in her male colleague's group. These processes and the assumptions underlying them thus seem distinctly gendered 'feminine'.

Rehman and Frisby (2000) note how little work considers the social construction of entrepreneurship, and they feel their study on women self employed as leisure industry consultants shows how they make very different business choices to men. Recent work by Bruni *et al.* (2004a, 2004b) has focused importantly on what women in business *do*. In studying women as entrepreneurs Bruni *et al.* (2004a) echo the earlier discussion of women and work, seeing research:

> reproduce[s] an androcentric entrepreneur mentality that makes hegemonic masculinity invisible. They portray women's organizations as "the other" ... thereby implicitly reproducing male experience as a preferred normative value. (2004a:abstract)

Bruni and colleagues see the entire concept of 'woman entrepreneur' as having therefore to be manufactured and asserted in the face of hegemonic masculinity, as inherently 'it is not an immediately shared and self-evident social value' (2004b:408). They critique previous work for assuming a 'sharp distinction' between public/private that ensures 'the emotional component necessary to manage inter-personal relations is ignored' (2004b:408). For them the literature on entrepreneurship:

> has never concerned itself with explorating [sic] the power relations comprised in economic structures, establishing instead an automatic relation between the qualities of an entrepreneur (leadership, risk-taking, rational planning) and a model of male rationality. (2004b: 409)

Their ethnographic studies of several women's and one gay man's business explore the lived experience of entrepreneurs outside the heterosexual male model and present an alternative to mas-culine models of entrepreneurship. Their participants value their business:

> for its significance in their private ... lives ...they deliberately reject certain assumptions about entrepreneurship as a male cor-porate performance, principally as the aggressive, competitive, solitary hero who aspires to the conquest of new markets. (2004b: 426)

For the authors this underlines the intertwined nature of entre-preneurship and gender, so that being an entrepreneur then 'involves a gender positioning.' This echoes both key elements seen in Table 9.1 and Moore and Buttner's findings that '[a woman's] decisions appear intricately linked with [her] decisions as an individual, as a house-hold member, at any given moment, over the course of her life.' (1997:15) One woman tells them: 'I think I am my business' (Moore and Buttner 1997:135). The women saw their businesses as 'inter-related parts of themselves'. Most 'viewed their work and life as a central point connected to an overlapping series of network rela-tionships that included family, business and society' (1997:126) and was highly valued. 'Gender and entrepreneurship are, therefore, a theoretical dichotomy whose dividing line is constantly blurred, crossed and denied ...' (Bruni *et al.* 2004b:415) as women bring their experiences and shifting selves to the work of running a (consulting) business.

The values of mutuality

The centrality to women of connection and relationships that is so vivid in this study links strongly to Miller's research (1982) on power, emotion and women:

> we women have been most comfortable using our powers if we believe we are using them in the service of others. Acting under those general beliefs, and typically not making any of this explicit.... (Miller 1982)

'The service of others' here echoes our values/assumptions in a discourse of 'worthwhile-ness', making a difference to the public sector and communities. Miller also echoes our struggle with power, in terms of our own agency and wanting to empower others. The women in the study take power where they can, but justify it through their focus on what is 'worthwhile' for them and for others in terms of the work in hand. The dangers of certainty and our frequent sense of being right are clear, despite our holding to public sector values; we avoid arrogance through an oscillation between certainty and self-doubt. As women our vulnerabilities may link to Miller's ideas on our ambivalence to 'power-over' and the privileging of emotional connection to others. Both underpin values of support and mutuality and to some extent echo the intercession for the weak of the premodern women advisers.

The development group of consultants featured in my study is much valued by us all, along with our individual, overlapping networks, echoing 'compelling support for the centrality of personal networks' and that 'forming cooperative networks' is key for women (Moore and Buttner 1997:118). Our informal group uses the network as 'the opportunity for teamwork without financial strings' (*op cit.*) in contrast to Martin's view of his network in Chapter 7. Networks of course offer sounding boards, idea exchange, support and training but crucially emotional support. One woman comments: 'I don't know why but women talk differently about the issues... we all network with women' (Moore and Buttner 1997:139). Respondents in Moore and Buttner's study also echo my findings about values; the women link up to 'make a difference' with most saying this is very important to them, especially to help other women succeed. They show how the women promote each other's businesses, not assuming a gain, but recognising this will create gains for them – directly enacting 'relational practice' in terms of mutual empowerment and self achieving as we saw in this study.[13]

A 'feminine' discourse of consulting

I now draw on all these ideas about power, emotion, values and the 'feminine' in relation to consulting interaction to elaborate the key elements of a 'feminine' discourse of consulting in contrast to the prevailing viewpoints of much contemporary literature about consulting. This discourse involves *the privileging of processes* and *of social purposes* and *the embracing of emotion*. In setting out this discourse I aim to re-animate a 'feminine' discourse visible in the premodern and subsequently 'disappeared' in the male discourse of organisations and management after the Industrial Revolution. Of course I acknowledge my 'interpretation is at best temporary, specific to the discourses within which it is produced and open to challenge.' (Weedon 1987:85) Readers must judge how far what follows illuminates aspects of consulting work for them.

This 'feminine' discourse draws on the discursive resources of the 'trusted adviser' but differs from its typical enactment in embracing the emotional dimension of apparently objective work, and privileging talk about values alongside the commercial frame. The 'feminine' discourse resists consulting work as a specified commodity and assumes the reciprocity of commercial relations. The notion of a 'feminine' discourse clarifies how the study's meta-themes are not a hierarchy, that is, neither power, emotion nor values simply contain the others, but dynamically shape them as they are shaped in turn. All three meta-themes entail (gendered) discursive resources related to relationships, identities and the commercial process. Thus the 'feminine' (re-)opens different discursive space in order both to carry out consulting interactions and to study them.

Privileging processes

The discussion has repeatedly emphasised the primacy of *relationships* in the 'feminine'. Here I connect this to a process based view of consulting and related discursive resources.

All the processes and 'projects' in consulting extend endlessly into the future and back into the past – there is always a trail of relationships and (inter)actions that led to the point of commissioning the consulting work. These cannot be artificially disconnected. Much of this for the women in this study links to close ties of colleagueship, friendship and common (political) cause over decades, as we saw with the premodern advisers. This extended notion of what is involved in the consulting process fundamentally undermines the 'transaction' or 'project' discourse which seeks to order and simplify the complex, often to exert traditional power relations of buyer and supplier in a market.

This process view is emphasised over and over in my material, consistently showing a consulting task at odds in its actual doing with that generally represented. It shows an *emergent* type of work enmeshed within a complex set of infinite processes, based on relationships, contrasted with a tightly managed, 'project'-based approach with clear start and end. The processes we see in the work portrayed in Chapters 6 and 7 are ongoing not discrete, they demonstrate the limits of a 'project' construction of the work. In this process based view, consulting may *change* the processes that come after the point of commissioning, but how far this represents an 'outcome' is debatable: such a term closes complex processes and interactions down to an object or clarity that we cannot see. From a process viewpoint, the result of consulting work is not as clear cut, nor as ambiguous, as is portrayed by many contemporary writers, especially in critical management quarters. An emergent processual view of consulting draws on a 'feminine' discourse of relationships and connection; privileging processes helps combat what is termed ambiguity by surfacing 'relational practice' as work in its own right, which contributes to results.

CDA highlighted this view of consulting through the concept of *intertextuality*: the chain of texts drawn on to achieve consulting work. These echo the multiple past and future processes referred to above. For my work such intertextuality includes not only relationships, but public policy development at many levels; it encompasses interactions in many organisations and domains to which consultants are simultaneously connected and to which they connect each other; it includes the multiple texts accessed within organisations and by professionals active in their own domains. Reducing consulting work to the 'brief', the 'contract', the 'deliverables', or 'impact' through performance measurement serves to underline these as discursive genres, developed to reduce complexity, but which cannot override it.

Intertextuality adds to the focus on relationships and networks. My analysis emphasises the networks of relationships that facilitate the work and within these the emotionality of the work itself: both reflecting the 'feminine'. Most writers see networks gaining the consultant entry to the work and the work itself as achieved through reliance on either rhetoric or proprietary models of 'effectiveness'. Only Ram (2000), Werr (2002) and especially Pellegrinelli (2002) challenge this from empirical study of consulting firms in action. They too see relationships as part of the work, and not simply the means to the end, of achieving an economic relationship. Here they are closer to Fletcher's 'relational practice' (2001) of 'preserving' work through relationships and achieving mutual empowerment.

The multiplicity of relationships and the different intensity of relationships have the effect of making the term 'client' quite elastic and in some ways quite meaningless – again we create an object to simplify what is going on. Consulting as 'relational practice' entails the work of constructing and maintaining mutually fulfilling relationships that enable growth as well as connection, and develop the trust for taboo-breaking and openness to doing things differently, within a re-definition of power as 'power with'. Immediately we then recognise the 'feminine' and the link of relationships to identity. Bruni and Gherardi (2002) comment that the performativity of identity has not been shown empirically. It seems this *is* visible in my material on women consultants, who perform their identities as women and as consultants, as they do their consulting work.

Privileging social purposes

A theme that has strengthened and deepened over the course of my work is that of enacting values in our consulting work: 'our ability to shape the meanings that define [our] communities ... the meanings that matter'. (Wenger 1998:188) This theme links strongly to the broader social and political context which frames consulting in the public and not-for-profit sectors. Arguably this theme synthesises CDA's three levels as values connect the individual to the broader society; they reflect power relations; they draw on a wealth of texts both old and contemporary. Foucault emphasises the individual dimension:

> the kind of relationship you ought to have with yourself, *rapport à soi*, which I call ethics and which determines how the individual is supposed to constitute himself as a moral subject of his own actions. (1984c:352)

The importance for women of integrating their sense of self with the exercise of power in relation to values of mutuality and the primacy of relationships was discussed earlier. The fragility of 'feminine' identity as shifting and 'other' is seen as undermining a sense of self worth.[14] My concerns at the outset of my study reflect this, as well as a concern to make a difference in terms of work in the public and not-for-profit sectors for public good. Repeatedly within the material women make the same point and take up the viewpoint of the service user or the public with those commissioning work or emphasise the democratic process of public policy rather than *realpolitik*. This too is identified with the 'feminine': through the notion of 'relational practice', through links to queenly intercession and to the earliest notion of the professional in premodern times. A discourse of 'worthwhile-ness' draws on values as the *basis for certainty* in advice, rather than a discourse of knowledge from the expert, whether 'trusted adviser' or 'objective professional'.

Deetz sees tension for consultants in worth being measured by money:

> Consulting, as the discursive self-conception, produces consent to worth's being determined by money ... the transforming of self into commodity. ... Rather than the self being an end with labour and money as means, the self becomes a means to money. (1998:158)

He seems here to sum up the tension women feel as consultants, which relates to 'feminine' imperatives identified by Miller (1976). Recent work by women about their consulting expresses those imperatives as 'pushing' their values (Fletcher and Beard 2005) and the 'quest to want to know' (Page 2005).

Embracing emotion

Emotion has been a theme in this inquiry from the start – which I later recognised as significantly gendered 'feminine'. Emotion is inflected with the 'feminine' and the private sphere. The public world of work assumes the rational, emotion-free or emotion-repressed. For professional work objectivity and rationality is a working principle. The CDA highlights throughout the strength of feeling in consulting interactions. The stuff of the pieces of work is acknowledged, often explicitly, as emotional labour where the consultants carry emotions for and with those commissioning them, they enact them in the work and 'backstage' together. The reflective discussions return time and again to pieces of work marred by negative emotions which redounded badly on relationships. The women struggle with the public and private as separate: for them they seem inextricable.

Fletcher's characterisation of the private sphere is a close description of the consulting work portrayed in this study: about work you want or choose to do; about emotion; concrete and situated yet over an ambiguous timespan. It 'produces people, relations, connection, community, attitudes, values and management of tension' (2001:29). Its elements are seen as innate to women and the work as not complex

– it looks easy and is therefore merely expected (of women) and/or is devalued. Fletcher also sees private sphere work as essentially unpaid: clearly consultants are not unpaid – although unpaid time features in a number of discussions in the study – but the focus on how women view the commercial process echoes the struggle of women to get what they feel is fair reward for work and the pre-occupation of women with finding a sense of their worth, from premodern times till today.

The embracing of emotion remains a double-edged sword, despite managerial fashion for 'emotional intelligence' in organisational theory (Goleman 1998). Women can be swamped by emotion as perhaps Madge was in her telephone call. The standing apart or avoidance seen in Martin's and Sam's words may be preferable to the angst of betrayal and the taking on of others' emotion work. We have to embrace the difficult paradox of privileging emotion (in processes) in order to connect public and private, while not idealising – or limiting – women as emotional beings.

Conclusion

Power has been a key concern here, problematic for women as habitual 'subordinates'. Exercising power comes to symbolise losing our identity. 'Relational practice' is concrete work often carried out by women invisibly that carries very different assumptions about power. It links to the notion of emotional labour (Guy and Newman 2004) and to values of mutuality. All of this is visible in the interactions I studied.

The discussion emphasises just how far my initial questions and concerns were indeed gendered 'feminine'. It also strengthens the links to historical antecedents of advice-giving and consulting, in terms of the discursive resources at our disposal. Placing my work within a broader frame of gender and work has emphasised the differences between my material and the perspectives of the contemporary literature discussed in Chapter 2:

- The discourse of 'trusted adviser' and close relationships dominate over any discussion of the 'objective professional'
- The discourses of change and of knowledge work are largely absent
- The discourse of consultant as expert and people commissioning work as deficient is muted
- The commodified view of the consulting process as transaction is resisted and is cast in the dynamics of relationships and emotion

- Notions of impression management affect professional women but ideas about consulting as rhetoric or magic are absent in favour of the aspiration 'to make a difference'.
- Women who commission work may reflect this approach or may take up the dominant discourses of consulting

My work echoes a similar set of issues as the sparse literature on women in consulting. Women consultants want autonomy not restriction in their work. However, autonomy and control entail issues of rejection and emotional investment for women. This results in independent women consultants seeing their work as both liberating and marginalising. This links clearly to Miller's views of women (1976, 1982), that we see power as double-edged and threatening our sense of identity.[15]

Alongside these issues, and stemming from them, new questions arise about the position of consultant in relation to commissioning organisations and its possible parallels with the position of women at work. The anomalous and provocative position of the 'other' has been charted along with its paradoxical results: both invisible and being on 'front stage'; the importance of impression management yet the 'disappearing' of 'relational practice'.[16]

The exploration of Fletcher's work also raises broader questions about what consultants do. Is what they do in fact this 'relational practice'? Relational practice is work: Fletcher shows how her respondents take time and effort to carry out 'preserving', 'mutual empowerment', 'self-achieving' and 'creating team' in order to achieve tasks/goals; and how in the prevailing organisational discourse this activity was 'disappeared'. If relational practice is key to consulting, might this explain the negative discourse? The link to gender/power dynamics may add to the strength of this explanation; that is, 'relational practice' is seen as women's work and not something 'real workers' or men do:

> 'interactional work is related to what constitutes being a woman, with what a woman is, the idea that it is work is obscured. The work is not seen as what women *do*, but as part of what they *are*.' (Fishman 1978:405 cited West and Zimmerman 2003:69 original italics)

West and Zimmerman conclude that while a woman may be respectfully worked with as a professional: 'Nonetheless she is subject to evaluation in terms of normative conceptions of appropriate attitudes and activities for her sex category and under pressure to prove that she is an "essentially" feminine being, despite appearances to the contrary.'

(2003:70) This echoes Acker's work on the 'ideal worker' as a male body (1990). It seems to me that consultants of both genders struggle with this requirement: a man has to look male despite being in a support or 'feminine' role and a woman is accepted in the support role but may therefore be ignored and undervalued.

The gender literature raises the question of the perceived value of women's work; this is especially relevant to consultants, whose work is continually questioned and often blatantly discounted. The notion of 'women's work' may go some way to explain how and why what consultants do is habitually disparaged publicly. Perhaps the consultant is enacting 'relational practice' and the 'disappearing act' is carried out on their work? If the consultant is female she embodies the problematic of 'relational practice' so her work may be more open to discounting. The resulting invisibility and silencing support the (male) norm (Simpson and Lewis 2005). Equally how easy is it to value 'relational practice' when men do it? Still it may be denied, as in 'I knew what the consultant said anyway, he added nothing new', or invisible, as in the secrecy around the trusted adviser and the emphasis on enabling the person commissioning to perform the public face unaided.

> So what consultants face in their daily work is what women face in life? (Comment from male student peer in PhD workshop, Lancaster, 22 March 2006)

I conclude that it is fruitful to characterise advisers and consultants as doing 'women's work' in the sense of 'relational practice' and to use the feminine lens to understand their work experience. For Fletcher, critical inquiry must 'disrupt the relationship between power and knowledge by bringing what are called "subversive stories" into the discourse.' (2001:21–22) In my study these stories are those of the women consultant and those (women) in the public and not-for-profit sectors, who commission her in small scale work. They help disrupt the existing consulting story and (re-)animate a 'feminine' consulting discourse, constituting a critical act. A 'feminine' consulting discourse thus helps take us towards a 'critical consulting' practice.

10
Toward a 'Critical Consulting' Practice: The Contribution of a 'Feminine' Discourse of Consulting

Introduction

I aimed from the start to illuminate the work my colleagues and I do, partly since we are paid from public money so everyone has an interest in this rather hidden aspect of consulting. I hoped to inform not only my own work and that of people who work with me, but also raise broader issues for a wider audience, both those commissioning and those consulting, as well as for researchers. Here I weave together the threads of this book to address the divergent interests of readers that I hope come together in concern for the implications of my work for our practice.

This chapter therefore reflects on the contribution of this study of small scale public sector consulting work by women – in contrast to previous studies of consulting based overwhelmingly on large scale work in the corporate sector. I focus my conclusions in three arenas: conceptualising consulting work; a 'feminine' discourse of consulting; and 'critical consulting' practice. I consider the implications of re-animating a 'feminine' discourse of consulting, for 'critical consultants' especially, but also for those commissioning consulting work. I end in critical mood reviewing possible limitations of my work and how further research could develop it. First I review the journey of the previous nine chapters and the issues that they together pose for the notion of 'critical consulting'.

Where has my work taken us?

'Live' consulting interactions from my work and the reflective material demonstrate the struggle of the consultant to meld the discursive resources of the contemporary world with advice-giving processes based substantially on pre-modern and 'feminine' approaches. She enacts a 'feminine' discourse of consulting that is potentially 'disappeared' by the dominant (masculine) discourses of consulting and of organisation more generally. The women in the study attempt to enact this discourse alongside dominant discourses, for example of transaction. This raises a series of *dilemmas and double-binds* for consultants:

- We resist the discourse of transaction and the commodified 'project' while retaining a commercial focus;
- We privilege close, mutual, trusting relationships, and the emotional labour they entail, while holding a clear view of our own values;
- We are certain of our views and advice despite working within a prevailing discourse of 'client is king' and despite searing personal vulnerability;
- We work for partnership with those commissioning us, yet we crave control and autonomy in our work and the power to make a difference through what we do.
- Our values are inclusive, about social justice and changing power relations in society, and our work nonetheless sustains public sector managerialism.

> **Reflection**
> *I break off in writing this to zap an email to a University manager about yet another piece of work for which I await payment, reminded again it's well overdue... I feel my inner rage rise at the endless time spent chasing money and the way in which people seem to commission work and feel no obligation to ensure it is paid! They pursue it 'if they have time'.*

These dilemmas ensnare us in asserting power from marginal positions; in needing to confront yet keep connections going; in expressing strong emotions and ethics yet needing to earn a living; in struggling to match our values with the values of people commissioning work; in 'delivering' work that nonetheless persists in emerging unpredictably.

Power, emotion and values

In Chapters 8 and 9, I explored the *meta-themes of power, of emotion, of values* in the commercial process. Power is enacted in interaction and constantly negotiated between actors; consultants assume power to act once commissioned and those commissioning assume power to control consultants' work. The resulting struggle challenges traditional notions of economic power and enables consultants to pursue their purposes based on values of 'making a difference'. Emotion is inherent to all the interactions and stories of the women studied. We expect and enact emotional labour. Emotion work is also resented and experienced as negative, a burden. The strength of emotions is striking when connected to issues of power/autonomy or to values and commerce. The commercial process is vividly a key framing of consulting for us, never far away in our talk. But while issues of (lack of) contracts and payment are constant, equally frequent is talk of 'worthwhile-ness' and our work making a difference. The ethics of the work, its link to our values, motivations and energies, colour our expectations of, and engagement with, the process of consulting. The interconnections of these meta-themes are demonstrated through complex links with issues of *identity, relationships* and prevailing assumptions about *the commercial process*, which all reflect and shape broader discursive forces of the political and social, such as gender, public policy and economics.

Consulting as a discursive practice

The argument for conceptualising consulting as a discursive practice is compelling. Other work has stopped short of identifying discourses of consulting or in exploring these through consulting interaction. This study has taken up this challenge and opened up a different framing to help study a phenomenon which most commentators agree is ambiguous and in need of further research. The surfacing of power as a meta-theme further confirms concepts of discourse as fundamental to consulting processes.

The power of critical discourse analysis (CDA)

My work focuses on 'live' interaction as well as reflective material and opens both to discourse analytic review. Such analysis enables a linking of local interaction to broad social, political and (inter-)discursive processes, thus connecting my conceptual framing to actual consulting work in action. Applying CDA to a substantial body of self-generated material is not only novel but enabled critical reflexivity and the grip to consider the notion of 'critical consulting' in practical terms for the first time.

The important CDA dimension of intertextuality also opens the 'bricolage' of consulting work to new scrutiny, revealing infinite chains of texts and interconnections woven to achieve the work. CDA has thus challenged the sharp boundaries[1] of the commodified consulting 'project' and demonstrated how this discourse seeks to reify and control consulting processes in the face of their inherent emergence from the actions of numerous densely networked agents. The interconnectedness of consulting with its broader context is explicated through the notion of intertextuality: we cannot see them as separate. This further develops our concepts of consulting.

Discourses of consulting

Within the broad discursive context I identified *discourses of consulting* that stem both from ancient, enduring concepts of advice-giving and more recent notions of management consulting. The discourse of the *transaction* in consulting, with its assumed power relations rooted in classical economics, underlies much contemporary work on effectiveness, on the 'client/consultant relationship' and on what the 'client' and consultant do. The dominant image is the clearly staged 'project' with defined aims, boundaries, roles and 'deliverables'. The paying client sets the frame for this and manages it firmly against the slippery consultant, keen to maximise the fee and exploit through rhetoric the inherent ambiguities of a professional service.

> **Reflection**
> *Towards the end of my research when doing this sense-making, I noted that I took a less deferential approach that challenged existing performative discourses of consulting in bidding for work. The commissioning group fed back that our bid was currently in the top two being considered but they felt we were not sufficiently lively and charismatic (!) to do the training they wanted with senior people. Instead of pointing to examples showing we indeed were effective with senior people, I chose to begin a conversation about how my colleagues and I saw the proposed work as about starting a process of learning & development, rather than a one-off training 'performance' and we would 'lead from the back' as facilitators. We talked some more about how we would work to support key people in achieving their intent and in the end we were awarded the contract.*

Yet the strange paradox of the certainty of the adviser in her/his advice alongside the need to defer to those commissioning work persists from the most ancient time to today (I constantly find this in my journal entries).

Alternatively the discourse of *trust* produces the 'trusted adviser' who works with the 'client', where the 'client is king' and the adviser enables them to act apparently unsupported. Trust and ambiguity together feed a further, powerful and competing discourse of the *profession*, where the 'objective professional' transcends the constraining relationship, offering transferable knowledge and expertise focused on measurable outcomes.

This links to discourses of the *knowledge intensive* economy and of *change*, which permeate management, producing managerial insecurity and promoting the (never-ending) search for answers through consultancy. This in turn feeds a discourse of *performativity* whereby the consultant's work is scrutinised 'front-stage', the consultant enacts emotional labour and others belittle the work and its impact. The discourse of *partnership* enables consultants to construct a relationship where joint work and ownership dilute that scrutiny. Nonetheless the relationship is reified and viewed as unitary and singular.

The 'feminine' in management consulting

These contemporary discourses draw on a worldview that privileges entities, assumes their power and explores subsequent exchange and interaction between them, rather than a *process* view which regards flux and movement as fundamental, *producing* (temporary, fragile) entities. My genealogical review in Chapter 2 shows such a process-based view of advice-giving, focused on relationship building, challenging and repairing, working on a constant flow of rather hidden interaction to sustain the fluctuating fortunes of those in power. These characteristics are reflected in Fletcher's 'relational practice', and the relational theory of Miller's work on women: the 'feminine' view of power, connection and mutuality.

In considering femininities and consulting, I trod a careful path through the minefields of gender, masculinities, power and identity to characterise as 'feminine' the core features of what has emerged. The premodern discourse of advice-giving reflects a 'feminine' sense of being Other, connected to the private realm, privileging relationships. Contemporary discourses of consulting stem primarily from a masculine view of the management domain, trapped in binary notions and competing discourses of consulting such as 'trusted adviser' or 'objective professional'. Exploration of the terrain of consulting thus documents a staged but distinct shift from 'feminine' advice-giving to a more masculine model.

My study of consulting work, however, shows consulting interactions of a 'feminine' character: we pay primary attention to relationships and connecting to others within an explicitly emotional and value-driven sense of self. While working within commercial processes we resist the commodification of consulting work. We build our autonomy within reciprocal relationships that aim to support progressive social purposes. Viewing women's consulting interaction shows a tussle of the 'feminine' or 'relational practice' with contemporary discourses such as performativity and rhetoric, but the 'feminine' remains clearly visible; it illuminates the complexity of power and values in the commercial process, connected to identity and relationships, and so to emotions

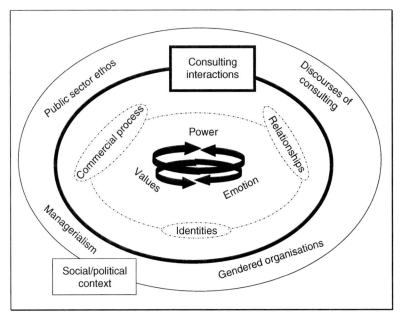

Figure 10.1   How we can view consulting interactions in the study

(see the mapping in Figure 10.1 reproduced here from Chapter 8 for convenience). In exploring femininities we see the impact of the 'separate spheres' tradition for both men and women in consulting. The 'feminine' discourse thus *privileges processes* and *social purposes* and *embraces emotion.*

The shift from 'feminine' approaches to the masculine in 'modern' consulting has led to 'disappearing' of 'feminine' approaches. Women are in a double-bind in enacting a 'feminine' discourse; men doing so may be perceived as doing women's work; both risk being discounted or held in contempt, unless those commissioning also enact a 'feminine' discourse. Women and men taking a more 'masculine' approach to consulting are either rivals for power, controlling people they advise (with mixed results positive and negative in my material), or engage in rhetoric, viewed as 'not action', again producing contempt.[2]

What can we learn from a 'feminine' discourse of consulting?

Contemporary literature, whether mainstream or in critical management vein, pursues an un-questioned characterisation of consulting as emerging in late 19th or early 20th century in relation to the growth of the corporate sector and especially of 'scientific management'. This book opens this view to question in offering the beginnings of a genealogical study of consulting as advice-giving. This has exposed a gradual discursive shift away from the 'feminine' of premodern advice-giving to the 'masculine' model of the contemporary image of consulting. In contrast, my empirical work found a 'feminine' discourse of consulting enacted presently in small scale consulting for public and not-for-profit sectors.

The (re-)animating of a 'feminine' discourse of consulting, 'disappeared' since premodern times, offers a renewed discursive space and discursive resources for women and men consultants to re-frame their practice and reconsider the implications of dominant discourses of consulting. The 'feminine' discourse of 'Other' may offer resources to work with the paradoxes of consulting rather than choose between the hierarchic binaries that stem from the assumption of 'separate spheres'. The discursive resources of values and 'worthwhile-ness' draw on the identities and commitments of those involved to help work with the tensions of power, emotion and the commercial process. They also reflect my starting concerns about worth. A 'feminine' discourse may highlight the (masculine) mainstream simply by becoming transgressively visible and so 'queer' (Sullivan 2003) the order of discourse.

At the least a 'feminine' discourse of consulting is now visible and can be explored rather than 'disappeared'; at best, it offers a path to expanding perspectives on consulting work in a critical vein through using a 'feminine' lens. This may represent a step to 'critical consulting' practice in offering ways to address the questions raised in Chapter 2.

Reflection

My discussions with broader audiences suggest approaching consulting from the 'feminine' produces interest, even excitement. On the other hand, practice remains tricky. I recently worked with a local authority in setting up a new network to create public involvement in health & social care using a process approach with no pre-determined agenda (in order to start with the widest possible set of views from the public). The men involved were so hostile to this and intent on their own agendas linked to existing entities that their negative emotions nearly obliterated progress toward the broader social purposes of the initiative. Thankfully the women involved, who commissioned me, stuck to their guns in supporting my approach (interesting military metaphor there!), but were clearly aware of the process, thanking me for taking the emotional flak instead of them.

Developing a 'critical consulting' practice

I began with aspiring to a notion of the 'critical consultant' and how such a person could act. At the end of Chapter 3 key questions were identified for the 'critical consultant' – are they now answered? Partly the notion of a 'feminine' discourse of consulting offers a different way to understand the questions, and partly it is a lens for developing answers – see Table 10.1.

Enacting the 'feminine' discourse, as a strategy to achieving a 'critical consulting' practice, will ensure that we keep broader purposes in view and make these explicit. This is the only path to achieving common ground with those we are working with and engaging our mutual energies. Consultants need to think how best to interact with those commissioning work in order to focus on 'relational practice' and how to achieve it. Perhaps we can ask Fairclough's question: 'how can I use

Table 10.1   Questions and opportunities for the 'critical consultant'

Initial questions from Chapter 3	Opportunities of a 'feminine' discourse of consulting
How to co-create progressive social change?	Privilege processes and relationships not entities
How to be credible and challenging while bringing knowledge & expertise to bear?	Focus on 'power with' not 'power over' Draw on values and 'worthwhile-ness' not 'knowledge'
How to develop and work in dynamic but mutual relations?	Work through 'relational practice': expect and nurture mutual growth and worth of the work; adopt a developmental and reflexive approach
How can consulting be a means to change/challenge power relations?	Break down 'separate spheres' assumptions, explicitly link political and personal, emotional/rational
How to live with and yet challenge the connection to management?	Hold to deep values, social purposes and ethics beyond 'knowledge' or 'skills' or 'change'
How to 'deliver' for those commissioning work while keeping a concern for society and goals of social justice?	Acknowledge the emotional work of consulting and express values and issues of 'worthwhile-ness'

language to constitute a different reality, one more in keeping with my values and beliefs?' (1997:158) This in turn requires our belief that we can help create new processes for people to develop their work and their organisations; we do not assume that existing enti-

> **Reflection**
> *This is the unhelpful assumption underlying all the endless restructuring in the public sector – changing the conversations would achieve more.*

ties must be put in different relation but that different relationships create new (temporary) entities. We need to operate in a 'both/and' world that embraces paradox and false binaries to bring emotions and social purposes rightfully into public and not-for-profit (consulting) work. The critical consultant must accept her power and take what agency she can to pursue progressive goals[3] but recognise this depends on being engaged to do the work – this is a commercial process. To do both involves emotional labour – and requires once more the expression of clear values and ethics throughout the work and its processes. All of this produces an identity of 'critical consultant' which remains fragile and contingent on all these elements holding together in each piece of work, with each person commissioning and with each consultant colleague involved. It is this fragility that leads to our sense of vulnerability and to the raft of negative emotions we saw in this study.

We may try to rearrange power relations as we work with the discursive resources we can access, but there are no 'pristine' places of power and resistance. We are caught in contradictions, constructing new arrangements of meaning and power as we craft our lives, but never 'authentically resisting' power to attain some emancipatory end (Kondo 1990). The linking of power, identity and resistance is a helpful

> **Reflection**
> *This reminds me of how Mel and I censor ourselves regarding politics and values, like challenging the private sector assumptions taking root in the public sector – 'contestability' in health is simply not contestable! We have to sneak things in, imply a critique and try to help managers at least voice how they feel about it.*

framing for 'critical consulting' by women. Surfacing the 'disappeared' femininities in consulting is one answer for a critical consulting – reanimating these is a critical act in problematising dominant perspectives. This is especially so as mainstream and critical management images of consulting are not so far apart as shown in Chapter 3.

In addition 'critical consulting' is more important than ever as private sector models of management and the concomitant discourses of consulting increasingly colonise the public and not-for-profit sectors. The dilemmas become sharper for the 'feminine' discourse – its 'disappearing' is even more a site of struggle as simply more is at stake: 'the ethico-political choice we have to make every day is to determine which is the main danger' (Foucault 1984c:343).

The resources that can help the 'critical consultant' include:

- Seeing consulting processes not as linear but iterative and net-worked, not transactional but reciprocal, and not starting and ending in specific 'projects'
- The close connection of values to 'knowledge' work and the emotionality of 'objective' work
- The dilemmas and contradictions identified – and noticing when they occur
- New ways to characterise how commercial relations are enacted in management consulting through a focus on explicit mutuality and trust
- The interdependence of the identities/values of managers and consultants and how this affects working processes; how common ground and reciprocal interests are established. What are the mutual interests of the actors? How can/do they emerge?

> **Reflection**
> *My recent work with a housing association showed me the value of focusing on purposes and modelling these in processes. Engaging tenants in shaping the organisation was the aspiration – not just 'involvement'. Pre-existing relationships helped overcome the reluctance of senior managers to agree a novel process that from the outset involved tenants & staff on an equal footing. The resulting event was for highly experienced staff 'the best meeting involving tenants we ever had'.*

But we also need people who commission work to help us understand the intertextuality of the process they are developing and be willing to work with the emergence that produces. People commissioning also need to recognise the limitations of the consulting discourse of transaction and commodity in achieving their purposes. They need to be open to the emotionality of the work and to their part in that. They should expect – or demand – an ethics from the consultant that includes stopping work where it is not going to make any difference, and back this up themselves.

So we need to find ways to privilege processes that do not provoke anxiety in those commissioning work (so used to 'specifying clear deliverables') but that enable them to act. We need to express social and political purposes and not hide them; we need to acknowledge and value the emotion work without taking it all on. We need to find ways to make sure we are genuine in 'relational practice' and not using it as a rhetoric. It is easy to assert reciprocity without ever hearing the other person's point of view, to talk mutuality while believing in their deficit. Our ethical commitment to 'critical consulting' must stand the test of others involved joining with us – we cannot achieve much alone.

In critical mood ...

Claims for any research are only sustained through critique. This book meets the task of critical research (Alvesson and Deetz 2000:18) to offer insight through:

- 'powerful exemplars'
- 'critique' to 'counteract the dominance of [the] taken-for-granted'
- 'transformative redefinitions' to achieve change and practical understandings

However of course it has limitations, not only as a relatively small study, but one where my closeness to most participants may limit the likelihood of enacting or identifying differences in practice. On the other hand it is legitimate to study such a 'community of practice' to unpack what is going on as autoethnographer.

CDA helped 'make strange' my material but my colleagues and I still had to complete the work in process. I was always within the commercial process I was studying – this limited what material I collected in some cases and may have narrowed my focus. However I think it helped emphasise the dilemmas. CDA is designed to focus on power relations and broad social/political issues such as gender, so it may have over-amplified these. My journal is full of entries about the difficulty of reflecting on my work and my research on it. I found it hard not to feel *'constantly I'm self-justifying when I find other work that supports my findings'* (Journal 2004). Putting my 'stuff' in the lead and clarifying my voice has been a (gendered?) struggle.

I remain hesitant about the assertion of a 'feminine' discourse for these reasons and others set out in Chapter 9: does it help apparently to set the 'feminine' against an assumed masculine if I want to escape essentialism? How can it avoid idealising the practice of women? My material contains numerous problematics of a 'feminine' discourse, such as a tendency to sublimate conflict, erroneously to assume shared values among women colleagues and to 'other' men just as hierarchically. Identifying such discourse and how it works, especially to draw conclusions about 'critical consulting' practice must remain careful, hesitant, exploratory work. However my critical discursive approach supports the importance of speaking from silence and relishing the space to talk differently about consulting work as a consequence.

While my work has addressed my starting concerns, these are inevitably not completely answered. The genealogy especially is a first attempt at exploring an enormous terrain, but fruitful nonetheless. The picture of consulting interaction in Figure 10.1 offers an image of its key components; it partially explains them and indicates how they may emerge for the actors. Further theoretical work linking the picture to other concepts could strengthen the explanation, for example 'communities of practice' (Wenger 1998) and situated learning, building on Handley *et al.* (2007). Examining concepts from queer theory would further illuminate 'feminine' discourse and its impact. Fletcher suggests more research 'to unpack the role of emotion' (2001:140) and help distinguish what is a growth-fostering interaction, combat idealised views of caring and affection that underlie our assumptions about relational practice and find new words to escape stereotypes.

Researchers in this field might therefore fruitfully extend the genealogical approach to explore especially the process of the shift away from the 'feminine' in advice-giving. Equally they might map the experience of men in public and not-for-profit consulting: what models or discourses do they draw on or are they too working within the 'feminine' discourse? Similarly inquiry into women working in the private sector and the discursive resources they draw on would add a great deal and I suspect would illustrate the 'disappearing' of the 'feminine' discourse of consulting.[4] The use of discursive resources by consultants and the identification of dominant and more marginal discourses across the heterogeneous field of consulting bears further study, along with the implications of doing consulting on identities of consultants, including issues of ethnicity, age, professional background. The power of using CDA as a tool in studying interaction should be noted here.

Connected further work on the centrality of gender to the interactions could fruitfully explore how far the 'disappearing' of relational practice may explain enduring (negative) perceptions of consultants, both men and women.

Final words ...

This book has given readers an inside view of a little-known arena of consulting, and how it is constructed as a discursive practice, that challenges contemporary portrayals of management consulting.

It has (re-)opened a space for a 'feminine' discourse of consulting absent from contemporary literature but present in the genealogy and in the interactions in my work. This is an important and different lens for considering consulting that may help explain the negativity and ambivalence surrounding consulting in terms of it being 'women's work', with consultants bearing the identity of woman, the helpmeet 'other'.

Both these contribute to exploring the notion of 'critical consulting' practice. While there is more to do and I have arguably raised more questions for research, the 'feminine' discourse may be one way in which 'critical consultants' work, as it challenges dominant discourses of consulting. As Michelle put it, in talking about working in the mental health system:

> every time you get that cold hard edge coming into something where cold hard edges don't need to be, you know you're up against a problem.' (Chapter 6)

This illustrates the trigger for the 'critical consultant' to work from her feelings and values in mutual relation with others to help create processes that make a difference.

Notes

Introduction

1. I first heard this story related by the Director of the Judge Institute at Cambridge University in an after dinner speech to delegates at the *Connecting Learning and Critique* conference held there in July 2002 and received by them with evident delight, cheering and applause.
2. This book is concerned exclusively with the *external* consultant, although the importance of internal consulting and advice to line managers within organisations is acknowledged.
3. I must also acknowledge being inspired by hearing Jonathan Gosling fearlessly present material at the *First International Critical Management Studies* conference in Manchester on his own dilemmas and concerns yet avoiding narcissism (Gosling 1999).
4. The term 'feminine' appears in inverted commas throughout to emphasise its contestability and to undermine any essentialist assumptions raised in the reader.
5. The plural (and masculinities similarly) signifies multiple, contested meanings, their socially constructed nature assuming unhelpful, either/or, gender binaries, that are not universally recognised nor enacted in everyday interaction between men and women.
6. See for example Alvesson and Wilmott 1996, Wilmott 2006, and www.aom. pace.edu/cms/About/Manifesto.htm
7. Harvey (2005) uses 'critical consulting' only in relation to the latter, a reflexive project focused on one's practice.

Chapter 1   Studying Consulting from the Inside: What Do I Mean By Consulting and How Did I Research It?

1. Such topics in the examples in this book include strategy development in mental health, tackling health inequalities, user-focused administrative systems, community cohesion, user involvement, supporting democratic scrutiny processes, innovation & development in services and partnership working.
2. The only exception I have found being Sturdy *et al.*'s study carried out 2005–2007 (see www.ebkresearch.org)
3. A term recently defined by Reynolds and Vince as 'a commitment to asking questions which may be neither comfortable or welcome... [and] capable of deconstructing [vested] interests and political processes.' (2004:4)

Chapter 2   Consultants, Confidantes and Consorts: A Genealogy of Consulting and Advice-Giving to Organisational Leaders

1. Mears (2005:97) describes this Renaissance view of 'counsel as a collaborative activity' focusing on its process and attending to the feelings of the advisee as much as on the business at hand, reflecting this study's concern with consulting interaction.
2. Kitsopoulos (2003) does refer to much earlier antecedents than the early 20th century but only extremely briefly and not in relation to a discourse analysis.
3. Plato's work (as with much in the pre-modern) is infused with assumptions about gender and class in ways we find unacceptable, and assumes trait theories of leadership. However he emphasises education and development in a much more modern view of leadership.
4. When the first printing press came to Florence in 1471 only 30,000 printed books existed; by 1500 this is estimated at 8 million (White 2004:30).
5. There were a few male exceptions, such as the salons of M. de la Poplinière, Helvétius, and the baron d'Holbach.
6. Urwick's personal papers held at Henley College are the source for this section.

Chapter 3   Images of Consulting: What Currently Shapes How We See Consulting and How It Works?

1. Indeed Alvesson and Johansson (2002) term it the 'pro-consultancy' literature.
2. In contrast, Cleverley (1971) sees management as 'post primitive', a culture not much more evolved than ancient Greek or Roman practice, so hinting at the value in examining the pre-modern, as in Chapter 2.
3. I have identified these images focusing on the material writers present rather than adopting the stereotypes that many offer, such as the consultant as 'trader in trouble' or 'agent of anxiety' (Alvesson and Johansson 2002).
4. His work is notable in actually recounting a live interaction in a workshop, where he posed as a participant.
5. He berates consultants for eschewing the rigour of scientific study: being self-critical, dealing with replicability, achieving generalisation from specific cases, which seems a strangely positivist analysis in such a critical management book!
6. The rhizome is a 'subterranean stem', not hierarchic but composed of decentred lines, multiplicities, random unregulated relationships, dynamic not static, and forming 'assemblages' (Best and Kellner 1991).
7. Legge's phrase in an unpublished paper (1994) much taken up in the critical management work.
8. Czerniawska (2002b) in reviewing Clark and Fincham's book (2002) is not convinced and suggests academics should carefully try not to throw stones in the glasshouse of their own position.

9. Little material exists outside a special edition in 1995 of the *Journal for Organisational Change Management* 8(1). Its editors (Covin and Harris) can only cite four earlier sources, which all concern North American consulting firms and female recruitment. Recent work in Finland and the UK researching gendered discourse and career paths focuses on women consultants, but only those in multi-national firms (Meriläinen *et al.* 2004).
10. King (2004, 2005) also presents an auto-biographical account of her work as a consultant but focuses overwhelmingly on her experiences in joining a major consulting organization and making sense of her work there, rather than a focus on solo practice as a woman as these accounts do.

Chapter 4   Consulting as a Discursive Practice

1. This ambiguity and multiplicity is echoed in the literature on discourse: the 'discursive paradox' that discourse both 'celebrates uncertainty' while 'generating meaning and constructing reality' (Grant *et al.* 1998:12–13). This paradox requires reflexive work and resisting too concrete a definition of either.
2. From this point on I shall treat 'client' as a constructed discursive term and show it in inverted commas, or use a process focused term such as: people commissioning work. This will help avoid assumptions and being entrammelled in discourses I am trying to explore and problematise.
3. In the most recent critical management collections of work (Clark and Fincham 2002; Kipping and Engwall 2002) no reference to discourse occurs in the indexes. In the former Sturdy makes passing reference to discursive reality, Legge considers Foucauldian power/knowledge but not discourse, preferring a focus on 'rhetoric' and Case examines discourses of virtual working but not in a consulting setting. Fincham (1999a) alludes briefly and broadly to consulting discourse.
4. Most recently tracked in Ernst & Young's stance using this exact term – see James (2005:10).
5. Grey (2003) cites historical material, for example concerning technological change in the 19th century, to suggest that little may have changed in the organisational environment.
6. Ethnographic work (Crucini 2002; Ram 2000) focuses on consulting firms and relies substantially on interviews; historical cases have given only a 'fragmentary picture of the client-consultancy interaction' (Kipping and Armbruster 2002:219); Werr uses a simulation of consulting work (2002).
7. He has since co-developed a study that observes live consulting meetings and interaction (Sturdy *et al.* 2006) This work nonetheless maintains the typical focus of extant studies in drawing on corporate settings with large consulting firms, and includes IT based assignments. See www.ebkresearch.org

Chapter 5   Researching Consulting Interactions: From Process Ontology to Critical Discourse Analysis

1. See for more insights the coherently argued article by Wilmott (2005) who draws on the discourse theory of Laclau and Mouffe, He sees *discourse,* rather than the 'seemingly pre-given' notions of structure and agency, actually

produces what these terms intend, and is required in order to understand them. Drawing on Laclau and Mouffe he acknowledges that every discursive structure also has material aspects; that is, 'language is embedded in material relations', both human and in 'the world of things, such as earthquakes and bricks.' (2005:765). For Wilmott, retaining dualistic concepts like agency and structure to explain the world serves only to strengthen hegemonic forces (2005:774).

2. See also Fox (2000) who reviews organisational learning as processes that produce the effects of power, competence, knowledge or whatever. He draws on the work of actor-network theorists (ANT) to add to his exploration of how this happens as does Chia (1996), who sees Law, and other ANT writers, as taking a becoming view of the world – 'How things come to be is a central concern [of their schema]'. Chia links Law's 'relational materialism' and Latour's 'infra-reflexivity' to his own commitment to the process position. This entails 'a commitment to recovering the concreteness of our brute experiences as they emerge ... to make *strange* what is familiar...' (1996:47 his emphasis) This echoes Foucault's genealogical approach to exploring discursive practice and confirms my need to study concrete processes of consulting as they happen.

3. Whittle (2006) draws on discourse as a concept to explore paradoxes she found in studying management consultants at work. Meriläinen *et al.* (2004) explore how male and female consultants in Finland and the UK discursively construct their careers and identities while 'embedded in a normalizing, gendered discourse of what it means to be an 'ideal' consultant.' (2004:539) They take a Foucauldian perspective on discourse but do not use a discourse analytic approach on their interview material, nor explore consulting interactions. Thomas (2003) draws on the role of consulting in management fashions, setting out how critical discourse analysis could help analyse the development of management thinking. However his analytic work is confined to management textbooks. Werr and Styhre's (2003) study, principally with those commissioning consulting work, examines the discursive construction of the 'client-consultant relationship' as it relates to the managerial discourses of the bureaucratic or the networked organisation. They draw on discourse as 'embedded institutional ideas and practices' (2003:50) in making sense of their interview material, but do not use discourse analysis.

4. As indicated by several recent special journal issues – *Organization Studies* in 2003, *Academy of Management Review* and *Organization* in 2004, *Organization Management Journal* 2005 – the recent 'handbook' (Grant *et al.* 2004) from Sage Publishing and the establishment of the journal Critical Discourse Studies in 2004 (Fairclough *et al.* 2004)

5. This concept helps explain the impact of comments, apparently trivial in others' eyes, that produce racism or are sexually harassing. The recipient experiences the power and weight of the freighted meanings and the accumulation of (past) negative results is vivid for them in the moment.

6. Nonetheless I have a duty of no harm to participants which has made some of my material unusable in the public domain.

7. I take email as interaction following Yates (2001) who researched internet interaction from a sociolinguistic perspective, that is, how far computer mediated communication (CMC) is more like talk or more like writing. He shows it

falls between the two and concludes 'a lack of visual communication [does not] prevent the complex expression of identity'. (2001:119) His research showed a high self reference and reference to others in CMC compared to other corpora of text. Regarding gender in CMC, his work suggests use of email is not only justified but a strength in terms of my aims.

8. The exceptions are the first piece of work chronologically, when I was perhaps least confident in seeking permission to tape and where there were few face-to-face interactions; and the Voluntary Sector work which did not involve me.

9. Leading training and development with individuals arguably produces different power relations; it also typically takes place away from the organisational context that produces the dynamics of management consulting processes in which I am interested.

10. All of the consultants in these pieces of work are white people (one identifying as Irish), except for one who is of dual heritage, are aged between 35 and 60 years old and have all lived in the UK for all or most of our adult lives. All of us would probably be viewed as middle class people, although at least three of us, including myself, have working class origins and are the first in family to go to university.

11. These included: my consultants' development network; a research seminar with public sector managers; discussion with PhD colleagues, who included consultants and people in management positions; co-leading a seminar for the University of West of England on researching consulting; presenting to the postgraduate cross-departmental History group, University of Lancaster; discussions with a women consultants group in Sussex.

12. An interview I held with a male consultant, who was not a direct colleague, formed a striking contrast. While he commented to others that he found the discussion stimulating, for me it felt stilted, not a two-way discussion at all. This was my only 'interview' during the study, that is, a process where I asked questions and the person responded. I felt then and, having analysed the notes and tape of this interview, continue to feel that this process was hierarchic and also produced a gendered interaction. The material generated is very different from that coming from women consultants, my direct colleagues, although it reflected themes from the contemporary literature. It emphasised to me the value of focusing the study on women and exploring our interactions as colleagues in achieving our work.

Chapter 8   What is Going On in Consulting Interactions?: Exploring Meta-themes of Power, Emotion and Values

1. Only King (2004) and Sturdy *et al.* (2008) deal with emotions other than in passing; the latter focuses on the use of humour in meetings rather than considering the broad role of emotion in consulting work as King does.

2. Sturdy *et al.* (2008) in reporting on their study of consulting interaction emphasise the role of humour/laughter as a strategy for making connection that may paradoxically embed difference. They do not refer to gender issues in relation to humour/laughter but their work is novel in explicitly exploring a dimension of emotion in live consulting interaction.

3. Ram's study of small consulting firms also found: 'a context in which the language of 'consultancy days', 'charge-out rates', 'billable' time was woven into daily interactions at work' (2000:660).
4. This links to notions of a 'community of practice' (Wenger 1998), where development of identity and meaning are core elements.

Chapter 9 Femininities and Consulting: (Re-)animating a 'Feminine' Discourse of Consulting

1. I also wish to avoid a simple, dualist construction of gender, recognising its endlessly complex, performative dimensions (Butler 1999)
2. This is often seen as primarily arising from the masculinisation of work following the Industrial Revolution (Crompton 1997; Harriman 1996; Smith 1988); it clearly predates that time given my genealogical findings of the importance of the private sphere for women advice-givers.
3. Parkin (1993) comments on how women in organisations are often on view and so surveilled. The front stage may be gendered space available to public gaze. Conversely the invisible woman may be in the 'back room' working as though she were not there. The front stage and back room are often gendered spaces giving men and women differential access to valued tasks and interactions. Law (2002) refers to 'the gendered buffer room that surrounds many sites of power' (2002:23). The work context is key: in some settings front stage work is valued, e.g. doctors, in others senior or important people avoid customer contact and are in the back room, e.g. bank managers.
4. It should be noted however that this literature is overwhelmingly predicated on work and organisations in the industrialised Northern hemisphere and assumes a homogeneous white cultural base in organisations and society.
5. Many have focused on distinguishing gender from sex, or biology (Crompton 1997; Gherardi 1994; Howard and Hollander 1997), on the problematics of gender differences and how far these are attributable to sex (Ahl 2002; Padavic and Reskin 2002; Powell and Graves 2003).
6. King's study of her own consulting work (2005) draws on similar concepts from Bakan's ethics of 'communion' and 'agency', concluding that 'unmitigated' pursuit of one or the other is not only gendered but unhelpful: integration of the two is required.
7. For example see Butler (1999 & 1993), Foucault (in Rabinow 1984), Giddens (1991), Kondo (1990), Marsella *et al.* (1985), Rose (1999), Sen (1999) who each discuss the imperative constantly to (re)create our self (selves) and the dynamics of history, power and culture in this process.
8. Barbara Czarniawska, Fiona Czerniawska, Karen Handley, Karen Legge and Patricia Shaw are the notable exceptions.
9. Interestingly in referring to Maddock's work on gendered cultures Collinson and Hearn change her terms to their 'discourses of masculinity' using less hostile words: for example 'authoritarianism' not the 'barrack yard' culture, 'informalism' not the 'locker room' culture.
10. It is important to stress Fletcher is using 'relational' in a highly specific way drawing on the relational theory of Miller, 'a feminine theory of growth

and effectiveness' (Fletcher 2001:30). Her 'relational practice' is therefore different in kind and meaning from other uses of the term in management literature, such as relational marketing, relational management.

11. Wenger (1998) also emphasises mutuality in his concept of 'communities of practice': 'At the core of processes of identification through engagement is the direct experience of mutuality characteristic of communities of practice. By recognising each other as participants, we give life to our respective social selves.' (1998:193)

12. Studies, such as Moore and Buttner's (1997) substantial survey of women entrepreneurs in the USA, Fenwick's (2002) study of learning in entrepreneurs' first few years or Warren's (2004) narrative cases, are more concerned with women making the move to self employment rather than with their practice once in business. Moore and Buttner (1997) see themselves filling 'the relative void of research [on women]' (1997:14).

13. Four fifths of their respondents name emotional support as the most important thing about networks, further echoing what I found. Two thirds said that making a difference to others, especially other women was most or next most important to them.

14. Importantly too this fragility extends to other gendered identities beyond the binary: gay, lesbian, transgender, bisexual.

15. Of course the changing landscape of women's issues affects how women act and interpret their world – thus our particular history in the UK is important and necessarily limiting, in terms of understanding the perceptions and assumptions we bring as women to our work, at this time and place, in the public sector. We have particular histories in terms of feminism, women's activism, women and work, women and management; which all affect us as consultants.

16. The impact of 'feminine' other has also been noted in different work settings, such as publishing and editing (Cameron 1987).

Chapter 10   Toward a 'Critical Consulting' Practice: The Contribution of a 'Feminine' Discourse of Consulting

1. Sturdy et al. (2006) comment on complex boundaries and how closeness and distance of actors are at once both over- and under-estimated.

2. Contempt, interestingly, is what Machiavelli most wishes his 'prince' to avoid provoking, in order to retain his position.

3. Readers may be reminded here of the 'tempered radical' concept advanced by Meyerson (2001) in referring to people working inside organisations for social change, not to the external consultant.

4. I am indebted to several women friends and colleagues working in the private sector whose reflections on their work in conversations with me addressed the 'feminine' in their approach but also raised differences in relation to values, assumptions and the prevailing (masculine) discourses of consulting that shaped their relationships at work.

References

Abolafia, M. (1998) Markets as cultures: an ethnographic approach, in M. Callon ed. *The Laws of the Markets*, pp.69–85. Oxford: Blackwell.

Acker, J. (1990) 'Hierarchies, jobs, bodies: a theory of gendered organisations', *Gender and Society*, 4, pp.139–158.

Ahl, H. (2002) The construction of the female entrepreneur as the Other, in B. Czarniawska and H. Hopfl (eds) *Casting the Other: the production and maintenance of inequalities in work organisations*, pp.52–67. London: Routledge.

Alvesson, M. (1993) 'Organisations as rhetoric: knowledge-intensive firms and the struggle with ambiguity', *Journal of Management Studies*, 30(6), pp.997–1015.

Alvesson, M. (2004) *Knowledge Work and Knowledge Intensive Firms*. Oxford: Oxford University Press.

Alvesson, M. and Deetz, S. (2000) *Doing Critical Management Research*. London: Sage.

Alvesson, M. and Johansson, A.W. (2002) Professionalism and politics in management consultancy work, in R. Fincham and T. Clark (eds) *Critical Consulting: new perspectives on the Management Advice Industry*, pp.228–246. Oxford: Blackwell.

Alvesson, M. and Karreman, D. (2000) 'Varieties of discourse: on the study of organizations through discourse analysis', *Human Relations*, 53(9), pp.1125–1149.

Alvesson, M. and Willmott, H. (1996) *Making Sense of Management: a critical introduction*. London: Sage.

Anglo, S. (1971) *Machiavelli: a dissection*. London: Paladin.

Ashford, M. (1998) *Con Tricks: the world of management consultancy and how to make it work for you*. London: Simon & Schuster.

Bacon, Sir Francis (1986) *The Essays*. London: Penguin.

Bakhtin, M. (1981) *The Dialogical Imagination*. ed. M. Holquist, trans. C. Emerson & M. Holquist. Austin: University of Texas Press.

Barker, J. (2005) *Agincourt: the king the campaign, the battle*. London: Little Brown & Co.

Barrett, F. (2002) Gender Strategies of women professionals: the case of the US Navy, in M. Dent and S. Whitehead (eds) *Managing Professional Identities: knowledge, performativity and the 'new' professional*, pp.157–173. London: Routledge.

Battersby, D. (1984) *Developing Effectiveness in a Training Consultancy Role*. MSc Thesis. Lancaster University.

Beattie, J. (1967) *The English Court in the Reign of George I*. Cambridge: Cambridge University Press.

Berglund, J. and Werr, A. (2000) 'The invincible character of management consulting rhetoric: how one blends incommensurates while keeping them apart', *Organization*, 7(4), pp.633–655.

Berry, J. (1996) 'Women and consulting – the downside', *Journal of Management Consulting*, 9(1), pp.34–38.

Best, S. and Kellner, D. (1991) *Postmodern Theory: critical interrogations*. Basingstoke: Macmillan.

Block, P. (2000) *Flawless Consulting: a guide to getting your expertise used*. 2nd ed. San Francisco: Jossey-Bass Pfeiffer.

Bloomfield, B.P. and Vurdubakis, T. (2002) The vision thing: constructing technology and the future in management advice, in T. Clark and R. Fincham (eds) *Critical Consulting: new perspectives on the management advice industry*, pp.115–129. Oxford: Blackwell Business.

Boden, D. (1994) *The Business of Talk – Organisations in Action*. Cambridge: Polity Press.

Bohm, S. (2003) 'The consulting arcade: walking through fetish-land', *Tamara: Journal of Critical Postmodern Organization Science*, 2(2) pp.20–36.

Bohmer, O. A. (1999) *The Philosophy Book*. London: Phoenix House.

Boje, D. (2001) *Narrative Methods for Organisational and Communication Research*. London: Sage.

Bolton, S. (2005) *Emotion Management in the Workplace*. Basingstoke: Palgrave Macmillan.

Bourdieu, P., Chamboredon, J-C., Passeron, J-C. 1991 [1968] *The Craft of Sociology*. trans. R. Nice. Berlin: De Gruyter.

Brown, E. (1999) 'Companion me with my mistress': Cleopatra, Elizabeth 1 and their waiting women, in S. Frye and K. Robertson (eds) *Maids and Mistresses, Cousins and Queens*, pp.131–145. Oxford: Oxford University Press.

Bruni, A. and Gherardi, S. (2002) Omega's story: the heterogeneous engineering of a gendered professional self, in M. Dent and S. Whitehead (eds) *Managing Professional Identities: knowledge, performativity and the 'new' professional*, pp.174–198. London: Routledge.

Bruni, A., Gherardi, S. and Poggio, B. (2004a) 'Entrepreneur-mentality, gender and the study of women entrepreneurs', *Journal of Organizational Change Management*, 17(3), pp.256–269.

Bruni, A., Gherardi, S. and Poggio, B. (2004b) 'Doing gender, doing entrepreneurship: an ethnographic account of intertwined practices', *Gender, Work and Organization*, 11(4), pp.406–427.

Burrell, G. (1998) Modernism, postmodernism and organizational analysis: the contribution of Michel Foucault, in A. McKinley and K. Starkey (eds) *Foucault, Management and Organisation Theory: from panopticon to technologies of self*, Chapter 2. London: Sage.

Butler, J. (1993) *Bodies that Matter: on the discursive limits of 'sex'*. London: Routledge.

Butler, J. (1999) *Gender Trouble: feminism and the subversion of identity*. 2nd edition (1st edn. 1990) London: Routledge.

Calas, M. and Smircich, L. (2003) Dangerous liaisons: the 'feminine-in-management' meets 'globalisation', in R. Ely, E. Foldy and M. Scully (eds) *Reader in Gender, Work and Organization*, Chapter 29. Oxford: Blackwell.

Callon, M. (ed.) (1998) *The Laws of the Markets*. Oxford: Blackwell.

Calvert, L.M. and Ramsey, V.J. (1992) 'Bringing women's voice to research on women in management: a feminist perspective', *Journal of Management Inquiry*, 1, pp.79–88.

Cameron, M. (1987) What the hell is feminist editing?, in G. Chester and S. Nielsen (eds) *In Other Words: writing as a feminist*, pp.119–125. London: Hutchinson.

Canback, S. (1998) 'The logic of management consulting pt 1', *Journal of Management Consulting*, 10(2), pp.3–11.

Carabine, J. (2001) Unmarried motherhood 1830–1990: a genealogical analysis, in M. Wetherall, S. Taylor, and S.J. Yates (eds) *Discourse as Data: a guide for analysis*, pp.267–310. Milton Keynes: Open University Press.

Case, P. (2002) Virtual stories of virtual working: critical reflections on ICT consultancy discourse, in T. Clark and R. Fincham (eds) *Critical Consulting: new perspectives on the management advice industry*, pp.228–246. Oxford: Blackwell Business.

Casey, C. (1995) *Work, Self and Society: after industrialism*. London: Routledge.

Cella, L. (2005) *Tensions in a Secondary English Classroom: an autoethnographic study of teacher Chang*, ed.D. dissertation New York: Columbia University Teachers College.

Chambers, R. (1997) *Whose Reality Counts? Putting the first last*. London: Intermediate Technology Publications.

Chia, R. (1996) 'The problem of reflexivity in organizational research: towards a postmodern science of organization', *Organization*, 3(1), pp.31–59.

Chia R. (1997a) 'Essai: thirty years on: from organisational structures to the organisation of thought', *Organisation Studies, Berlin*, 18(4), pp.685–707.

Chia, R. (1997b) Process philosophy and management learning: cultivating 'foresight' in management education, in J. Burgoyne and M. Reynolds (eds) *Management Learning: integrating perspectives in theory and practice*, pp.71–88. London: Sage.

Clark, P. and Rowlinson, M. (2004) 'The treatment of history in organisation studies: towards an "historic turn"?' *Business History*, 46(3), pp.331–352.

Clark, T. (1995) *Managing Consultants: consultancy as the management of impressions*. Buckingham: Open University Press (Managing Work and Organisations series ed. G. Salaman).

Clark, T. (1996) 'Managerial consulting skills: a practical guide / consultant's journey: a professional and personal odyssey' (book review), *Human Resource Management Journal London*, 6(4), pp.93–95.

Clark, T. and Fincham, R. (eds) (2002) *Critical Consulting: new perspectives on the management advice industry*. Oxford: Blackwell Business.

Clark, T. and Greatbatch, D. (2002) Collaborative relationships in the creating and fashioning of management ideas: gurus, editors and managers, in M. Kipping and L. Engwall (eds) *Management Consulting: emergence and dynamics of a knowledge industry*, pp.129–145. Oxford: Oxford University Press.

Clark, T. and Salaman, G. (1998a) 'Creating the right impression: towards a dramaturgy of management consultancy', *The Service Industries Journal*, London, 18(1), pp.18–38.

Clark, T. and Salaman, G. (1998b) 'Telling tales: management gurus' narratives and the construction of managerial identity', *Journal of Management Studies*, 35(2), pp.137–161.

Clegg, S. (1998) Foucault, power and organisations, in A. McKinley and K. Starkey (eds) *Foucault, Management and Organisation Theory: from panopticon to technologies of self*. Chapter 3. London: Sage.

Clegg, S., Kornberger, M. and Rhodes, C. (2004) 'Noise, parasites and translation: theory and practice in management consulting', *Management Learning*, 35(1), pp.31–44.

Cleverley, G. (1971) *Managers and Magic*. London: Longman.

Coghlan, D. (2001) 'Insider action research projects: implications for practising managers', *Management Learning*, 32(1), pp.49–60.

Coghlan, D. and Brannick, T. (2005) *Doing Action Research in Your Own Organisation*, 2nd edn. London: Sage.

Collins Concise Dictionary (1989) P. Hanks (ed.) 2nd edn. London: William Collins Sons & Co Ltd.

Collinson, D. and Hearn, J. (eds) (1996) *Men as Managers, Managers as Men: critical perspectives on men, masculinities and managements*. London: Sage.

Collinson, D. and Hearn, J. (2003) Breaking the silence: on men, masculinities and management, in *Reader in Gender, Work and Organisation* (eds) Ely, R., Foldy, E. and Scully, M. Oxford: Blackwell, pp. 75–78.

Conroy, M. (2007) *MacIntyre and the Manager: virtue to virtue combat for the moral high ground of the UK NHS*. Unpublished PhD thesis, University of Lancaster.

Cooper, D. (1994) 'Productive, relational and everywhere? Conceptualising power and resistance within Foucauldian feminism', *Sociology*, 28(2), pp.435–454.

Covin, T. and Harris, M. (1995) 'Viewpoint: perspectives on women in consulting', *Journal of Organisational Change Management*, 8(1), pp.7–11.

Crawford, A. (ed.) (1994) *Letters of the Queens of England 1100–1547*. Stroud: Sutton Publishing.

Crick, B. (ed.) (1970) *Machiavelli: the discourses*. Harmondsworth: Penguin Classics.

Crompton, R. (1997) *Women and Work in Modern Britain*. Oxford: Oxford University Press.

Crossley-Holland, K. (ed. trans.) (1984) *The Anglo-Saxon World: an anthology*. Oxford: Oxford University Press.

Crucini, C. (2002) Knowledge management at the country level: a large consulting firm in Italy, in M. Kipping and L. Engwall (eds) *Management Consulting: emergence and dynamics of a knowledge industry*, pp.109–128. Oxford: Oxford University Press.

Czarniawska, B. and Hopfl, H. (eds) (2002) *Casting the Other: the production and maintenance of inequalities in work organisations*. London: Routledge.

Czarniawska, B. and Mazza, C. (2003) 'Consulting as a liminal space', *Human Relations*, 56(3), pp.267–290.

Czerniawska, F. (2002a) *Management Consultancy: what next?* Basingstoke: Palgrave.

Czerniawska, F. (2002b) 'Book review: critical consulting: new perspectives on the management advice industry', *Consulting to Management*, 13(3), pp.56–58.

Czerniawska, F. (2003) 'Book review: McKenna, 2003 Ferguson, 2002; and Kipping and Engwall, 2002', *Consulting to Management*, 14(2), p.55.

Czerniawska, F. (2004) *Storm Clouds Ahead*. Brighton: University of Sussex, available at: http://www.sussex.ac.uk/spru/documents/czerniawska_slides.ppt#256,1 Fiona Czerniawska [accessed 10.08.2005].

Czerniawska, F. and May, P. (2004) *Management Consulting in Practice*. London: Kogan Page.

Czerniawska, F. and Toppin, G. (2005) *Business Consulting: a guide to how it works and how to make it work*. London: Economist Books.

Davison, R. (2002) *Salons*. Available at http://www.oup.com/us/brochure/0195104307/salons.pdf [accessed 05.05.2008].

Davies, C. (1995) *Gender and the Professional Predicament in Nursing*. Buckingham: Open University Press.

Deetz, S. (1998) Discursive formations, strategised subordination and self-surveillance, in A. McKinley and K. Starkey (eds) *Foucault, Management and Organisation Theory: from panopticon to technologies of self.* Chapter 9. London: Sage.

Dent, M. and Whitehead, S. (eds) (2002) *Managing Professional Identities: knowledge, performativity and the 'new' professional.* London: Routledge.

Denzin, N. (2003) 'Performing [auto] ethnography politically', *The Review of Education, Pedagogy and Cultural Studies*, 25, pp.257–278.

Denzin, N. and Lincoln, Y. (eds) (1998) *The Landscape of Qualitative Research.* London: Sage.

Diehl, D. and Donnelly, M. (2002) *How Did They Manage? Leadership Secrets from History.* London: Spiro Press.

Dunford, R. and Palmer, I. (1998) Discourse, organisations and paradox, in D. Grant, T. Keenoy and C. Oswick (eds) *Discourse and Organisation*, pp.214–221. London: Sage.

Ellis, C., Kiesinger, C., Tillman-Healy, L. (1997) Interactive interviewing: talking about emotional experience, in R. Hertz (ed.) *Reflexivity and Voice*, Chapter 6. London: Sage.

Ely, R., Foldy, E. and Scully, M. (eds) (2003) *Reader in Gender, Work and Organization.* Oxford: Blackwell.

Emerson, C. (1997) Section on M.M. Bakhtin, in M. Groden and M. Kreiswirth (eds) *The John Hopkins Guide to Literary Theory and Criticism.* Baltimore: John Hopkins University Press, available at: http://www.press.jhu.edu/books/hopkins_guide_to_literary_theory/g-index.html [accessed 04.08.2005].

Esprit Consulting (1992) *UK Management Consultants and the Small/Medium Firm, study of the Business Growth Training option 3 programme.* London: The HRD Partnership.

Everything2: open source web encyclopaedia available at: http://everything2.com/index.pl?node_id=1272019 [accessed 05.05.2008].

Fairclough, N. (1989) *Language and Power.* Harlow: Longman.

Fairclough, N. (1992) *Discourse and Social Change.* Cambridge: Polity Press.

Fairclough, N. (2001) The discourse of New Labour: critical discourse analysis, in M. Wetherall, S. Taylor, S.J. Yates (eds) *Discourse as Data: a guide for analysis*, pp.229–266. Milton Keynes: Open University Press.

Fairclough, N. (2003) *Analysing Discourse: textual analysis for social research.* London: Routledge.

Fairclough, N. (2005) 'Discourse analysis in organization studies: the case for critical realism', *Organisation Studies*, 26(6), pp.915–939.

Fairclough, N. and Hardy, G. (1997) Management learning as discourse, in J. Burgoyne and M. Reynolds (eds) *Management Learning: integrating perspectives in theory and practice*, pp.144–160. London: Sage.

Fairclough, N., Graham, P., Lemke, J. and Wodak, R. (2004) 'Introduction', *Critical Discourse Studies*, 1(1), pp.1–7.

Fairclough, N. and Thomas, P. (2004) The discourse of globalisation and the globalisation of discourse, in D. Grant, C. Hardy, C. Oswick and L. Putnam (eds) *The SAGE Handbook of Organizational Discourse*, pp.379–396. London: Sage.

Faust, M. (2002) Consultancies as actors in knowledge arenas: evidence from Germany, in M. Kipping and L. Engwall (eds) *Management Consulting: emergence and dynamics of a knowledge industry*, pp.146–166. Oxford: Oxford University Press.

Fenwick, T. (2002) 'Lady, Inc.: women learning, negotiating subjectivity in entrepreneurial discourses', *International Journal of Lifelong Education*, 21(2), pp.162–177.

Ferree, M. (2003) 'Practice makes perfect? A comment on Yancey Martin's gendering practices, practicing gender', *Gender & Society*, 17(3), pp.373–378.

Fincham, R. (1999a) *Rhetorical Narratives and the Consultancy Process*. Paper presented to the British Academy of Management Conference, Manchester 1–3 September.

Fincham, R. (1999b) 'The consultant: client relationship: critical perspectives on the management of organisational change', *Journal of Management Studies*, 36(3), pp.335–352.

Fincham, R. (2000a) *Knowledge Work as an Occupational Strategy: the cases of IT and management consultancy in the UK*. Paper presented to 16th EGOS Colloquium Helsinki 2–4 July (published 2006 as 'Knowledge work as occupational strategy: comparing IT and management consulting', *New Technology, Work and Employment*, 21(1), pp.16–28).

Fincham, R. (2000b) Divergence or convergence? Reengineering and the search for business salvation, in D. Knights and H. Wilmott (eds) *The Re-engineering Revolution: critical studies of corporate change*, pp.174–191. London: Sage.

Fincham, R. (2002) Charisma vs. technique: differentiating the expertise of management gurus and management consultants, in T. Clark and R. Fincham (eds) *Critical Consulting: new perspectives on the Management Advice Industry*, pp.191–205. Oxford: Blackwell Business.

Fincham, R. (2003) 'The agent's agent: power, knowledge, and uncertainty in management consultancy', *International Studies of Management & Organization*, 32(4), pp.67–86.

Fincham, R. (2006) 'Knowledge work as occupational strategy: comparing IT and management consulting', *New Technology, Work and Employment*, 21(1), pp.16–28.

Fincham, R. and Clark, T. (2003) 'Management consultancy: issues, perspectives, and agendas', *International Studies of Management & Organization*, 32(4), pp.3–18.

Fincham, R. and Evans, M. (1998) 'The consultants' offensive: re-engineering – from fad to technique', *New Technology, Work and Employment*, 14(1), pp.50–62.

Finch-Lees, T., Mabey, C. and Liefooghe, A. (2005) 'In the name of capability': a critical discursive evaluation of competency-based management development', *Human Relations*, 58(9), pp.1185–1222.

Fineman, S. (ed.) (2000) *Emotion in Organisations*. 2nd edition, London: Sage.

Fineman, S. (2003) *Understanding Emotions at Work*. London: Sage.

Fineman, S. and Sturdy, A. (1999) 'The emotions of control: a qualitative exploration of environmental regulation', *Human Relations*, 52(5), pp.631–663.

Fleetwood, S. (2005) 'Ontology in Organization and Management Studies: A Critical Realist Perspective', *Organization*, 12(2), pp.197–222.

Fletcher, J.K. (1998) 'Relational practice: a feminist re-construction of work', *Journal of Management Inquiry*, 7(2), pp.168–186.

Fletcher, J.K. (2001) *Disappearing Acts: gender, power and relational practice at work*. Cambridge, Mass.: MIT Press.

Fletcher, J.K. and Beard, S.B. (2005) *Practical Pushing: creating discursive space in organisational narratives*. Paper presented to the 4th International Critical Management Studies conference, Cambridge, UK.

Follett, M.P. (1926–27) *Letters to Lyndall Urwick*, Urwick Papers held at Powergen Library, Henley College, box 14, ref 12/1/12.

Foucault, M. (1984a) Truth and power, in P. Rabinow (ed.) *The Foucault Reader: an introduction to Foucault's thought*, pp.51–75. London: Penguin.

Foucault, M. (1984b) Nietzsche, genealogy, history, in P. Rabinow (ed.) *The Foucault Reader: an introduction to Foucault's thought*, pp.76–100. London: Penguin.

Foucault, M. (1984c) On the genealogy of ethics: an overview of work in progress, in P. Rabinow (ed.) *The Foucault Reader: an introduction to Foucault's thought*, pp.340–372. London: Penguin.

Foucault, M. (1984d) Politics and ethics: an interview, in P. Rabinow (ed.) *The Foucault Reader: an introduction to Foucault's thought*, pp.373–380. London: Penguin.

Foucault, M. (2002) *The Order of Things*. London: Routledge Classics.

Fournier, V. (2002) Keeping the veil of otherness: practicing disconnection, in B. Czarniawska and H. Hopfl (eds) *Casting the Other: the production and maintenance of inequalities in work organisations*, pp.68–88. London: Routledge.

Fox, S. (2000) 'Communities of practice, Foucault and actor-network theory', *Journal of Management Studies*, 37(6), pp.853–867.

Franko, E. (2004) *Coffee, Discourse and Democracy*, paper from her thesis. Available at http://www.elizabethfranko.com/coffee.pdf [accessed 05.05.2008].

Fullerton, J. and West, M. (1992) *Management Consultancy: dimensions of client-consultant relationships*, ESRC research centre discussion paper 99, London: LSE Centre for Economic Performance.

Gabriel, Y. (2004) Narratives, stories and texts, in D. Grant, C. Hardy, C. Oswick and L. Putnam (eds) *The SAGE Handbook of Organizational Discourse*, pp.61–77. London: Sage.

Gammelsoeter, H, (2002) Managers and consultants as embedded actors: evidence from Norway, in M. Kipping and L. Engwall (eds) *Management Consulting: emergence and dynamics of a knowledge industry*, pp.222–237. Oxford: Oxford University Press.

Gealy, J., Larwood L. and Elliott, M.P. (1979) 'Where sex counts: effects of consultant and client gender in management consulting', *Group and Organization Studies*, 4(2), pp.201–211.

Gherardi, S. (1994) 'The gender we think, the gender we do on our everyday organizational lives', *Human Relations*, 47(6), pp.591–611.

Giddens, A. (1991) *Modernity and Self-Identity: self and society in the late modern age*. Cambridge: Polity Press.

Gini, A. (1998) 'Work, identity and self: how we are formed by the work we do', *Journal of Business Ethics*, 17(7), pp.707–714.

Goleman, D. (1998) *Working with Emotional Intelligence*. New York: Bantam Books.

Gosling, J. (1999) *Murder in the Chapel*. Paper presented to the First International Critical Management Studies Conference, Manchester.

Graham, P. (1991) *Integrative Management*. London: Blackwell.

Grant, D., Hardy, C., Oswick, C. and Putnam, L. (eds) (2004) *The SAGE Handbook of Organizational Discourse*. London: Sage.

Grant, D., Keenoy, T. and Oswick, C. (eds) (1998) *Discourse and Organisation*. London: Sage.

Greiner, L.E. and Metzger, R.O. (1983) *Consulting to Management: insights to building and managing a successful practice*. Englewood Cliffs NJ: Prentice Hall.

Grey, C. (2003) 'The fetish of change', *Tamara: Journal of Critical Postmodern Organization Science*, 2(2), pp.1–19.

Griffin, A.C. (2001) 'Maintaining credibility and authenticity', *Consulting to Management*, 12(3), pp.21–24. Book review.

Grimm, Baron de (1815) *Historical and Literary Memoirs and Anecdotes*, Vol. 3, pp.400–405. London: Henry Colburn, available at: http://www.fordham.edu/halsall/mod/18salons.html [accessed 05.05.2008]

Guy, M.E. and Newman, M.A. (2004) 'Women's jobs, men's jobs: sex segregation and emotional labour', *Public Administration Review*, 64(3), pp.289–298.

Hackley, C. (2000) 'Silent running: tacit, discursive and psychological aspects of management in a top UK advertising agency', *British Journal of Management*, 11, pp.239–254.

Hall, S. (1996) Who needs identity?, in S. Hall and P. du Gay (eds) *Questions of Cultural Identity*, Chapter 1. London: Sage.

Hall, S. (ed.) (1997) *Representation: cultural representation and signifying practices*. London: Sage.

Handley, K., Clark, T., Fincham, R. and Sturdy, A. (2007) 'Researching situated learning: participation, identity and practices in client-consultant relationships', *Management Learning*, 38(2), pp.173–191.

Hardy, C. and Phillips, N. (2004) Discourse and power, in D. Grant, C. Hardy, C. Oswick and L. Putnam (eds) *The SAGE Handbook of Organizational Discourse*, pp.299–316. London: Sage.

Harriman, A. (1996) *Women/Men/Management*, 2nd edn. Westport CT: Praeger.

Harris, L.C. (2002) 'The emotional labour of barristers: an exploration of emotional labour by status professionals', *Journal of Management Studies*, 39(4), pp.553–584.

Harris, M. (1995) 'What has it been like to be a woman consultant over the last two decades?', *Journal of Organizational Change Management*, 8(1), pp.32–43.

Harvey, B. (2005) *Caught in 'No-Mans Land? Consultancy and critique*. Paper presented to 4th International Critical Management Studies Conference, Cambridge, UK.

Hatcher, C. (2003) 'Refashioning a passionate manager: gender at work', *Gender, Work and Organization*, 10(4), pp.391–412.

Hayano, D.M. (1979) 'Auto-ethnography: paradigms, problems and prospects', *Human Organization*, 38(1), pp.99–104.

Heller, F. (2002) What next? More critique of consultants, gurus and managers, in T. Clark and R. Fincham (eds) *Critical Consulting: new perspectives on the Management Advice Industry*, pp.260–272. Oxford: Blackwell Business.

Hertz, R. (ed.) (1997) *Reflexivity and Voice*. London: Sage.

Hirst, A. (2003) *The Art of Cross-Dressing: Spanning social distance in public services management*. MPhil thesis University of Lancaster.

Hochschild, A. (1983) *The Managed Heart: commercialisation of human feeling*. Berkeley, CA: University of California Press.

Hodgson, D. (2005) 'Putting on a professional performance: performativity, subversion and project management', *Organization*, 12(1), pp.51–68.

Hoggett, P. (2006) 'Conflict, ambivalence, and the contested purpose of public organizations', *Human Relations*, 59(2), pp.175–194.

Holmes, G. (1982) *Augustan England: professions, state and society 1680–1730*. London: George Allen & Unwin.

Howard, J. and Hollander, J. (1997) *Gendered Situations, Gendered Selves: a gender lens on social psychology*. London: Sage.

Howell, M. (1998) *Eleanor of Provence: queenship in thirteenth century England*. Oxford: Blackwell.

Hughes, C. (1999) 'Learning to be intellectually insecure: the dis/empowering effects of reflexive practice', *International Journal of Social Research Methodology*, 1(4), pp.281–296.

Institute of Management Consultancy (2008) *Introducing the New Management Consultancy Competence Framework*. Available at http://www.imc.co.uk/ our_standards/competence_framework.php [accessed 10.02.2008].

Jackall, R. (1988) *Moral Mazes – the world of corporate managers*. New York: Oxford University Press.

Jackson, N. and Carter, P. (1998) Labour as dressage, in A. McKinley and K. Starkey (eds) *Foucault, Management and Organisation Theory: from panopticon to technologies of self*, Chapter 4. London: Sage.

James, M. (2005) 'Could we be witnessing a transformation in the consulting industry?', *Consulting Times*, November available at: http://www.consulting-times.com/November2005/1.aspx [accessed 15.04.2006].

Jarrett, M. (2001) 'Consulting to the Public Sector', in *Management Consultancy: A Handbook for Best Practice*. P. Sadler (ed.) 2nd edn, pp.383–397. London: Kogan Page.

Kamen, H. (1997) *Philip of Spain*. New Haven, Ct: Yale University Press.

Kaplan, K. (1995) 'Women's voices in organizational development: questions, stories and implications', *Journal of Organizational Change Management*, 8(1), pp.52–80.

Kent, Princess Michael of (2004) *The Serpent and the Moon: two rivals for the love of a renaissance king*. New York: Touchstone.

Kerfoot, D. (2002) Managing the 'professional' man, in M. Dent and S. Whitehead (eds) *Managing Professional Identities: knowledge, performativity and the 'new' professional*, pp.81–95. London: Routledge.

Kets de Vries, M.F.R. (1990) 'The organisational fool: balancing a leader's hubris', *Human Relations*, 4(3), pp.751–770.

Kieser, A. (1994) 'Why organisational theory needs historical analyses – and how this should be performed', *Organization Science*, 5(4), pp.608–620.

Kieser, A. (2002) On communication barriers between management science, consultancies and business organisations, in T. Clark and R. Fincham (eds) *Critical Consulting: new perspectives on the management advice industry*, pp.206–227. Oxford: Blackwell Business.

King, K. (2005) *Towards Relational Consulting*, Paper presented to SOLAR Co-Inquiry Forum 26 April, Bristol.

King, K. (2004) *Relational Practice in Organization Consulting*, PhD thesis, University of Bath, available at: http://www.bath.ac.uk/carpp/publications/doc_theses_links/k_king.html [accessed 31.03.2008].

Kipping, M. (2002) Trapped in their wave: the evolution of management consultancies, in T. Clark and R. Fincham (eds) *Critical Consulting: new perspectives on the management advice industry*, pp.28–49. Oxford: Blackwell Business.

Kipping, M. and Armbruster, T. (2002) The burden of otherness: limits of consultancy interventions in historical case studies, in M. Kipping and L. Engwall (eds) *Management Consulting: emergence and dynamics of a knowledge industry*, pp.203–221. Oxford: Oxford University Press.

Kipping, M. and Engwall, L. (eds) (2002) *Management Consulting: emergence and dynamics of a knowledge industry*. Oxford: Oxford University Press.

Kitsopoulos, S. (2003) 'Consulting's origins', *Consulting to Management*, 14(1), pp.16–17.

Klat-Smith, A. (2005) 'Anthony Buono (ed.): current trends in management consulting (Research in management consulting Vol. 1) 2001 Greenwich CT: Information Age Publishing' (book review), *Organization Studies*, 26(6), pp.959 –966.

Knights, D. and Kerfoot, D. (2004) 'Between representations and subjectivity: gender binaries and the politics of organizational transformation', *Gender, Work and Organization*, 11(4), pp.430–454.

Kolb, D. (2003) Gender and the shadow negotiation, in R. Ely, E. Foldy and M. Scully (eds) *Reader in Gender, Work and Organization*, pp.129–134. Oxford: Blackwell.

Kondo, D. (1990) *Crafting Selves: power, gender and discourses of identity*. Chicago: University of Chicago Press.

Kristeva, J. (1986) Word, dialogue and novel, in T. Moi (ed.) *The Kristeva Reader*. Oxford: Blackwell, pp. 24–33.

Kubr, M. (ed.) (2002) *Management Consulting: a guide to the profession*, 4th edition. Geneva: International Labour Office.

Law, J. (1994) *Organising Modernity*. Oxford: Blackwell.

Legge, J. (trans) (1895) *The Chinese Classics, Volume II, The Works of Mencius*. Oxford: The Clarendon Press, available at http://www.humanistictexts.org/mencius.htm#_Toc483368133 [accessed 06.05.2005].

Legge, K. (1994) On knowledge, business consultants and the selling of Total Quality Management, unpublished paper. University of Lancaster.

Legge, K. (2002) On knowledge, business consultants and the selling of Total Quality Management, in T. Clark and R. Fincham (eds) *Critical Consulting: new perspectives on the management advice industry*. Oxford: Blackwell Business.

Levy, G.R. (1956) *Plato in Sicily*. London: Faber & Faber.

Lewis, H. (1992) *Age of Enlightenment*. available at http://history-world.org/age_of_enlightenment.htm [accessed 06.06.2005].

Lewis, P. (2005) 'Suppression or expression: an exploration of emotion management in a special care baby unit', *Work, Employment and Society*, 19(3), pp.565–581.

Leyser, H. (1995) *Medieval Women: a social history of women in England 1450–1500*. London: Weidenfeld & Nicholson.

Lieblich, A., Tuval-Mashiach, R. and Zilber, T. (1998) *Narrative Research: reading, analysis and interpretation*. London: Sage.

Linstead, A. and Brewis, J. (2004) 'Editorial: beyond boundaries: towards fluidity in theorizing and practice', *Gender Work and Organization*, 11(4), pp.355–362.

Lippitt, G. and Lippitt, R. (1986) *The Consulting Process in Action*. San Francisco: Jossey-Bass/Pfeiffer.

Lister, J. (2005) *Health Policy Reform: Driving the wrong way?*, London: Middlesex University Press.

Lorbiecki, A. and Jack, G. (2000) 'Critical turns in the evolution of diversity management', *British Journal of Management Special Issue*, 11(3), S.17–S.31.

Lutz, C. (1996) Engendered emotion: gender, power, and the rhetoric of emotional control in American discourse, in R. Harre and W.G. Parrot (eds) *The emotions*, pp.152–170. Thousand Oaks, CA: Sage.

Macalpine, M. and Marsh, S. (1999) *Can You Have Critical Management as well as Improve Services?* Paper presented at the First International Critical Management Studies Conference, Manchester, UK.

Macalpine, M. and Marsh, S. (2005) 'On being white: 'there's nothing I can say' exploring whiteness and power in organisations', *Management Learning*, 36(4), pp.429–450.

Machiavelli, N. (2001) [1513 written/1532 pub] *The Prince*. Q. Skinner and R. Price (eds) Cambridge: Cambridge University Press.

Maddock, S. (1999) *Challenging Women: gender, culture and organisation*. London: Sage.

Maister, D.H., Green, C.H. and Galford, R.M. (2000) 'What is a trusted advisor?', *Consulting to Management*, 11(3), pp.36–41.

Mangham, I. (1990) 'Managing as a performing art', *British Journal of Management*, 1, pp.105–115.

Mangham, I. (1998) Emotional discourse in organizations, in D. Grant, T. Keenoy and C. Oswick (eds) *Discourse and Organisation*, pp.51–64. London: Sage.

Marsella, A.J., DeVos, G. and Hsu, F.L.K. (eds) (1985) *Culture and Self: Asian and Western perspectives*. London: Tavistock Publications.

Marsh, S. (1992) *The Purchase Decision of Clients in Management Consultancy and its Impact on the Marketing of Small Consulting Firms*. unpublished MBA dissertation, University of Warwick.

Marsh, S. (1996) 'Cautionary tales of managing in the internal market: a comparative look at public and private sector experiences of support services', *Journal of Management Development*, 15(2), pp.69–79.

Marsh, S. and Macalpine, M. (2002) 'Perversity and absurdity in "high" managerialism: the role of management educators'. Paper presented at the Connecting Learning and Critique Conference, Cambridge, July. Available at: www.swampyground.org [accessed 05.05.2008].

Marshall, J. (1994) Re-visioning organizations by developing female values, in R. Boot, J. Lawrence and J. Morris (eds) *Managing the Unknown: By creating new futures*, pp.165–183. London: McGraw Hill.

Martin, P.Y. (2003) '"Said and done" versus "saying and doing": gendering practices, practicing gender at work', *Gender & Society*, 17(3), pp.342–366.

Martin, P.Y. and Collinson, D. (2002) 'Over the pond and across the water: developing the field of "gendered organizations"', *Gender, Work and Organization*, 9(3), pp.244–265.

Mason, A.G. (2001) [1891] *The Women of the French Salons*. Available as e-book at: http://www.fullbooks.com/The-Women-of-the-French-Salons5.html [accessed 20.12.04].

Mason, J. (1996) *Qualitative Researching*. London: Sage.

Matthews, P. and Satsangi, M. (2007) 'Planners, developers and power: a critical discourse analysis of the redevelopment of Leith Docks, Scotland', *Planning Practice & Research*, 22(4), pp.495–511.

McHoul, A. and Rapley, M. (2005) 'A case of attention-deficit/hyperactivity disorder diagnosis: Sir Karl and Francis B. slug it out on the consulting room floor', *Discourse and Society*, 16(3), pp.419–449.

McKenna, C. (2001) 'The world's newest profession: management consulting in the twentieth century', *Enterprise and Society*, 2, pp.673–679. (Also published as *The World's Newest Profession: Management Consulting in the Twentieth Century*. New York: Cambridge University Press, 2003).

McKinley, A. and Starkey, K. (eds) (1998) *Foucault Management and Organisation Theory: from panopticon to technologies of self*. London: Sage.

McLachlin, R.D. (1999) 'Factors for consulting engagement success', *Management Decision*, 37(5), pp.394–402.

Mears, N. (2005) *Queenship and Political Discourse in the Elizabethan Realms*. Cambridge: Cambridge University Press.

Meriläinen, S., Tienari, J., Thomas, R. and Davies, A. (2004) 'Management consultant talk: a cross-cultural comparison of normalizing discourse and resistance', *Organization*, 11(4), pp.539–564.

Metzger, M.J. (1990) 'Double Gestures: feminist critiques and the search for a usable practice' (review essay), *Hypatia*, 5(3), pp.118–124.

Meyerson, D. (2001) 'Radical change, the quiet way', *Harvard Business Review*, 79(9), pp.92–100.

Miller, J.B. (1976) *Toward a New Psychology of Women*. Boston: Beacon Press.

Miller, J.B. (1982) *Women and Power: some psychological dimensions*, Work in Progress paper 1. Wellesley MA: Wellesley Centers for Women (Stone Center).

Mills, S. (2003) 'Third wave feminist linguistics and the analysis of sexism', *Discourse Analysis Online*, available at: http://www.shu.ac.uk/daol/articles/open/2003/001/mills2003001-paper.html#citation25 [accessed 05.05.2008].

Mirchandani, K. (2003) 'Challenging racial silences in studies of emotion work: contributions from anti-racist feminist theory', *Organization Studies*, 24(5), pp.721–742.

Moore, D.P. and Buttner, E.H. (1997) *Women Entrepreneurs: moving beyond the glass ceiling*. London: Sage.

Morales-Lopéz, E., Prego-Vásquez, G. and Domínguez-Seca, L. (2005) 'Interviews between employees and customers during a company restructuring process', *Discourse and Society*, 16(2), pp.225–268.

Morris, J. and Feldman, D. (1996) 'The dimensions, antecedents, and consequences of emotional labor', *The Academy of Management Review*, 21(4), pp.986–1011.

Mumby, D. (2004) Discourse, power and ideology: unpacking the critical approach, in D. Grant, C. Hardy, C. Oswick and L. Putnam (eds) *The SAGE Handbook of Organizational Discourse*, pp.237–258. London: Sage.

Mumby, D. and Putnam, L. (1992) 'The politics of emotion: a feminist reading of bounded rationality', *The Academy of Management Review*, 17(3), pp.465–487.

Mutch, A. (2005) 'Discussion of Wilmott: critical realism, agency and discourse: moving the debate forward', *Organization*, 12(5), pp.781–786.

Nayak, A. (2008) 'On the way to theory: a processual approach', *Organization Studies*, 29(2), pp.173–190.

Nederman, C.J. (2001) The monarch and the marketplace: economic policy and royal finance', in William of Pagula's *Speculum regis Edwardi III' History of Political Economy*, 33(1), pp.51–69.

Neumann, J., Kellner, K. and Dawson-Shepherd, A. (eds) (1997) *Developing Organisational Consultancy*. London: Routledge.

O'Day, R. (2000) *The Professions in Early Modern England, 1450–1800*. Harlow: Pearson Education Ltd.

Otto, B. (2001) *Fools Are Everywhere: The Court Jester Around the World*. Chicago: University of Chicago Press. Extract, pp.233–247 available at: http://www.press.uchicago.edu/Misc/Chicago/640914in.html [accessed 05.08.2005].

Padavic, I. and Reskin, B. (2002) *Women and Men at Work*, 2nd edn. London: Sage (*Sociology for a new century* Series at Pine Forge Press).

Page, M. (2005) *Silences and Disappearing Acts: the politics of gendering organisational practice*. Paper presented to the 4th International Critical Management Studies conference, Cambridge, UK. (Published in T. LeTrent-Jones, M. Vonorov, D. Weir and J. Wolfram-Cox (eds) (2009 forthcoming) *Critical Management Studies at Work: multidisciplinary approaches to negotiating tensions between theory and practice*. London: Edward Elgar).

Parker, M. (2002) *Against Management: organisation in the age of managerialism*. Cambridge: Polity Press.

Parkin, W. (1993) The public and the private: gender, sexuality and emotion, in S. Fineman (ed.) *Emotion in Organisations*, pp.167–189. London: Sage.

Pellegrinelli, S. (2002) 'Managing the interplay and tensions of consulting interventions: the consultant-client relationship as mediation and reconciliation', *Journal of Management Development*, 21(5/6), pp.343–367.

Perren, L. and Jennings, P. (2005) 'Government discourses on entrepreneurship: issues of legitimization, subjugation, and power', *Entrepreneurship Theory and Practice*, 29(2), pp.173–184.

Perriton, L. (2001) 'Sleeping with the enemy: exploiting the textual turn in management research', *International Journal of Social Research Methodology*, 4(1), pp.35–50.

Plato (1976) [c380 BCE] *The Republic*. Trans. A.D. Lindsay, intro. R. Bambrough. London: Dent.

Plato (2006) *7th Letter*. Trans. J. Harward, available at http://evans-experientialism.freewebspace.com/plato_seventh_letter01.htm [accessed 05.06.2006].

Poulfelt, F. and Paynee, A. (1994) 'Management consultants: Client and consultant perspectives', *Scandinavian Journal of Management*, 10(4), pp.421–436.

Powell, G. and Graves, L. (2003) *Women and Men in Management*, 3rd edition. London: Sage.

Pratt, J. Gordon, P. and Plamping, D. (1999) *Working Whole Systems: putting theory into practice in organisations*. London: King's Fund.

Pritchard, C., Jones, D. and Stablein, R. (2004) Doing research in organisational discourse: the importance of researcher context, in D. Grant, C. Hardy, C. Oswick and L. Putnam (eds) *The SAGE Handbook of Organizational Discourse*, pp.213–236. London: Sage.

Putnam, L. and Cooren, F. (2004) 'Alternative perspectives on the role of text and agency in constituting organizations', *Organization*, 11(3), pp.323–333 [introduction to special issue].

Putnam, L. and Kolb, D. (2003) Rethinking negotiation: feminist views of communication and exchange, in R. Ely, E. Foldy and M. Scully (eds) *Reader in Gender, Work and Organization*, pp.135–150. Oxford: Blackwell.

Rabinow P. (ed.) (1984) *The Foucault Reader: an introduction to Foucault's thought*. London: Penguin.

Ram, M. (2000) 'Hustling, hassling and making it happen: researching consultants in a small firm context', *Organization*, 7(4), pp.657–677.

Rawson, E. (1989) Roman rulers and the philosophic adviser, in M. Griffin and J. Barnes (eds) *Philosophia Togata: essays on philosophy and Roman society*, pp.233–257. Oxford: Clarendon Press.

Reed-Danahay, D. (1997) *Auto/Ethnography*. Oxford: Berg.

Rehman, L. and Frisby, W. (2000) 'Is self-employment liberating or marginalising? The case of women consultants in the fitness and sport industry', *Journal of Sport Management*, 14, pp.41–62.

Rescher, N. (1996) *Process Metaphysics: an introduction to process philosophy*. Albany: State University of New York Press.

Reynolds, M. and Vince, R. (eds) (2004) *Organising Reflection*. Aldershot: Ashgate Publishing.

Ritchie, A. (2001) *Alcuin of York*. Available at: http://www.bbc.co.uk/history/ancient/vikings/alcuin_04.shtml [accessed 05.05.2008].

Robillard, A. (1997) Communication problems in the ITU, in R. Hertz (ed.) *Reflexivity and Voice*, Chapter 12. London: Sage.

Rose, N. (1996) Identity, genealogy, history, in S. Hall and P. du Gay (eds) *Questions of Cultural Identity*, Chapter 25. London: Sage.

Rose, N. (1999) *Governing the Soul*. 2nd edn. London: Free Association Books.

Ross-Smith, A. and Kornberger, M. (2004) 'Gendered rationality? A genealogical exploration of the philosophical and sociological conceptions of rationality, masculinity and organization', *Gender, Work and Organization*, 11(3), pp.280–305.

Sadler, P. (ed.) (2001) *Management Consultancy: a handbook for best practice*. London: Kogan Page.

Saint-Martin, D. (2000) *Building the New Managerialist State: consultants and the politics of public sector reform in comparative perspective*. Oxford: Oxford University Press.

Salacuse, J.W. (2000) *The Wise Advisor: what every professional should know about consulting and counseling*. Westport, Conn: Praeger. Available at: http://www.netlibrary.com/Reader/ [accessed as e-book 16.10.2004].

Salaman, G. (2002) Understanding advice: towards a sociology of management consultancy, in T. Clark and R. Fincham (eds) *Critical Consulting: new perspectives on the management advice industry*, pp.247–259. Oxford: Blackwell Business.

Samra-Fredericks, D. (2005a) 'Strategic practice, "discourse" and the everyday interactional constitution of "power effects"', *Organization*, 12(6), pp.803–841.

Samra-Fredericks, D. (2005b) *Strategic Practice and Researching 'the Everyday'*, Paper presented to the 4th International Critical Management Studies conference, Cambridge, UK.

Sass, J.S. (1997) 'Emotional labor as cultural performance: the communication of care-giving in a nonprofit nursing home', *Western Journal of Communication*, 64(3), pp.330–358.

Sayer, A. (2000) 'Moral economy and political economy', *Studies in Political Economy,* Spring, pp.79–103.

Sayer, A. (2005) Approaching moral economy, in N. Stehr, C. Henning, and B. Weiler (eds) *The Moralization of the Markets,* pp.77–97. New Brunswick, New Jersey: Transaction Books.

Scarbrough, H. (1995) 'Blackboxes, hostages and prisoners', *Organisation Studies,* 16(6), pp.991–1019.

Schein, E. (2002) Consulting: what should it mean?, in T. Clark and R. Fincham (eds) *Critical Consulting: new perspectives on the management advice industry,* pp.21–27. Oxford: Blackwell Business.

Sen, A. (1999) *Reason before Identity, The Romanes Lecture for 1998.* Oxford: Oxford University Press.

Senge, P., Roberts, C., Ross R.B., Smith, B.J. and Kleiner, A. (1994) *The Fifth Discipline Fieldbook: strategies and tools for building a learning organisation.* London: Nicholas Brealey.

Shaw, P. (1997) 'Intervening in the shadow systems of organisations: consulting from a complexity perspective', *Journal of Organizational Change Management,* 10(3), pp.235–250.

Simpson, R. and Lewis, P. (2005) 'An investigation of silence and a scrutiny of transparency: re-examining gender in organization literature through the concepts of voice and visibility', *Human Relations,* 58(10), pp.1253–1275.

Smith, D.E. (1988) *The Everyday World as Problematic: a feminist sociology.* Milton Keynes: Open University Press.

Smith, R. (2000) *Mind for Hire: a practitioner's guide to management consulting,* Nedlands: University of Western Australia Press.

Sorge, A. and van Witteloostuijn, A. (2004) 'The (non)sense of organizational change: an Essai about universal management hypes, sick consultancy metaphors, and healthy organization theories', *Organization Studies,* 25(7), pp.205–1231.

spirit hawk collective (Schor, S., Kane, K. and Lindsey, C.) (1995) 'Three women's stories of feeling, reflection, voice and nurturance: from life to consulting', *Journal of Organizational Change Management,* 8(1), pp.39–57.

St Clare Byrne, M. (ed.) (1985) *The Lisle Letters.* Harmondsworth: Penguin.

Sturdy, A. (1997a) 'The consultancy process – an insecure business', *Journal of Management Studies,* 34(3), pp.389–413.

Sturdy, A. (1997b) 'The dialectics of consultancy', *Critical Perspectives on Accounting,* 8, pp.511–535.

Sturdy, A. (1998) 'Customer care in a consumer society: smiling and sometimes meaning it?', *Organization,* 5(1), pp.27–53.

Sturdy, A. (2002) Front-line diffusion: the production and negotiation of knowledge through training interactions, in T. Clark and R. Fincham (eds) *Critical Consulting: new perspectives on the management advice industry.* Oxford: Blackwell Business.

Sturdy, A. (2003) 'Knowing the unknowable? A discussion of methodological and theoretical issues in emotion research and organization studies', *Organization,* 10(1), pp.81–105.

Sturdy, A., Clark, T., Fincham, R. and Handley, K. (2004) 'Silence, procrustes and colonization – a response to Clegg *et al.*'s "Noise, parasites and translation: theory and practice in management consulting"', *Management Learning,* 35(3), pp.337–340.

Sturdy, A., Clark, T., Fincham, R. and Handley, K. (2006) *Boundary Complexity in Management Consultancy Projects – re-thinking potentials for knowledge flow*. EBK Working Paper 2006/06, available at: www.ebkresearch.org [accessed 18.05.2006].

Sturdy, A., Clark, T., Fincham, R. and Handley, K. (2008) Management consultancy and humour in action and context, in S. Fineman (ed.) *The Emotional Organization*, pp. 134–153. Oxford: Blackwell.

Sullivan, N. (2003) A critical introduction to queer theory. Edinburgh: Edinburgh University Press.

Tannen, D. (1992) *You Just Don't Understand: women and men in conversation*. London: Virago Press.

Taylor, M. (1999) 'Unwrapping stock transfers: applying discourse analysis to landlord communication strategies', *Urban Studies*, 36(1), pp.121–135.

Taylor, S. (2001a) Locating and conducting discourse analytic research, in M. Wetherall, S. Taylor and S.J. Yates (eds) *Discourse as Data: a guide for analysis*. pp.5–48. Milton Keynes: Open University Press.

Taylor, S. (2001b) Evaluating and applying discourse analytic research, in M. Wetherall, S. Taylor, S.J. Yates (eds) *Discourse as Data: a guide for analysis*, pp.311–330. Milton Keynes: Open University Press.

Teo, P. (2000) 'Racism in the news: a critical discourse analysis of news reporting in two Australian newspapers', *Discourse & Society*, 11(1), pp.7–49.

Thomas, P. (2003) 'The recontextualisation of management: a discourse-based approach to analysing the development of management thinking', *Journal of Management Studies*, 40(4), pp.777–801.

Tisdall, P. (1982) *Agents of Change: the development and practice of management consultancy*. London: Heinemann, in association with Institute of Management Consultants.

Tonn, J. (2004) *Mary P. Follett: creating democracy, transforming management*. New Haven: Yale University Press.

Turnbull, N. (1999) *Get a Grip on Philosophy*. London: Weidenfeld & Nicholson.

Tyldesley, J. (1998a) *Daughters of Isis: women of ancient Egypt*. London: Penguin.

Tyldesley, J. (1998b) *Nefertiti: Egypt's sun queen*. London: Viking.

Urwick, L. (1950) *Letter 21st March in Urwick Papers*, Henley College Box 14 ref 12/47.

van Dijk, T. (1993) 'Principles of critical discourse analysis', *Discourse and Society*, 4(2), pp.249–283.

van Es, R. (2002) 'From impartial advocates to political agents: role switching and trustworthiness in consultancy', *Journal of Business Ethics*, 39(1/2), pp.145–151.

Van Maanen, J. (1988) *Tales of the Field*. London: University of Chicago Press.

Waclawski, J., Church, A. and Burke, W. (1995) 'Women in organization development: a profile of the intervention styles and values of today's practitioners', *Journal of Organizational Change Management*, 8(1), pp.12–22.

Waldron, V. (2000) 'Relational experiences and emotion at work', in *Emotion in Organizations*, ed. S. Fineman, 2nd edition, Ch. 4. London: Sage.

Warren, L. (2004) 'Negotiating entrepreneurial identity – communities of practice and changing discourses', *International Journal of Entrepreneurship & Innovation*, 5(1), pp.25–35.

Weedon, C. (1987) *Feminist Practice & Poststructuralist Theory*. Oxford: Blackwell.

312 *References*

Weick, K. (1995) *Sense-making in Organisations.* London: Sage.

Weick, K. (2004) A bias for conversation: acting discursively in organisations, in D. Grant, C. Hardy, C. Oswick and L. Putnam (eds) *The SAGE Handbook of Organizational Discourse,* pp.405–412. London: Sage.

Weiss, A. (2003) 'That unpleasant image in the mirror', *Consulting to Management,* 14(2), p.14.

Wenger, E. (1998) *Communities of Practice: learning, meaning and identity.* Cambridge: Cambridge University Press.

Werr, A. (1998) *Managing Knowledge in Management Consulting.* Paper presented at the Academy of Management Meeting, San Diego (Winner of the William Jerome Arnold Meritorious Paper Award).

Werr, A. (2002) The internal creation of consulting knowledge: a question of structuring experience, in M. Kipping and L. Engwall (eds). *Management Consulting: emergence and dynamics of a knowledge industry,* pp.91–108. Oxford: Oxford University Press.

Werr, A. and Styhre, A. (2005) 'Management consultants – friend or foe? Understanding the ambiguous client-consultant relationship', *International Studies of Management & Organisation,* 32(4), pp.43–66.

West, C. and Zimmerman, D. (2003) Doing gender, in R. Ely, E. Foldy and M. Scully (eds). *Reader in Gender, Work and Organization,* pp.62–74. Oxford: Blackwell.

Wetherall, M., Taylor, S. and Yates, S.J. (eds) (2001) *Discourse as Data: a guide for analysis.* Milton Keynes: Open University Press.

White, M. (2004) *Machiavelli: a man misunderstood.* London: Little, Brown & Co.

Whittle, A. (2006) 'The paradoxical repertoires of management consultancy', *Journal of Organizational Change Management,* 19(4), pp.424–436.

Whyte, D. (2002) *Crossing the Unknown Sea: work and the shaping of identity.* London: Penguin.

Wildavsky, A. (1979) *Speaking Truth to Power: the art and craft of policy analysis.* Boston: Little, Brown & Co.

Willard, C. (1984) *Christine de Pizan: her life and works.* NY: Persea Press. Available at: http://www.pinn.net/~sunshine/book-sum/pizan1.html [accessed 12.01.2006].

Williams, A.P.O. and Woodward, S. (1994) *The Competitive Consultant: a client-oriented approach for achieving superior performance.* Basingstoke: Macmillan.

Williams, C. (2003) 'Sky service: the demands of emotional labour in the airline industry', *Gender, Work and Organization,* 10(5), pp.513–550.

Willmott, H. (2005) 'Theorizing contemporary control: some post-structuralist responses to some critical realist questions', *Organization,* 12(5), pp.747–780.

Willmott, H. (2006) 'Pushing at an open door: mystifying the CMS manifesto', *Management Learning,* 37(1), pp.33–38.

Wood, L.A. and Kroger, R.O. (2000) *Doing Discourse Analysis: methods for studying talk and text.* London: Sage.

Yates, S.J. (2001) Researching internet interaction: sociolinguistics and corpus analysis, in M. Wetherall, S. Taylor, S.J. Yates (eds) *Discourse as Data: a guide for analysis,* pp.93–146. Milton Keynes: Open University Press.

Index

Discourse
  and interaction, 131, 132
  and knowledge, 115
  and power, 130
  consulting as discourse, *see also*
    Consulting as discursive
    practice, 24, 115, 128
  discourse theory, 128
Discourse analysis, 131
  email material, 142
  genres, 69, 119, 135, 150, 152, 153,
    170, 173, 180, 188, 213, 270
  growth in, 113
  modality, 138
  passive voice, 132, 155, 196, 197
  sense-making process, 145
Discourses of consulting
  'client is king', 116, 117, 119, 120,
    158, 159, 189, 245, 259, 277, 279
  'objective professional', 95, 107,
    111, 116, 117, 189, 211, 220,
    222, 223, 236, 237, 239, 259,
    261, 273, 279, 280
  transaction and commodified
    'project', 107, 113
  'trusted adviser', 34, 46, 60, 66, 78,
    79, 80, 95, 107, 111, 116–117,
    120, 165, 173, 189, 221, 223,
    233, 245, 259, 261, 269, 272,
    273, 275, 279, 280
Dominant/subordinate, *see also* Power
  and women, 258
Duchess of Kendal, confidante of
  George I of England, 58–59

Egypt
  pharaonic advisers, 33, 34, 53
  power of queens, 34, 53, 54
Eleanor of Provence, queen of
  Henry III of England, 53, 54, 56
Elizabeth I, queen of England, 33, 53,
  59, 60
Email, *see* Discourse analysis
  email material, 142
Emotion
  absence from consulting literature,
    117
  betrayal, 195, 229, 235, 256, 259,
    273

doubt, 2, 4, 59, 127, 197, 212, 214,
  222, 251, 252, 268
'emotional intelligence', 273
emotional labour, 98, 117, 159,
  166, 180–181, 189, 193, 220,
  232, 234, 236, 237, 240, 254,
  272, 273, 278, 280, 284
empathy, 4, 159, 186, 198, 255
feelings expressed, 2, 37, 43, 105,
  151, 158, 164, 165, 168, 171,
  180, 181, 186, 194, 201, 203,
  204, 211, 233–236, 241, 243,
  244, 260, 261, 264, 288
guilt, 35, 199, 201
research into, 234, 237
Empress Matilda, 56
'Entanglement' (Michel Callon), *see
  also* Consulting as economic
  transaction, 213, 239
Entrepreneurs, 10, 121, 222, 241, 247,
  254, 265, 266, 267
  emotional support, 295
  sole traders, 15, 266
Equal opportunities, 201
Ethics and practice, 5, 17, 30, 80, 81,
  82, 107, 108, 120, 147, 170, 195,
  199, 200, 201, 202, 222, 233,
  240–242, 251, 271, 277, 278,
  283–286, 294
  in research, 147
Ethnicity, 258, 261, 287
Ethnography, 139, 141, 143, 144,
  147, 252, 267

Fairclough, Norman, 24, 25, 111, 128,
  129, 130, 131, 133, 134, 135, 136,
  137, 138, 139, 142, 146, 188, 283,
  292
Feminine, 3–5, 26–27, 66, 67, 112,
  117, 166, 188, 234, 246–254, 256,
  260–266, 269–277, 280–289, 294,
  295
  hierarchic binaries, *see also*
    'Separate spheres' concept, 117,
    248, 282, 284, 289
Feminine discourse of consulting,
  269–273
Feminist research, 22, 26, 27, 126,
  246, 248, 251, 260

318